"The odds would seem long against finding [...] various skills to tranquilize wild East Af[...] explain the scientific implications of his wor[...] primate power struggles (especially those of H. sapie[...], and write about it all with great wit and humanity. But *A Primate's Memoir* is such a book, and Robert M. Sapolsky is such a writer."

—George Packer, author of *The Village of Waiting* and *Blood of the Liberals*

"A witty concoction blending field biology, history, hilarious cross-cultural mishaps, and hair-raising adventure. What Jane Goodall did for chimpanzees, Birute Galdikas for orangutans, and Dian Fossey for gorillas, Sapolsky does in spades for baboons."

—*Kirkus Reviews* (starred)

"Mr. Sapolsky has been to the end of the road and come back with some of the best stories you will ever hear, and, in the process, has put his finger on some vast, comic common denominator. What you have in your hands is the reason to read books."

—Pete Dexter, author of *Paris Trout* and *The Paperboy*

"For all its high spirits and black humor, *A Primate's Memoir* is a powerful meditation on the biological origins of baboon and human misery, as well as a naturalist's coming-of-age story comparable to Jane Goodall's and E. O. Wilson's. . . . As a memoirist, Sapolsky is a mensch, a prince among primates."

—Caroline Fraser, *Outside*

"This engrossing account of Robert Sapolsky's life in science, set down with style and force, is brilliantly informative (baboons have long memories, and seek vengeance!) and heartbreakingly acute in its rendering of African lives, terrains, fates."

—Norman Rush, author of *Mating*

"A gem . . . sidesplitting vignettes about monkey politics alternate with equally hilarious tales of misadventure on the backroads of East and Central Africa. . . . *[A Primate's Memoir]* will keep you chuckling from start to finish."

—Unmesh Kher, *Time*

"*A Primate's Memoir* is witty, erudite, and full of baboons. What could be bad?"

—Allegra Goodman, author of *Kaaterskill Falls*

"A tale of adventure, science—and corruption. Four stars."
—Sharon Begley, *Newsweek*

"At the end of *A Primate's Memoir*, I felt as though I'd been on a guided tour of Africa with a wise, soulful, funny, generous, and deeply intelligent guide. Loved him, loved his insights about these strange and distant cultures, loved his baboons."
—Caroline Knapp, author of *Pack of Two*

"Filled with cynicism and awe, passion and humor, this memoir is both an absorbing account of a young man's growing maturity and a tribute to the continent that, despite its troubles and extremes, held him in its thrall."
—*Publishers Weekly* (starred)

"Touching . . . Honor is a word that echoes in the reader's consciousness throughout this funny, often elegiac rendering of a remarkable place and some magnificent creatures that call it home."
—Margaria Fichtner, *The Miami Herald*

"Powerful . . . He tells fascinating stories that run an emotional gamut from absurdly hilarious to profoundly troubling, and those stories compel the kind of response that great stories always elicit—you can't stop thinking about them. . . . [The stories] will stick with you long after you've put down *A Primate's Memoir*."
—Jim Ericson and Patty Griffin Jensen, *Minneapolis Star Tribune*

"What Jane Goodall's work might be like if she had a sense of humor."
—*Talk*

"Engaging . . . Sapolsky's storytelling gifts make this book difficult to put down . . . his scientific references [are] straightforward but enlightening . . . poignant."
—John Freeman, *The Plain Dealer*

"Ceaselessly brilliant . . . wonderful . . . there is surprise and great drama."
—Arthur Salm, *The San Diego Union-Tribune*

"To his credit and our benefit, Sapolsky's depiction of the African bush isn't shrouded in either gauzy, neocolonial paternalism or harsh, anticolonial righteousness. His stories are told with the hilarious realism of someone who'd been there. . . . When the book is finished, we wish it wasn't."
—Rodger Brown, *Atlanta Journal-Constitution*

A Primate's Memoir

ROBERT M. SAPOLSKY

SCRIBNER

New York   London   Toronto   Sydney   New Delhi

To Benjamin and Rachel

SCRIBNER
An Imprint of Simon & Schuster, Inc.
1230 Avenue of the Americas
New York, NY 10020

This Scribner trade paperback edition March 2002

SCRIBNER and design are registered trademarks of The Gale Group, Inc., used under license by
Simon & Schuster, Inc., the publisher of this work.

For information about special discounts for bulk purchases, please contact Simon & Schuster
Special Sales at 1-866-506-1949 or business@simonandschuster.com.

The Simon & Schuster Speakers Bureau can bring authors to your live event.
For more information or to book an event, contact the Simon & Schuster Speakers Bureau at
1-866-248-3049 or visit our website at www.simonspeakers.com.

Interior design by Erich Hobbing

Manufactured in the United States of America

27   29   30   28   26

The Library of Congress has cataloged the Scribner edition as follows:
Sapolsky, Robert M.
A primate's memoir/Robert M. Sapolsky.
p. cm.
1. Baboons—Behavior—Africa, East—Anecdotes.
2. Sapolsky, Robert M.
I. Title

QL737.P93 S27 2001
599.8'6515'09676—dc21.
00-063522

ISBN 978-0-7432-0247-3
ISBN 978-0-7432-0241-1 (pbk)
ISBN 978-1-4165-9036-1 (ebook)

The names and other identifying characteristics of some people have been changed.

CONTENTS

Acknowledgments   9

Part 1. The Adolescent Years:
When I First Joined the Troop

1. The Baboons: The Generations of Israel   13
2. Zebra Kabobs and a Life of Crime   25
3. The Revenge of the Liberals   37
4. The Masai Fundamentalist and My Debut as a Social Worker   47
5. The Coca-Cola Devil   57
6. Teaching Old Men About Maps   65
7. Memories of Blood: The East African Wars   71

Part 2: The Subadult Years

8. The Baboons: Saul in the Wilderness   95
9. Samwelly Versus the Elephants   105
10. The First Masai   117
11. Zoology and National Security: A Shaggy Hyena Story   121
12. The Coup   127
13. Hearing Voices at the Wrong Time   135
14. Sudan   139

Part 3: Tenuous Adulthood

15. The Baboons: The Unstable Years   169
16. Ol' Curly Toes and the King of Nubian-Judea   177
17. The Penguins of Guyana   187
18. When Baboons Were Falling Out of the Trees   197
19. The Old White Man   209
20. The Elevator   213
21. The Mound Behind the 7-Eleven   219

Part 4: Adulthood

22. The Baboons: Nick   233
23. The Raid   243
24. Ice   249
25. Joseph   255
26. The Wonders of Machines in a Land Where They Are Still Novel:
    The Blind Leading the Blind   259
27. Who's on First, What's on Second   263
28. The Last Warriors   269
29. The Plague   275

ACKNOWLEDGMENTS

This is a memoir of my more than twenty years spent working intermittently in a national park in East Africa. The stories are true but, as is often the case in such retellings, subject to a bit of literary license that I want to describe here. The story of Wilson Kipkoi is true in most details. However, names and some other details have been changed to protect anonymity. The final chapter, unfortunately, is true in all its devastating details; however, here, too, I have changed names and certain characteristics. The chronology of the various chapters has been expanded in some places, truncated in others. In a few cases, the sequence of some stories has been changed; the sequence of all events in the lives of the baboons, however, is unchanged. Finally, a number of humans, and a number of baboons, represent composites of a few members of their species. This was done to keep down the cast of characters coming and going—for example, within the human realm, a particular game-park ranger, British tour operator, or tourist-lodge waiter may be a composite of a few individuals. All of the major baboon figures are real individuals, as are the major human characters—Richard, Hudson, Laurence of the Hyenas, (the late) Rhoda, Samwelly, Soirowa, Jim Else, Mbarak Suleman, Ross Tarara, and, of course, Lisa are all real people. I, to the best of my knowledge, am not a composite.

A number of individuals helped me with fact checking, reading part or all of this book or, in the case of Soirowa, who cannot read, having sections in it related, in order to confirm the accuracy of facts as they remember them. As such, I thank Jim Else, Laurence Frank, Richard Kones, Hudson Oyaro, and Soirowa. I also thank Colin Warner for some formal fact checking in the library, and John McLaughlin, Anne Meyer, Miranda Ip, and Mani Roy for help in proofreading the manuscript. Thanks also to Robert Shanafelt for pointing out an error in the finished volume. Dan Greenwood and Carol Salem shared stories with me of their travels in East Africa, and I thank them for that. I thank Jonathan Cobb, Liz Ziemska, and Patricia Gadsby for their priceless editorial advice when reading what was a proto-version of this book, a number of years ago.

Funding for this work was made possible by the Explorer's Club, the Harry Frank Guggenheim Foundation, the MacArthur Foundation, and the Templeton Foundation. I thank them not only for their generosity but for their extraordinary flexibility in recognizing the peculiar exigencies of fieldwork— at the very least, I thank them for accepting receipts and budget summaries on waterlogged, moth-eaten (literally) accounting notebooks. I thank the Institute of Primate Research, National Museums of Kenya, for my association with them, and the Office of the President, Republic of Kenya, for permission to conduct my research all these years. Two colleagues—Shirley Strum of the University of California at San Diego, and Jeanne Altmann, of Princeton University, have opened their field sites to me as part of our collaborations, and I thank them for that experience. And I thank a number of individuals who taught me aspects of doing fieldwork or helped me with data collection during some of the early seasons—Davie Brooks, Denise Costich, Francis Onchiri, and Reed Sutherland.

I thank my agent, Katinka Matson, for her tremendous support and expertise in making this book a reality, and Gillian Blake, my editor, and Rachel Sussman, her assistant—you have been remarkably graceful in pointing out problems in this manuscript that anyone but a scientist should have learned back in Creative Writing 101. It has been a pleasure working with you all.

And finally, I thank my wife, Lisa, the love of my life, who has shared so many of these moments in Kenya with me.

A final note: The depredations and plunderings of colonialism in Africa are now a thing of the past. However, the West often continues to exploit Africa in far subtler ways, even on those occasions when intentions are the best. I have now spent more than half my life connected with Africa, and I have intense feelings of warmth, respect, and gratitude for the place and my friends there. I deeply hope that I have not inadvertently been exploitative in any way in these writings. This was the last thing I would have intended.

Part 1

The Adolescent Years:

When I First Joined the Troop

1

The Baboons:
The Generations of Israel

I joined the baboon troop during my twenty-first year. I had never planned to become a savanna baboon when I grew up; instead, I had always assumed I would become a mountain gorilla. As a child in New York, I endlessly begged and cajoled my mother into taking me to the Museum of Natural History, where I would spend hours looking at the African dioramas, wishing to live in one. Racing effortlessly across the grasslands as a zebra certainly had its appeal, and on some occasions, I could conceive of overcoming my childhood endomorphism and would aspire to giraffehood. During one period, I became enthused with the collectivist utopian rants of my elderly communist relatives and decided that I would someday grow up to be a social insect. A worker ant, of course. I made the miscalculation of putting this scheme into an elementary-school writing assignment about my plan for life, resulting in a worried note from the teacher to my mother.

Yet, whenever I wandered the Africa halls in the museum, I would invariably return to the mountain gorilla diorama. Something primal had clicked the first time I stood in front of it. My grandfathers had died long before I was born. They were mythically distant enough that I would not be able to pick either out in a picture. Amid this grandfatherly vacuum, I decided that a real-life version of the massive, sheltering silverback male gorilla stuffed in the glass case would be a good substitute. A mountainous African rain forest amid a group of gorillas began to seem like the greatest refuge imaginable.

By age twelve, I was writing fan letters to primatologists. By fourteen, I was reading textbooks on the subject. Throughout high school, I finagled jobs in a primate lab at a medical school and, finally, sojourning to Mecca itself, volunteered in the primate wing of the museum. I even forced the chairman of my high school language department to find me a self-paced course in Swahili, in preparation for the fieldwork I planned to do in Africa. Eventually, I went off to college to study with one of the deans of primatology. Everything seemed to be falling into place.

But in college, some of my research interests shifted and I became focused on scientific questions that could not be answered with gorillas. I would need to study a species that lived out in the open in the grasslands, with a different type of social organization, a species that was not endangered. Savanna baboons, who had struck no particular chord in me before, became the logical species to study. You make compromises in life; not every kid can grow up to become president or a baseball star or a mountain gorilla. So I made plans to join the baboon troop.

I joined the troop in the last year of the reign of Solomon. In those days, the other central members of the troop were Leah, Devorah, Aaron, Isaac, Naomi, and Rachel. I didn't plan beforehand to give the baboons Old Testament names. It just happened. A new adult male, leaving the troop he grew up in, would transfer into the troop, and during the few weeks when he'd vacillate about joining permanently, I would hesitate about giving him a name. I'd just refer to him in my notes as the new adult transfer, or NAT, or Nat, or, by the time he decided to stay forever, Nathanial. Adam was first known as ATM, for adult transfer male. The small kid who was first abbreviated as the SML kid then turned into Samuel on me. At that point I just gave up and started handing out the prophets and matriarchs and judges left and right. I would still occasionally stick with a purely descriptive name— Gums or Limp, for example. And I was way too insecure in my science to publish technical papers using these names—everyone got a number then. But the rest of the time, I wallowed in biblical names.

I have always liked Old Testament names, but I would hesitate to inflict Obadiah or Ezekial on a child of mine, so I ran wild with the sixty baboons in the troop. Plus, clearly, I was still irritated by the years I spent toting my Time-Life books on evolution to show my Hebrew school teachers, having them blanch at such sacrilege and tell me to put them away; it felt like a pleasing revenge to hand out the names of the patriarchs to a bunch of baboons on the African plains. And, with some sort of perversity that I suspect powers a lot of what primatologists do, I couldn't wait for the inevitable day that I could record in my field notebook that Nebuchanezzar and Naomi were off screwing in the bushes.

What I wanted to study was stress-related disease and its relationship to behavior. Sixty years ago, a scientist named Selye discovered that your emotional life can affect your health. It struck the mainstream doctors as ludicrous—people were perfectly accustomed to the idea of viruses or bacteria or carcinogens or whatnot getting you sick, but your emotions? Selye found that if you got rats upset in all sorts of purely psychological ways, they got sick. They got ulcers, their immune systems collapsed, their reproduction went to hell, they got high blood pressure. We know now exactly what was happening—this was the discovery of stress-related disease. Selye showed that stress was what you were undergoing when emotional or physical disturbances threw your body's balance out of whack. And if it went on for too long, you got sick.

That last piece has been hammered home with a vengeance—stress makes all sorts of things in the body go bad, and in the years since Selye, people have documented numerous diseases that can be worsened by stress. Adult onset diabetes, muscle atrophy, high blood pressure and atherosclerosis, arrested growth, impotency, amenorrhea, depression, decalcification of bones. You name it. In my laboratory work, I was studying how, on top of all that, stress can kill certain brain cells.

It seemed a miracle that any of us survived. But clearly we did. I decided that, in addition to my laboratory work on neurons, I wanted to study the optimistic side of it—how come some of us are more resistant to stress than others? Why are some bodies and some psyches better at coping? Does it have something to do with your rank in society? If you have lots of relatives, if you hang out with friends? If you play with kids? If you sulk when you're upset about something or if you find someone else to take it out on? I decided to go study this in wild baboons.

They were perfect for it. Baboons live in big, complex social groups, and the population I went to study lived like kings. Great ecosystem, the Serengeti. Grass and trees and animals forever, Marlin Perkins country. The baboons work maybe four hours a day to feed themselves; hardly anyone is likely to eat them. Basically, baboons have about a half dozen solid hours of sunlight a day to devote to being rotten to each other. Just like our society—few of us are getting hypertensive from physical stressors, none of us are worrying about famines or locust plagues or the ax fight we're going to have with the boss out in the parking lot at five o'clock. We live well enough to have the luxury to get ourselves sick with purely social, psychological stress. Just like these baboons.

So I would go out and study the behavior of baboons, see who was doing what with whom—fights, trysts and friendships, alliances and dalliances. Then I would dart them, anesthetize them, see how their bodies were doing—blood pressure, cholesterol levels, rate of wound healing, levels of stress hormones. What would individual differences in behavior and psychological patterns have to do with the individual differences in how their bodies were working? I wound up studying only the males. You wouldn't want to anesthetize females when they were pregnant, or when they had a dependent nursing kid, and that's most of the time for most of the females. Thus, I settled in with the males and planned to get to know them very well.

It was 1978; John Travolta was the most important human alive, white suits were sweeping our proud nation, and Solomon was in the final year of his rule. Solomon was good and wise and just. Actually, that's nonsense, but I was an impressionable young transfer male at the time. Nevertheless, he was a pretty imposing baboon. For years, the anthropology textbooks had been having a love affair with savanna baboons and their top-ranking male, the alpha male. According to the books, the baboons were complex social primates living in open grasslands; they had organized hunts, a hierarchical rank system, and at their core was the alpha male. He led the troop to food, spearheaded the hunts, defended against predators, kept the females in line, changed the lightbulbs, fixed the car, blah blah blah. Just like our human ancestors, the textbooks ached to say, and sometimes even did. Most of that turned out to be wrong, naturally. The hunts for food were disorganized free-for-alls. Furthermore, the alpha male couldn't lead the troop to food during a crisis, as he wouldn't know where to go. The males transferred into the troops as adolescents, while the females spent their whole lives in the same troop. Thus, it would be the old females who remembered the grove of olive trees past the fourth hill. When predators attacked, the alpha male would be in the thick of it, defending an infant. But only if he was absolutely certain that it was his kid who was at risk of becoming someone's dinner. Otherwise, he had the highest, safest spot in the tree to watch the action. So much for Robert Ardrey and 1960s anthropology.

Nevertheless, within the small, parochial, self-interested, unreflective, petty world of male baboons, being alpha was hot stuff. You might not really be the troop leader, but you got to do about half the matings, sit in the shade when it was hot, enjoy the best food with a minimum of effort merely by ripping off someone else's lunch box. And Solomon excelled at all of this. He had been alpha male in the troop for three years, an inordinately long time for a male's tenure. The grad student who preceded me with the troop said that Solomon had been a ferocious and canny fighter back when he defeated his predecessor, but by the time I got there (and secretly instituted the name Solomon—his boring published identification number I will never divulge), he was in his silver years and resting on his laurels, persisting out of sheer psychological intimidation. He was damn good at it. He hadn't had a major fight in a year. He would just glance at someone, rouse himself from his regal setting and saunter over, at the most swat him, and that would settle things. Everyone was terrified of him. He swatted at me once, knocked me off a rock, shattered my going-away-to-Africa-gift binoculars, left me terrified of him as well. I immediately dropped any plans I might have had of challenging him for the alpha position.

Most of his days he spent lounging with the many infants who he felt certain were his kids (i.e., no one else went near the female baboon during the part of the cycle she conceived), stealing the occasional tuber or root that someone else had dug up, being groomed, consorting with new females in heat. As of late, the hot number in the troop was Devorah, daughter of Leah, who was probably the oldest member of the troop, the alpha female, and one incredibly tough cookie. Male baboon ranks shift over time; as someone grows into his prime, someone else snaps a canine and is out of business. Females, on the other hand, inherit their rank from their mothers; they get the rank below mom, kid sister gets one below that, and so on, until the next lower-ranking family starts. So Leah had been sitting on top of that pile for at least a quarter of a century. Leah would harass Naomi, around her age and the matriarch of a much lower-ranking family. Old Naomi would sit down to a midday rest in some nice spot in the shade, and Leah would bash on over and boot her out. Naomi, unruffled, would find someplace else to sit, and, unable to resist, Leah would do it again and again. I would marvel at the antiquity of it. Some years before, Jimmy Carter was jogging at the White House, people were buying Pet Rocks and trying to look like Farrah Fawcett-Majors, and the aging Leah was giving Naomi grief. Even further back, the My Lai massacre occurred, people were wearing cranberry bell-bottoms and dancing on waterbeds, and the prime-aged Leah was forcing Naomi to groom her. Further back, Lyndon Johnson was showing off his gallbladder scar while the adolescent Leah was waiting for Naomi to fall asleep during her midday nap before hassling her. And way back when people were still protesting the Rosenbergs' being executed and I was positioned in my grandmother's lap in her nursing home for us to be photographed with the Brownie camera, Naomi, the toddler, had to give the branch she was playing with to Leah. And now they were two decrepit old ladies still playing musical chairs in the savanna.

Leah had given birth to a whole line of strapping, confident sons. In various social species of animals, either males or females pick up and move to a different social group around puberty—one of those incest avoidance deals. Among baboons, it's the males who get this undefined itch of wanderlust, and Leah's sons were raising havoc far and wide throughout the troops of the northeast

Serengeti. Devorah was her first daughter in quite some time, maybe even ever. She was just hitting puberty, and Solomon was going wild about her. Devorah was highly desirable by any male baboon's standards. She was well fed, in good health, and thus very likely to conceive and carry through her pregnancy. And once the kid was born, no one was going to mess with it; it would survive. From the standpoint of evolutionary theory, of leaving as many copies of your genes in future generations as possible, all that jazz, this was one highly desirable young primate. I never thought that Devorah was a big deal (unlike Bathsheeba, whom I had a crush on, and who was soon to meet a tragic end at the canines of that bastard Nebuchanezzar), but she certainly did not lack for confidence. When male baboons who are getting along well run into each other and want to say howdy, they yank on each other's penises. I think it is, in effect, their way of saying, "We're getting along so well, I trust you so much for this one second, that I'm gonna let you yank on me." Like dogs rolling on their backs to let each other sniff at their crotches. Among male primates, this means trust. All the guys did it to the other guys that they were pals with. And in addition, Leah and Devorah would do penis-grab greetings on males. Only females I ever saw do it. I saw Devorah pull this off on Nebuchanezzar, around the time he first joined the troop. He comes sauntering along, having just spent the morning causing trouble and feeling pretty good about himself, passes this little ol' lady and her young daughter, Leah and Devorah, coming the other way, don't reckon he knows them yet, but he does the male baboon equivalent of tipping his hat—flashing his eyebrows—and this young thing reaches over, and, well, she just yanks his balls, good solid heft, and goes walking on with the old biddy. Nebuchanezzar actually crouched to get a better view of her departing rear end, perhaps to be certain that she wasn't really some fella who just came past.

Thus, Devorah was sailing through puberty without a care, without a hint of acned insecurities, Solomon just waiting for her to smell a little sexier, get a slightly larger estrus swelling, perhaps, before starting to squire her around. Such was not the destiny, however, of poor Ruth, also going through puberty at that time. Hers was the more usual adolescence. She was from an obscure, low-ranking lineage and had the constant, swiveling, nervous movements of someone who gets dumped on a lot. Years later, in middle age, she would still have an anxious hyperadrenal look, and her umpteen kids would have the same frazzled edge to them. But this year, her major problem was that she was slowly being driven mad by estrogen. Puberty had hit, and she was getting estrus swellings and steroids were poisoning her brain, and all she could think of was male baboons—but no one was interested in her. For about the first six months when they start cycling and getting estrus swellings, female baboons are probably not yet really ovulating; the system's just warming up. Almost certainly, to the males, this translates as the female just not quite yet smelling sexy enough, the estrus swelling on her rear not quite yet having that irresistible glint in the African twilight.

Meanwhile, poor Ruthie was in hormonal limbo and going bonkers. She was after all the big guys, and no one would even look at her. Solomon would step from out of the bushes and sit down in the field, and Ruth would be up in a flash, scurrying over from whatever she was doing to stick her tush in his face, as per the custom of female baboons in estrus, in the hope that he would do something more than sniff. No dice. Or ol' Aaron, another adult male, would be trying to accomplish the simple task of walking over to the fig tree, and Ruth would be all over him, running two steps ahead to stop and present; he'd pass, she'd spring again and try it from a different angle. How I remember Ruth best is from the summer of 1978: standing, preening, presenting her behind, arching her back every which way, looking back over her shoulder to gauge the effect, trying to get that perfect irresistible pose, panting with the sheer pleasure of the proximity to Solomon, who sits there, the thug, distractedly picking his nose and ignoring her.

Eventually, Ruth had to settle for Joshua, a young lanky kid who had transferred into the troop the year before. Quiet kid, didn't make trouble, had a serious, unflappable look about him. Masturbated a lot in the bushes. By October 1978, Joshua had developed a crush on Ruth, who was none too pleased. For two months he pursued her ardently. He'd lope after her and she'd run away with her adrenaline twitches. He'd sit next to her and she'd get up. He'd groom her carefully, pulling ticks off of her, and she'd scoot off the second he'd stop, to go moon around some hunk male. Once, while she preened and presented to Aaron, Joshua sat watching and got an erection.

Such shows of male devotion occasionally do move even the most crazed of adolescent female baboons, and by December, Joshua was with her constantly during her estrus swellings. They were not particularly adept at the whole business, and even years later, Ruth's incredible nervousness when any male actually did attempt to approach her had probably cut into her reproductive success considerably. Nevertheless, in May, she gave birth to Obadiah.

This was one weird-looking kid. He had a narrow head and long stringy hair that formed an elongated wing in the rear; he looked like a dissipated fin de siècle Viennese neurotic. Ruth was a nervous wreck of a mother, retrieving him when he got two steps from her, scampering off with him whenever another female approached. Joshua turned out to be a rarity among male baboons, a superb, devoted father. This actually makes sense to people who worry about such things. Your average female—more desirable than Ruth but less so than Devorah—will mate with perhaps five or six different males over the week of her estrus. A low-ranking guy on the first day, when she is least likely to be ovulating. By a day later, he's forced away by someone higher ranking, and so on, until a very high ranking male (perhaps the alpha) is with her on her peak day. Thus, five months later if a kid shows up, all anyone can do is get out his calculator and decide that he has a 38 percent chance of being the father. Expect no help from him in that case. In the case of Joshua, however, the sole suitor of Ruth for her months of young, blushing estrus swellings, he was 100 percent sure. To use the harsh economic terms of sociobiologists, it was in his evolutionary interests to parentally invest in the kid.

He carried Obadiah around when Ruth was tired, helped him climb up trees, nervously stood by him when lions were spotted. There was a hint of overprotection, perhaps; Joshua clearly didn't understand child play. Obadiah would be in there wrassling with his buddies, having a fine time, when Joshua would suddenly pounce into the center, defending his child from his menacing playmates, bowl the kids over, tossing them every which way. Obadiah would look confused, perhaps the nonhuman equivalent of the excruciating embarrassment kids feel when parents prove how lame they are. The kids would run screaming to their moms, who'd give Joshua grief, even chase him at times. But he never learned. Years later, when he was the alpha male, Joshua would still be breaking up Obadiah's adolescent wrestling matches with his friends.

Around the same time that Joshua joined the troop, Benjamin showed up. They were contemporaries, although Joshua came from the troop on the eastern mountain, and Benjamin came from the troop on the Tanzanian border. Still just emerging from my own festering adolescent insecurities, I had a difficult time not identifying utterly with Benjamin and his foibles. His hair was berserko. Unkempt, shocks of it sticking out all over his head, weird clumps on his shoulders instead of a manly cape that is supposed to intimidate your rivals. He stumbled over his feet a lot, always sat on the stinging ants. He had something odd going on with his jaw so that every time he yawned, which was often, he had to adjust his mouth manually, pull his lips and cheeks back over his canines. He didn't have a chance with the females, and if anyone on earth had lost a fight and was in a bad mood, Benjamin would invariably be the one stumbling onto the scene at the worst possible moment. One day, early in that first year in the troop, I was observing Benjamin. When collecting behavioral data, you pick someone randomly (so as not to bias the data by picking only those who are doing something exciting), and follow him for an hour, recording every behavior. It was midday, and two minutes into the sample, Benjamin took a nap under a bush. An hour later, at the end of that riveting sample, everyone had moved off. When he awoke, he didn't know where the troop was, and neither did I. We were lost together. I stood on the roof of the Jeep and scanned with my binoculars. We looked at each other. I finally spotted them, little black specks a few hills over. I drove off slowly, he ran after me, happy ending. After that, he would sit next to me when I worked on foot, sit on the bonnet of the Jeep when I worked out of the vehicle. It was around then that I decided he was my favorite baboon and bestowed upon him my favorite name, and everything he ever did subsequently reinforced that feeling. Many years later, long after he is gone, I still keep his picture with me.

Even younger than Joshua and Benjamin were David and Daniel. They had just joined the troop, still seemed frazzled by the trauma of their first transfer, the months of being outsiders in a new troop, away from friends and family, amid hassling strangers, on the edge of the troop and exposed to predators. They hadn't come from the same natal troop, but they were lucky enough to have shown up at the same time, and lucky enough to have temperaments that caused them to cling to each other instead of harass each other. They were inseparable, little more than kids, and spent their time playing and wrestling. One afternoon, I discovered the two of them off in the field near the forest, managing to panic an entire nursery herd of baby giraffes, stampeding them back and forth across the savanna. Each giraffe probably weighed fifty times as much as Daniel or David and could have stomped them easily. Instead, the disconcerted baby giraffes ran away from these strange tiny furball devils yapping at their feet.

There was one adult male who I felt certain had grown up in the troop, had never transferred out. Of the hundreds of baboons I would eventually know, Job had to have been dealt the worst set of cards. Savanna baboons are gorgeous animals; muscled, contoured woolly bears. Job was rail thin and had far too large a head for his body. He had tremors and spasms and palsies and seizures. His hair fell out intermittently, and each rainy season, his orifices would bloom with fungi. He had long fragile limbs and mange on his tail. As far as I could tell, he'd never hit puberty: undescended testes, no secondary sexual characteristics like large canines or cape hair or a deep voice or muscles. He was no idiot, though, and went about life with the alert canny vigilance of someone honed by constant fear. I had all sorts of theories as to what was wrong with him, gleaned from endocrinology textbooks that swam with disturbing pictures of glandular disasters, people standing naked in front of height charts, their eyes blacked out with a rectangle. Hypothyroid cretins and acromegalic freaks, exophthalmic nightmares and card-carrying hermaphrodites. Kleinfelter syndrome was my leading guess for Job, but I never found out. He was undiagnosed, beyond being certifiably weird and sad.

Predictably, he was tortured, chased, harassed, beaten, mauled, slashed, and terrorized by every male in the troop who needed an outlet (and more than once by both Leah and Devorah). New transfer males, pipsqueak adolescents, would be shocked and pleased to find that there was at least one individual lower ranking than they in their new troop. In the years that I knew him, I never saw him win a single dominance interaction. His only solace was Naomi's family—old Naomi, daughter Rachel, and grandkid Sarah. To use technical lingo, Naomi's family were mensches, and they soon became my favorite lineage. There was no mistaking them or their relatedness. They all had short bowlegs and little round tugboat torsos, and these crazy muffy faces that made them look like a family of barn owls. They were a middle-ranking lineage, had many friends, and helped each other. And helped Job. I could never prove it, but I felt sure that Job was Naomi's son, the troubled sick one who could never have survived a transfer to another troop and never had the androgenic drive to try, that adolescent male itch to pick up and try one's luck in the New World of another baboon troop. Naomi fretted over him, Rachel would ferociously defend him from harassing juvenile males, Sarah groomed him. One morning, Job, on the periphery of the troop, was cut off from the rest when he was surrounded by a herd of grazing female impalas. Nearly Bambis, for god's sake, innocuous as you can get, things that baboons *hunt*. But Job became frightened of them, started giving alarm barks until old Naomi and Rachel waded through the impalas to sit with him till they had gone and he felt safe.

In addition to matriarchs such as Naomi, the troop had some august older males as well. For example, there was Aaron, definitely past his prime, but still a force to be reckoned with. He was decent, quiet, had a lot of affiliative friendships with the females, didn't beat up on anyone too much. He still walked with a limp resulting from his moment with destiny. A few years earlier, Solomon was number 3 in the hierarchy, a young kid on the way up. Aaron was number 2, great shape, on the edge of his primacy, breathing down the neck of the then alpha, someone merely recorded in the archives as Male 203. One memorable morning, Aaron and 203 had their showdown, a stupendous fight that seesawed for hours. And at a critical moment, showing the strategic brilliance that would serve him in good stead for years to come, Solomon entered the fight, ably taking on both while they were preoccupied and exhausted. Result: number 203 dead, Aaron badly injured, Solomon settling in to his reign.

While the troop consisted of sixty-three members in 1979, these were the ones around whom the central events swirled. There were others, of course. Isaac, a young adult male a few years from his prime who was already having the good style to hang out with Rachel's family. Poor bedraggled Miriam, who had an endless string of colicky kids. The young sisters Boopsie and Afghan, who were so slinky and hypersexual, so salacious in the way that they would present to males by sticking their left foot over the guy's face, that I couldn't bring myself to give them matriarchal names from the Good Book.

It was during my first season in the troop that time no longer stood still for Solomon, that the inevitable shadow of mortality finally took form as Uriah. Uriah was a young kid, big as a barn, who transferred into the troop that spring and without any regard for precedent, for history, for the powers of intimidation, went about overthrowing Solomon. I've always suspected that Uriah was simply too dim to be intimidated by a stylist like Solomon, to appreciate the almost Oriental minimalism with which Solomon sent waves of nervous displacements, controlled the flow of tubers, matings, groomings. Uriah bowled over Joshua and Benjamin, quickly defeated Aaron, Isaac, some of the other big males. On one audacious morning while Solomon was consorting with the estrual Devorah, Uriah stepped between them and attempted to mate with her. Solomon had his first fight in years. Solomon trashed Uriah, gave him a deep canine slash to the shoulder, ripped his upper lip, sent him running with a fear grimace and his tail up in the air (the baboon equivalent of the tail between the legs). And then the next morning, Uriah challenged Solomon all over again.

Over and over it went throughout the spring, Uriah repeatedly being defeated and, apparently incapable of detecting a pattern, coming back again and again. He'd threat-yawn in Solomon's face, fight him over a carcass, scare away females when they groomed Solomon. Getting thrashed repeatedly. And slowly, he was wearing Solomon down. The latter was losing weight, looking more punchy in each fight. When male baboons fight, they lunge at each other openmouthed, flailing with the knife-sharp canines that are longer than those of adult lions. One morning, for the first time, Solomon backed up as the two fenced in this way. This was the first time he had ever given up ground, even for an instant. He ultimately won the fight, but got a facial slash in the process. More challenges, more time spent looking over his shoulder. Uriah was the nightmare of those who age—an opponent too young to know yet what fatigue feels like. One afternoon, between fights with Uriah,

Solomon was challenged by another high-ranking male, who, two months earlier, shrank before Solomon's gaze. Solomon won, but it involved more fencing and a sustained chase where the male reversed on him a few times. The threads were unraveling.

The next morning, Solomon sat next to Devorah, who was not in estrus that week, not sexually receptive. Obadiah had just taken his first few steps; Rachel was sitting near Job; Miriam, two months pregnant, was grooming her youngest kid, who was throwing a tantrum. A quiet, small-town morning. Uriah appeared and stood a dozen yards from Solomon, staring, town no longer big enough for the two of them. And Solomon, like the script specified, looking neither left nor right, walked toward Uriah, turned around, and groveled, belly in the grass, rear end stuck in the air, a male gesture of submission. The transition had occurred.

During that day, Uriah sat and groomed with Leah, Naomi, some of the other females. Solomon, without provocation, attacked Benjamin, mauled Job repeatedly, broke up the play of Daniel and David, chased the terrified Ruth and Obadiah. I would come to recognize this as the typical behavior of a male baboon with problems who wants someone else to pay for them. And Solomon did something else, a behavior I would see only once afterward, again on the day that an alpha male lost his primacy. Debates rage among animal behaviorists as to the appropriateness of using emotionally laden human terms to describe animal behaviors. Debates as to whether ants really have "castes" and make "slaves," whether chimps carry out "wars." One group says the terms are a convenient shorthand for lengthier descriptions. One group says they are the same thing as human examples of these behaviors. Another group says that they are very different, and that by saying that all sorts of species take "slaves," for example, one is subtly saying that it is a natural, widespread phenomenon. My bias is to agree somewhat with this final group. Nevertheless, Solomon did something that day that I think merits the emotion-laden term that is typically used to describe a human pathology. Solomon chased Devorah, seized her near an acacia tree, and raped her. By this I mean that she had not presented to him, was not behaviorally receptive or physiologically fertile at the time, that she ran like hell, tried to fight him off, and screamed in pain when he entered her. And bled. So ended the reign of Solomon.

2

Zebra Kabobs and a Life of Crime

When I went off to Africa for the first time to join the baboons, I had an array of skills and experiences that would prepare me for anything I'd encounter in that new world. I knew a great deal about the subway system in New York City and, to top that off, had even obtained a driver's license a week before leaving for my trip. I had been to a few of the Mid-Atlantic states, as well as to New England. I had backpacked extensively in the Catskill Mountains in New York and once had to lie very still while a porcupine waddled past my sleeping bag. I had managed to make a campfire once, allowing me to melt my Velveeta cheese on my crackers, instead of eating them cold, as was my typical meal on a backpacking trip. I had even broadened my food horizons in other ways, preparing myself for the novelties about to come—I had recently escaped the dietary restrictions of my Orthodox religious upbringing, and thus, in the prior year, had had my first slice of pizza, first Chinese meal, and first Indian food (although, admittedly, in the last case, I ate only the rice, denouncing everything else as too spicy to possibly be safe). Best of all, in case there were any fronts in which I was lacking in useful experiences, I had read a book on almost any subject that could possibly be relevant to my new life ahead. I'd be able to handle anything thrown at me.

Arriving at the airport in Nairobi at dawn, I had rejected the taxis waiting for the tourist groups, instead taking the city bus into town. Jammed into a crowd, barely holding on to my overstuffed backpack and duffel bag, I stared out the window, trying to absorb every detail. There were volcanic mountains in the distance, open plains spotted with acacia trees, there were men out in the fields already, women walking alongside the road with baskets of food balanced on their heads. I couldn't believe it—everyone was *black*. I was in *Africa,* it had actually happened. It took me a while to be drawn back to events in the bus, to notice that a middle-aged man, seated nearby, was offering to hold my bag amid our lurching over the potholes. Actually, he was forcefully commandeering my bag, repeatedly saying, "My arms are strong, white man, my arms are strong," in English, with an intensity that puzzled me. Gingerly, I let him hold it, feeling half grateful and half distrustful. When the time came for him to leave, he returned my bag with apologies that he couldn't help further, pushed his arms against the bus seat so as to lift his torso into the air, and dropped to the floor of the bus on his hands and knees. Crab-walking down the stairs and onto the Nairobi street, he turned once to shout over his shoulder, "My arms are strong," chuckling, delighted. I had just met my first street beggar crippled by polio.

So I settled in to Nairobi for the week it took to arrange permits and transportation out to the park. Almost immediately, it became apparent that I was speaking the wrong kind of Swahili. I had learned it from a Tanzanian law student at my university. As part of Tanzania's socialist experiment, tribalism was being slowly eradicated, and everyone learned rich, complex, elegant Zanzibari Swahili as a first language. In neighboring Kenya, a chaotic tribalism prevailed, where you were raised with your tribal language, along with those of your closest tribal ally and closest tribal enemy, and where Swahili might only be acquired later. Most people spoke some Swahili, and almost everyone spoke it horribly, especially in Nairobi, where it had taken on a broken, slangy, urban form. I had done the equivalent of showing up in the Bronx, speaking the Queen's English. Nobody understood a word I was saying, nor I them.

Despite the communication problem, I still managed to have my share of first-day experiences. Within rapid order, I was billed for a fake government tax by the clerk at the hotel I had been directed to, was overcharged by the proprietor of the first food kiosk I went into, and was hustled for money by a university student from Uganda. He explained to me that his family had been killed by Idi Amin, he had escaped as a refugee, he was trying to get the money to go back and take part in the revolution. We had a long discussion about this, sitting in the shade of some trees on the grounds of the national museum, as he spoke with fervor about his desire to bring a Western-style democracy to his homeland. I gave him an absurdly large amount of money. In the years to come, he would become a familiar face to me, working the tourists on the museum grounds as a refugee from whatever African country whose recent political turmoils had managed to catch briefly the awareness of the West.

By the end of that first day, I had concluded that everything was going just fine. I had learned about an interesting government tax on lodging. I had learned that I needed to pay more attention to the posted prices in the food kiosks, as I had mistakenly thought the prices were less than they actually were, forcing the poor proprietor into the uncomfortable position of having to tell me I owed him more money. And best of all, I had done my part to help bring a two-party democratic system to Uganda.

So went my first week in Nairobi, and it should have been dizzying, making my way through this tumult-filled Third World city, not knowing a soul, every food, every face, every gesture, utterly alien, more alien than anything I'd ever encountered. But instead, it was kind of a blank for a simple reason. I didn't even know which direction to face, but throughout, I had the same thought, over and over—somewhere out there, beyond the spanking new skyscrapers, beyond the shantytown, beyond the immaculate colonial Brit suburbs, it all melted away and the bush began. Everything else was just me holding my breath until I could get there, to the place I had been planning for most of my life.

Finally, the day came. I had made my way in town to the office of the wildlife conservation group, where I had a "contact." This overstated the connection considerably—a secretary there had merely been notified from the States that some kid with my name was going to show up, and she should help me out a bit. It was wonderfully exciting. The mere existence of my name on a piece of paper in this office, even horribly misspelled and with my fore- and surnames reversed, was immensely thrilling, made me feel like an old Africa hand. I was given instructions about how to catch a bush plane out to the game park, and the name of the bush pilot—up to two contacts now in Africa! I was supposed to hook up with two grad students in the game park, and to overlap with them for a few months while I learned the ropes. The secretary somewhat convincingly promised to radio-call them, to make sure they'd eventually come fetch me from the airstrip.

And so there I was on a tiny plane bouncing in a rainstorm cutting across the Rift Valley, the cloud layer too low to allow the slow emergence of this new world below me. Instead, we swam in clouds until the last thirty seconds of descent. With a sudden burst of visibility, I got a glimpse of scrub plains and zebras and wildebeests sprinting off the runway to avoid our plane, and I found myself in the diorama.

I will forever ache with the knowledge that I can never again spend my first weeks out in the bush—a first introduction to the baboons, a first afternoon spent meeting the nearby villagers, the first realization that behind every bush and tree there was an animal. Each night in my tent, I would fling myself down in exhaustion at all the novelty, with the fatigue of looking and listening and smelling at everything so intently.

The first, most potent lesson that I got, naturally, was that things were not as I had anticipated. I had steeled myself for years in expectation and acceptance of the dangers I would face in the bush, had bid farewell to my loved ones at home as if I might not return. I had fully prepared myself for predators and buffalo and poisonous snakes. Instead, a far bigger problem was the constant bugs in the food.

I had learned that the local tribespeople were formidable—the warlike Masai, famous for their plundering and raiding; fearsome, intimidating neighbors. I had not anticipated that the biggest difficulty that the Masai would pose would be the mamas sitting around camp each afternoon, snickering and gossiping and chortling at seemingly anything I did, crowding around in curiosity with no concept of privacy or personal space, endlessly trying to cadge my possessions as gifts.

I had accepted that I stood the risk of some appalling tropical disease, would be braving malaria, bilharzia, or schistosomiasis. Instead, my ill health soon took the form of having low-grade nonspecific runs for a year nonstop, plus lying awake for hours each night, scratching between my maddeningly itchy toes at the mildewy fungus that had bloomed there.

Most of all, I had dwelled on the psychological challenges I was likely to face in that sort of isolation, knowing no one on the continent, working and living alone much of the time, being isolated from the outside world except for a mail drop once every few weeks. I was quite familiar with the phenomenon of most Peace Corps volunteers sinking into a depression somewhere around the tenth month of their first year, just when friends got bored sending letters, when the rainy season was at its peak, when the loneliness and alienness began to feel intolerable. I was prepared for that. Little did I know that I would think that I was cracking up from the isolation in the very first month.

The trouble was elephants. Did you know that female elephants have breasts? By this, I do not mean rows of teats, a mama elephant lying on her side with dozens of little piglet elephants nursing with their eyes still closed. I mean *breasts,* two huge voluptuous billowy mounds, complete with cleavage. I bet you had no idea, did you? Nor did I—it is a subject rarely broached in our public schools. I'm out in the bush that first month, armed with binoculars and stopwatch and notepad, spending the days carefully watching baboons mating left and right. And then, suddenly, some pachyderms come cruising past, and I see some elephant with these, well, breasts. And the natural first reaction is to think, Oh, great, I'm such a horny lascivious pathetic adolescent that after a mere month of isolation in the bush I've already cracked, I'm hallucinating breasts the size of Volkswagens on the elephants. Horrors, to have one's psychotic break occur so soon, and to have it take the form of a puerile sexual obsession many embarrassing steps below gawking at *National Geographic* nudies. I was greatly relieved to eventually discover that the elephant's breasts were real, that I was not having some Marlin Perkins wet dream.

It was shortly after my epiphany concerning the elephants that I had one of even greater consequence. The grad students had left and I was alone at the field site, a beautiful mountain overlooking the baboons' plains below. It was late afternoon and I was relaxed, fairly pleased with myself—I was beginning to be able to differentiate the various baboons from one another with some consistency. That morning, the aggressive Nebuchanezzar, whom I already disliked, had had a fight with a coalition of the aging Aaron and young Joshua. It was a complex, sustained battle in which the outcome had flip-flopped repeatedly, bursts of tight snarling and lunging among the three of them interspersed with high-speed chases over the field and through the bushes. The fight had lasted a couple of minutes until Joshua and Aaron prevailed by a narrow margin, and I had managed to follow the sequence and write down the details in my notebook. I was beginning to get the hang of this observational stuff.

I was lounging in front of my tent, watching the harem of impalas that lived in the nearby bushes, when a Land Rover belonging to the rangers down at the park gate bounced over the crest of the mountain's ridge and came along the dirt road into camp. I passed through their gate daily and made a point of always stopping to chew the fat with these guys. This was my first community in which one has the archetypally African experience of spending fifteen minutes merely exchanging greetings and salutations: My friend, how are you today? How was your night? How is your work? What do you think the weather will be tonight? What news of the cows of the parents of your sister's husband? And so on.

The vehicle pulled up. There were three rangers squeezed into the front and something big in the back. They opened up the back doors, and I saw that it was a dead zebra.

The senior ranger approached me with the usual greetings, while one of the junior guys went to work on the zebra with a machete. That's a dead zebra, I said, interrupting his inquiries about my parents' health. Yes, of course. Where did it come from? We shot it. You shot it!? Hunting was illegal in Kenya, banned from top to bottom, a source of great pride and self-congratulation in luring tourists to come see Kenya's game parks rather than those of its neighbors, a measure of the country's commitment to conservation and the Edenic preservation of its parks. Why were these game park rangers shooting game?

As we spoke, another ranger approached me with the handiwork of his machete, the back leg of the zebra. He tossed it to me, a huge muscular shank of leg, with bits of grass still clinging to the hoof. Was the zebra sick? I asked, hoping they would explain that they had killed it out of mercy. The ranger misunderstood what I was implying—"No, of course it was not sick, we wouldn't bring meat from a sick animal, this was a big strong male." He was a bit indignant.

They were getting back in the vehicle, probably miffed at my diffidence about their gift. As they started the engine, I managed to ask, Isn't it against the law to shoot zebras? The senior ranger looked at me coolly and said, The warden has not paid us in weeks, he is keeping our money for himself, we have no meat.

I sat there cradling the zebra leg in my arm for some time, consumed with my multiple layers of confusion. At age thirteen, I had become vegetarian in some sort of addled gesture to test my self-discipline and irritate my parents. Both motives had succeeded handsomely, and with the passing years, I had become even more doctrinaire about the whole thing and had added on some sensible reasons for the restrictiveness—animal suffering, an ecological consciousness, a health awareness. I had decided that I would eat whatever I had to in Africa, had accepted that as part of my adventure, but I had still managed, a few months into my time there, to avoid any actual meat. So here was my reintroduction to carnivory.

The other problem was a practical one. How the hell did you prepare this? The last meat I had eaten was no doubt a pastrami sandwich at a delicatessen in junior high school, or my mother's stuffed cabbage meatballs. I had spent all of college in the dormitories subsisting on the horrid purple-flavored yogurt that was their sop to the vegetarians, and during the vacation breaks when I had stayed in the dorm, my forays into preparing food on my own had consisted of going to the local grocery to buy purple-flavored yogurt. I was living on rice and beans and cabbage in camp, occasionally even managing to cook them adequately. I hadn't a clue what to do with the zebra leg.

Mostly, there was this yawning moral question. Those rangers had killed this zebra, just because they wanted some meat. They were *poachers,* and here I was with part of their spoils. Should I report them to the warden? But the warden was stealing their salaries. Whom should I report the warden to? Should I go and confront all of them, reason with them, convince them of their error? Who the hell was I to judge them? I could barely wipe my nose. And these rangers had brought me a gift. But they had killed a zebra. But why should a zebra be more valuable than the cows they were allowed to kill? It seemed immoral to actually eat the thing. But it seemed more immoral to waste it, to just toss it in the bushes.

I sat there paralyzed, the moral quandary beginning to coalesce into a term paper, when I noticed that the open muscle of the leg was already covered with flies. Without being aware of quite how I arrived at the decision, I carefully began to skin the leg with my Swiss army knife, and to then hack off pieces of muscle, chopping them into little squares. I made a complete mess of it, with blood and tissue everywhere; that night, hyenas were all over that spot just outside my tent, rooting out the scraps. I began to cook the chunks, letting them molder over the fire for hours, burning the hell out of them, transforming them into tasteless leather, unrecognizable as something that that morning had helped a zebra thunder across the savanna.

It was not possible to "eat" those chunks or, to frame it even more mechanically, to "chew" them. I was feeling so detached, starting to consume these leathery crisps, that it occurred to me that this was the textbook definition of "mastication," using my primate incisors to cut and shear, and my broad molars to grind repeatedly at this inedible mass.

As I sat there masticating away on the first few pieces of what would be my meals for days to come, eating this illegal meat, a sudden realization swept over me from out of nowhere. I actually stopped chewing, openmouthed, half from the fatigue of all this primate mastication and half with the sheer weight of my sudden knowledge. With a shock, I thought: That Ugandan student . . . that Ugandan student the other week at the museum . . . the one I gave that huge amount of money to . . . *that guy wasn't really a Ugandan student.* It was as if my vision had suddenly cleared. It dawned on me as well that I had been ripped off repeatedly by the guy at the food kiosk where I had returned each day, and by the clerk with the imaginary government tax at the lodging place. All this swept over me in a sudden, sagging realization, this sense of, What the hell is with this place, is everything some sort of scam? If it wasn't a case of the snake bringing me an apple from the Tree of Knowledge, it was at least the rangers bringing me poached zebra kabobs from the Tree of Wising Up.

I spent a horrible, sleepless night, suffering from the synergistic effects of being at a moral crossroads coupled with stupefyingly acidic gas from the charred zebra. The next day, it happened—I lied for the first time in the Garden of Eden. I passed through the park headquarters, as I did most days. I had somehow fallen into the habit of having to give a ride way out of my way to a particular ranger. I would deliver him to a village at the far end of the park's boundary, out of which, after a period of incoherent shouting, he would emerge silently, in order for me to return him to the headquarters. He was rather brusque and aggressive with me, and in the weeks during which this odd chauffeuring had evolved, I repeatedly reminded myself that I had to be more understanding, that this was no doubt a sort of crudeness found in men from the bush, that he was unused to dealing with someone from a foreign culture. Sometime during that sleepless night, it instead occurred to me that he was an asshole who was exploiting me, and that he was doing some sort of shakedown of the villagers to which I blithely squired him. As usual, he waved me down with his rifle, and in response to his demand that we leave immediately for that village, I took a deep breath and lied. In the careful, offhanded way that I had rehearsed half the night, I said that I had to do something first, and that I'd be back in a few minutes. And instead, I high-tailed it through a back track up to my mountain where I sat, glowing with a sense of triumph, picking zebra from my teeth.

There was no turning back. Oh, it wasn't as if I was out robbing banks under an assumed name by the next day. It wasn't even so much a behavioral change on my part. Instead, it was the start of my perceiving that things here worked utterly differently than anything I'd previously known. It was a constant source of confusion to me. People were generally far friendlier than any from my world, people with next to nothing were achingly generous with the little they had. But it was all within this framework of someone constantly being up to something. People with uniforms and weapons victimizing those without. People running shops who tallied the bills constantly bilking the customers who couldn't read or add numbers. Jobs that were available only for certain tribes, that were available only for those who agreed to kick back parts of their salaries to the boss. Health officials who stole the monies for vaccines, relief officials who pocketed the food monies, endless buildings or roads sitting uncompleted because some contractor or other had run off with the funds. Soon I saw one of the whitey versions of it. My next supply trip into Nairobi, I switched to staying at a rooming house run by Mrs. R, an elderly Polish settler, a place filled with white hitchhikers and overlanders boasting of smuggling and bribings at border posts, with tips on black-marketing illegal cash and where to have fake visa stamps made. I saw my first police shakedown: it was on a city bus that was stopped for inspection of IDs. The cops methodically worked their way down the aisle, relieving people of cash, until they spotted me gawking in the back and abruptly sent us on our way. A few days later, I got to see an event classic to an African or Indian city—a thief caught by a crowd and beaten into a coma in a joyous, frenzied outburst.

There was no shortage of explanations for the endless scams and maneuvers and cheatings and victimizations amid a world of people of intense decency. The desperation of being desperately poor. The raw tribal animosities that made "us's" and "them's" in ways I couldn't begin to detect. The most venal of corruption. A Wild West mentality, small-town boredom, unbridled selfish capitalism without even the pretense of regulations and restraint. Maybe this was how my own world worked, if I had ever bothered to experience anything outside of my ivory tower. Maybe this was also how the ivory tower worked, if I wised up a little there as well. But it was a startling revelation, as the animals continued to graze in the museum diorama I thought I had gone to live in. And it was remarkably preparative for my own minor descent a few months later.

Basically, the professor who sent me out there forgot that I existed. It was four or five months into that first season. I came to Nairobi to call him in the States, at great expense, politely reminding him that money was due. Oh, right, sorry about that, I forgot, money will be cabled to the game park within the week. I'd hitch back and go back to work, only to have a few weeks go by with no money. Back to Nairobi, a slightly more desperate call, Oh damn, sorry, completely slipped my mind, money will be cabled in the next few days. Soon, I was utterly broke and stranded in Nairobi. I couldn't afford to call this guy anymore, and there were no such things as collect calls from Africa in those days. I would never have contacted my parents for help—my independence was of paramount importance, and I rationed my shrinking funds to include the postage for the cheerful weekly aerograms I sent. The U.S. embassy turned out to be useless for Americans in Nairobi unless they were wealthy businessmen. I knew no one in Kenya who had any money. In fact, I basically knew no one in Kenya. Out of desperation, I took to a life of crime. And it worked.

The first scam I worked out was astonishingly simple. In the land of ex–British colonialism, of whites pouring in with their tours and vacations, the last thing *any* Kenyan would expect from a white guy would be that he was trying to rip off a meal, or a loaf of bread, or 20 shillings. It's not that whites were considered above larceny. It's just that they had proven themselves more concerned with stealing far larger things (e.g., your ancestral land, your nation).

First, getting more money. I had inadvertently entered the country with 50 undeclared dollars in 10-dollar bills. I had it in my knapsack, separate from my stash of travelers' checks, and I had simply forgotten to declare it at customs. In future years, I would do cartwheels to smuggle in undeclared cash for emergency black-marketing. But that first season, I had simply forgotten to declare the cash. Once I discovered my error, I even went to the government bank to try to declare it and fill out the appropriate legal forms. The clerk was utterly perplexed by me—at first, he made a halfhearted attempt to steal the money from me, to hold it there for presumed safekeeping, but seeing my insistence that he come up with some nonexistent form for me to do after-the-fact declaring of foreign currency, he finally brusquely told me to get lost.

So I had some undeclared cash and decided to try to black-market it, piecemeal. Normally, as I was slowly learning from the overlanders at the rooming house, this was done with careful, paranoid, silent Hindu businessmen with terrible complexions who owned the downtown electronics shops, part of the Indian middle class of East Africa. These are the credible businessmen who would give you, perhaps, 10 shillings to the dollar, instead of the going rate of 7 in the banks. Instead, I'd put on my backpack, walk down the main street of Nairobi, gawking at the people like a newcomer. Street sharps would instantly approach me, offering to change money at outlandish rates—change money? Change money? One dollar, 25 shillings. As I had learned, these were, of course, thieves. They normally get you in an alleyway and, if you are lucky, merely shout in a panic about how the "police" have found us, everyone run, and in the tussle, you lose your money. The less articulate fellows merely bash your head in in the alleyway and take your money.

This time, instead of telling the con artists to screw off, I say, Oh great, just got here to Nairobi, looking for someone to change money with, 25 shillings, what a great rate, glad to meet you. Tell him I only have 10 American dollars with me right now, but at the hotel where I'm staying (mention a fancy one), I have *five hundred dollars* that I want to change. Can you change the 10 right now and then meet me later for the 500?

Gulp, says the thief. Even thieves are sometimes disciplined, and he does a quick calculation—if he gives me 250 shillings for the 10 dollars now, this dumb-ass kid is going to come back with 500 bucks and *then* I bash his head in. Money is exchanged, friendship is sworn, a follow-up meeting time is arranged. Avoid that street thereafter, working a different one with the next 10-dollar bill.

This worked fine for making the money stretch. As the crisis worsened, even that money was finished. I sold my camera and film at awful prices. I lived for days on nothing but starch, which made me dizzy and stupid. I left the rooming house, took to sleeping in the city park, stole toilet paper from a downtown hotel. Four years earlier, in my first year of college, I had once traveled a great distance to see someone I barely knew who I felt sure would allow me to kiss her at the end of the day. Now, I hitchhiked two days to offhandedly drop in on a near-stranger of a researcher who I felt sure might feed me.

Eventually, I evolved my next scam. I would go to the city market, where there was a labyrinth of vegetable stalls. Sellers plead with you to buy their cabbages. When you are closer to them, they also try to sell you pot if you look like a plausible customer. I am told that some even do sell it, rather than merely rip you off or inform on you to the police, who then blackmail you.

You line up to buy vegetables with money you do not possess. Slick seller inquires whether you want pot. Yes, you betcha, what price. He names some silly price, you agree, proclaiming what a bargain it is. You arrange to return later with the money, he insists that you, his good friend, leave with free vegetables. Naturally, you avoid that stall thereafter. Critical thing is to start with the stall in the very back, and work your way forward with each day, so that you never encounter one of your disappointed friends again, who presumably now wants to slit your throat.

Finally, a number of days into not eating, I made the decision to just plain steal. The strategy seemed to be to simply walk into a middling-class hotel, sit down at the dining room table, and act colonial and confident, giving the number of your supposed room for billing when asked. No Kenyan waiter would dream of challenging you, I assumed. I had targeted the YMCA, planning to pass myself off as a young Christian man who had paid for a room. And on the very day that I intended to execute my plan, the cabled money appeared, the professor finally remembering my existence. Somehow, in my dizzied, food-deprived state, the YMCA seemed to me to have played some role in my salvation. And I would not forget this. A year later, as Uganda was in the middle of a war to overthrow Idi Amin, I would sleep in a bombed-out, roofless YMCA in a small Ugandan town and would give the proprietor what he considered to be an immense sum of money toward rebuilding the roof, thus atoning for my life of crime.

3

The Revenge of the Liberals

I am the angel of death. I am the reign of terror, the ten plagues, I am a case of the clap, I am the thing that goes bump in the night, De Shadow, death warmed over. I am the bogeyman with cat eyes waiting until midnight in every kid's clothes closet, I am leering slinky silent quicksilver baboon terror, I am Beelzebub's bill collector. Another baboon successfully darted. Euphoria. Today I darted Gums, the last baboon on earth I would have ever thought of getting. Wily old bugger, knew my every trick, had eluded me for months. I was near despair at ever getting a blood sample from him, and today, he screwed up. Surrounded himself in presumed safety in a crowd of females, figured he was safe, figured they would take the fall if there was a rubout, figured I'd never dare shoot into a crowd, but he was wrong! They all had their heads turned, he miscalculated the space between two closely spaced trees, and, *ffft*, I sent an anesthetic dart sailing from the blowgun into his ass. Unconscious in four minutes. Musk triumph power loins dawn-of-man science. It was all I could do to keep from savaging his soft underbelly with my canines while he was down.

Darting. As I said, the main thing I wanted to learn when I first joined the troop was what a baboon's social behavior, his social rank, his emotional life, has to do with what diseases he gets, especially stress-related diseases. Why are some bodies, and some psyches, more susceptible to such diseases than others? So you watch the animals like crazy, carefully document the whole soap opera. Then dart them with an anesthetic blowgun and find out how their bodies are working. Theoretically simple. Approach a baboon you typically walk up to twelve times a day while you're doing behavioral observation, except *this time,* your walking stick turns out to be a blowgun and you zip a dart into him. The only problem is that you have to dart everyone at the same time of day, to control for daily fluctuation in blood hormones. And you can't dart someone if he's sick that day, has had a fight, an injury, mated—because

37

those will throw off the normal values of the hormones. Finally, and here's the real pisser, you can't dart someone if he knows it's coming. If I'm trying to see what stress hormone levels in the bloodstream are like under normal unstressed resting conditions, I have to get the baboons when they are quiet, unsuspecting. I must sneak up on them. No witnesses. To wit, I dart baboons in the back for a living. And then get a first blood sample as fast as possible before normal values are thrown off by the stress of being darted.

What I actually wind up doing for a living is trying to act nonchalant around baboons, get them to turn around, forget about me. Which is a lot trickier than you'd think, even with a college education.

You wake up at five in the morning, tense as hell, get things ready in the dark. Anesthetic, darts, blowgun, syringes, vacutainers, centrifuge, liquid nitrogen tanks, needles, vials, burlap to cover the animal, instant ice bags, cages, scales, emergency medicines if there's an accident, powerverters to run everything off of the Jeep batteries, pipettes, slides, test tubes, endless crap. Find the baboons by six-thirty, as they come down off their rocks or trees that they slept in. Pick someone, start stalking, start calculating—which way will he run when hit, up a tree? Up the rocks? How do you get him down if he does that so that he doesn't pass out and fall? What if he attacks someone else, what if he gets attacked—who's pissed off at him these days and would love to slash his throat while he's staggering around half-conscious? What if he attacks you? Which direction is the wind going, how much do you have to compensate in the shot, shit, can't shoot, some weasly kid is looking right at you, go stalk from a different position, he's not looking, no one else looking, ready for a shot, fabulous, fabulous, this is going to be perfect, get ready, feel absolutely sick to your stomach with tension, realize you're hyperventilating so much that you can't blow the blowgun properly—you'll either accidentally inhale the dart or shoot it two feet because of shallow breath. Shit, shit, he's moved again, reposition, control your breath, he's looking straight at you now, act nonchalant, how the hell do you act nonchalant in front of a baboon anyway? He's in a perfect position now, but turned sideways, too much peripheral vision. Crouch and wait, tense, not moving a muscle, near to cramping, there's some goddamn bug biting your calf, but you don't want to move, keep still still still until you realize you just want to scream and run amok and bowl him over, then perfect, a fight breaks out elsewhere, irresistible to baboon voyeurs, he turns around, cranes his neck to look at the action elsewhere, full clear beautiful meaty rear end, zip!, dart in his ass, and he's off.

Panic, heavy breathing, heart racing: you, not him. He ambles off, thinking he's only been stung by a bee. After him, trying not to chase him, trying not to lose him in the bush. Minutes, *minutes,* endless time, three minutes and he gets wobbly, staggers a bit, decides to sit down and take it easy a bit because the drugs are beginning to work and the acacia trees probably have a purple aura and are beginning to spin around, the zebras are all doing some dance number from *The Lion King.* He's getting woozier, everything is under control, perfect darting, when some rival bastard comes up to hassle him while he's hallucinating. Shoo the rival guy away, just in time, because, *splot,* your guy's out cold. Run over, throw a burlap bag over him, take a fast, surreptitious blood sample, and adrenaline city, androgenic triumph, you've successfully darted a wild baboon—stalked him in the bush and took him out—perfect to shore up your precarious sense of manhood and, *best of all,* you're not even doing something appalling like hunting, you're doing it all in the name of science and conservation. You can wipe out innocent beatific baboons and still be a liberal. Oh, joy.

The rush is over with, and you have to get him out of there. The Jeep is half a kilometer away over a ridge, you have to spirit him away without anyone else in the troop seeing you or else they'll freak and rip you to shreds. Seventy-pound baboon wrapped in burlap, and you're *tiptoeing* through the middle of the troop, arms aching, trying not to run or giggle or collapse from exhaustion. The guy's snoring and you try to shush him. Get up over the ridge, nearing the Jeep, feel like you're going to die, but you're almost there. You begin to plan the rest of the day—what time do you have to take the subsequent blood samples, what other tests will you do on him, what time will he be awake enough to release him back to the troop, which seven baboons are you going to dart flawlessly tomorrow. He's bouncing along on your shoulder like a sack of potatoes, and suddenly he burps. You are unspeakably charmed by that and thus let your guard down, and ten seconds later he throws up down your back, a thick lava flow.

So goes a darting; there's nothing I enjoy more in the world. I learned how to dart baboons in a dormitory room in Manhattan. It was on my first break back in the States after I had joined the troop. I was boiling with schemes about the research. The biggest problem was how to dart on foot, to work on foot in general, and not get smeared by some buffalo. There was a guy from Berkeley named Laurence who lived over on the next mountain who studied hyenas. Laurence of the Hyenas had just gotten a donation of an old pair of infrared light-enhancing night-viewing goggles from the military, which allowed him to drive around in pitch darkness and follow his hyenas, all the while with the twenty-pound contraption strapped to his head. I decided I needed a similar high-tech solution; I would get a Flash Gordon jet pack from the army. I knew they existed, and figured if I could lumber around the

Serengeti with one, I'd be safe. Buffalo comes at me, and I'd be gone, into the air, a god to the local Masai tribesmen. I called the Pentagon, got shuffled through a dozen of their R & D groups, finally found a colonel who thought the problem was fascinating. He confirmed that the jet packs existed, would check into it for me, generously offered to call back. A week later he had the bad news—he was afraid that I'd have to go to something bigger than the U.S. military for my jet pack—the Disney people had the only working model on earth. I called them, was told by someone far less courteous than the colonel that the jet packs weighed ninety pounds, took a minute to warm up, required asbestos pants, and were not available for loan to some zoologist. End of that idea; instead, I merely had to look out for buffalo and use some common sense in where I wandered in the bush.

Next, I had to figure out what to dart the baboons with. I checked out some long-distance, gas-powered anesthetic rifles, but they all cost a fortune, and had all these moving parts that would gum up in the field, and required replacement gas cylinders, and mostly made too much noise. I checked into tasers, which are guns that shoot an electrode on a wire into the target. Zap the guy, press a button, and some insane number of volts shoots through his body and he goes down like a sack of creamed spinach. Dandy, but apparently prone to giving the subject cardiac arrest, as a number of police forces were apparently discovering. I thought of feeding the animals drugged meat, using drugged snares, spraying a mind-clouding gas over the entire troop, and so on. Finally, I stumbled on a small Southern company that sold anesthetic blowguns to canine control units. Their brochure featured pictures of the executives who were all good ol' boys with tobacco chaws in their mouths and John Deere caps on, they sold a cheap blowgun that shot out a 1cc syringe with a contact explosive, and it sounded terrific. The package arrived, and I was as excited as I was in second grade when the We-Like-to-Read book club would send the cartons of books with the shiny smell. The gun was a narrow reinforced tube, with little dart syringes, each with a formidable needle and some sort of explosive that I didn't understand. I set up my Arm and Hammer detergent box across the room, loaded up, fired, and blew detergent all over my bookshelf.

I practiced relentlessly in my room. Angled shots, pointing down, pointing up, fast spinning shots, over the shoulder, in the wind (with the fan turned on). Allan, a stolid graduate school friend with a low center of gravity who had been a standout lineman on his Fredonia, Kansas, high school football squad, consented for me to practice wrestling him as if he were a darted baboon. This was done in the dorm basement next to the Gene Cloners club room.

Time went by and I improved. I could have darted a baboon anywhere in my room, in or out of Groucho Marx's pajamas. Two fantasies dominated my darting then. I wanted to dart Fritz Lipmann. Lipmann was an incredibly famous biochemist, got the Nobel Prize decades ago, and now was an august octogenarian who would spend his day shuffling around the campus in his running shoes, endlessly passing my first-floor dorm window. I would get him in my blowgun sights from behind my biochemistry textbooks (which were half about him), choose between his rear end and shoulders, try to calculate his body weight for a proper dosage. I refrained from darting, however. The other fantasy was to sneak into Central Park and dart some random people. While they were down, I would quickly Magic Marker some Mayan hieroglyphic on their bellies and leave them to wake up soon thereafter underneath the *Alice in Wonderland* statue. I figured three such cases and the newspapers would be screaming, TV pundits would lecture on Mayan rituals of sacrifice, Jimmy Breslin would beg for me to give myself up, frenzied angry crowds would form around police stations in which jobless PhD archaeologists would try to come up with feeble alibis about how they weren't the Mayan Darter.

The months passed and it was time to return to the field. I spent the entire night before my first darting awake and tossing, feeling queasy. By dawn, I was sick to my stomach, convinced I was about to pass out, all an excuse to get out of it. Finally, I headed out. And within a few minutes, I walked up to dear Isaac, who was watching some giraffe walk past, controlled my desire to scream a warning to him, and darted him. And he passed out. And none of the other baboons saw. I was so excited that I kissed him on the forehead, and then spent the rest of the day fretting with guilty concern every time he groaned or shifted or farted—heart attack, allergic reaction, darting-induced flatulence? We both recovered from the darting just fine.

And I darted more and more baboons, thought like a baboon, had baboon on my breath, was soon up to my ears in baboon blood samples and fecal smears and dental casts and all sorts of neat things. Then, expectedly, the process got harder and harder. The darting itself turned out to be trivial, the process of pointing a blowgun at someone's rear and causing the dart to reach there. It was getting to the point of darting. The baboons just got more and more wily. I could no longer just walk up to someone and dart him. Instead, I had to become increasingly surreptitious, so that the baboons didn't know it was coming, didn't have an anticipatory stress response. The baboons began to differentiate between a blowgun and a walking stick. They could tell if I was inhaling to dart or to sneeze, and hit the dirt for the former. I started to have to dart from behind bushes. They would start doubling back on me, we'd circle around a tree, the target one step ahead. They figured out my darting range, knew it was shorter in the wind. They could probably tell if I had a chest cold and was taking shallower breaths. It was uncanny.

Things got increasingly complicated. I took to darting from vehicles. I would have to switch vehicles when they learned one. Soon, I would have friends drive the Jeep, while I hid in the back. Decoys, extra vehicles. Southern-sheriff sunglasses to keep the baboon from seeing where you're looking, trying to look out the side of your head. Ski masks, a plastic Halloween mask that made it nearly impossible to use the blowgun. Complex schemes, hiding behind tourist cars, stakeouts hours in advance, hoping the baboons would pass by me before nightfall. On one memorable day's darting, I came up to Joshua, sitting behind a bush on top of a mound. I rolled the Jeep to the front of the bush, he moved to the back end. I moved the Jeep to the back, he shifted to the front. This went on for a while. Finally an inspiration—rolled the Jeep to the back, he moved front. Put the Jeep in neutral, slithered out the far side, went to the back, and pushed. The Jeep rolled forward down the mound, he moved backward straight into my trap. One baboon darted, one Jeep hood dented from rolling into a tree.

A peculiar thing happens under these sorts of circumstances. You find yourself, a reasonably well educated human with a variety of interests, spending hours and hours each day and night obsessing on how to outmaneuver these beasts, how to think like them, how to think better than them. Usually unsuccessfully. Your mind runs wild with unlikely schemes, using hang gliders, hot air balloons, mannequins, being wheeled through the forest hidden in a perambulator. During those difficult times, at least I could take p.ide in what I consider to be one of my greatest points of professionalism in this venture: I have yet to take out an innocent bystander—I've never darted the wrong baboon. People get their money's worth when they hire me for a contract.

Oddly, people started hiring me to do just that—come to their research site, collaborate in their studies by darting their baboons. Suddenly, a whole new pressure—assembly-line darting. Instead of having an entire season to lollygag around with the baboons and pick them off in between days of just collecting behavioral data, you show up at some new research site, don't know a baboon there or the terrain, and have to get twelve in the next week. Big complex productions involving teams of people from the new research site. In one place, we would follow the baboons off cliffs where they slept down to the plains where they foraged each day—the researchers at that site whom I had trained to dart and I going after baboons on the plain, spotters up on the cliffs, waving flags to indicate where in the bush the darted animals had gone. Walkie-talkies, semaphores, great fun.

So I was on my way to honing my life's vocation. And it was right around that time that I had my most disastrous darting ever.

It was a perfect darting of Uriah, shortly before he laid siege to Solomon. He was snoozing in the forest, back to me, long good shot, had the gun away before he could turn around. He jumped up, ran about ten steps, and sat down again. Everything going fine. Then, suddenly, twenty feet to the right, Joshua knocked over an impala, a small one, grazing in the forest. Impalas are usually too big for a single death bite to the neck. Instead, the typical game plan is to just knock them down and hold them while you eat them alive, everyone else all over you for a piece, so you'd better be more concerned about your compatriots than bothering to kill the impala; it's not going anywhere. Joshua brings down the impala and Uriah is up in a shot, wrestles Joshua, and comes up with the impala. Shit, disaster. He's off and running into the forest with four big guys after him. They all wrestle, I'm praying that he loses it so the pressure is off him, he can just go and get stupid on the anesthetic quietly. Instead, he holds on to the impala—I'm panicked, the minute he starts weakening from the anesthetic, he's going to get ripped apart; males are unbelievably aggressive fighting over a kill. He wrestles, runs with it, and barrels into this tiny corner of the riverbed, into a thick clump of thorn bushes that has only a single entrance—effectively, a small enclosed cave with one opening, a bunch of branches with about a one-foot clearance on the bottom. He holes up in there, you can hear the impala screaming bloody hell inside, and any of the males who go near the entrance get Uriah flinging himself at them. They have to squeeze through on their bellies into the cave, which puts them at a major disadvantage; Uriah'd be on them before they'd even get up.

So here's the problem: I have to get Uriah out of his little bush cave soon, because if the other males can get at him, they're going to rip him apart if he's half-conscious. But if I go into that cave when he's more than half-conscious, he's going to rip me apart, as he's in an aggressive frenzy himself. Everyone is standing around outside, agitated, threatening me as I go near the entrance. The impala is still screaming, so I finally decide if it's yelling so healthfully, Uriah must be asleep in there, hasn't killed it yet. I jump up and down, yelling and gesticulating, to scare away everyone else. Clutching my syringes and catheters for blood sampling, I psych up and slowly slide into the cave on my back, waiting to be attacked. Get inside the tiny space, about three feet high, and find that Uriah is sound asleep, slumped down on the thoroughly alive impala, whose stomach has been ripped open.

Now that I'm inside, safe and sound with the snoozing Uriah, it occurs to me that there is no way either of us is coming out safely unless the impala goes out the sole exit to the waiting dinner crowd first. I ponder the moral implications of my being a central actor in that particular drama for a while as the male tumult begins to build up outside again. The shaft of light coming into the cave is occluded—someone is beginning to crawl in. I hoot loudly once and the shadow disappears. This seems likely to be only a temporary respite; I'd better do something. In the middle of all these worries, I suddenly become concerned about saving my stupid experiment on Uriah, i.e., getting a blood sample from him before it is too late to use the data. With assured and calm movements, I roll Uriah over for a sample, completely forgetting something critical—the impala. It's up in a shot, kicking, flailing, sharp goddamn hooves. It kicks me in the forehead, knocking me back, opening up a big gash. I can't believe it—I'd forgotten about the impala. Here I am, figuring out a way to avoid all this craziness with these mad aggressive male baboons and I'm about to be killed by Bambi. The impala is bellowing, all the males immediately outside start screaming bloody hell, I give up my composure and start yelling my head off also. The impala is trying to bash through the other side of the thorn bush, no luck, kicking again at my face. Finally, I freak out, convinced it's about to kill me, which is not out of the question in that small a space. I jump on it and I believe I actually strangle it. I was so frantic I was definitely flailing it around, bashing its head on the ground. Then a profoundly chilling moment: I had to get the impala out of there. Start pushing it on the ground, now a dead weight, under the branches through the opening. Heavy, lots of friction, as it moves along the thorny ground, and suddenly, as I am slowly, slowly pushing it out—the sensation of its heavy body moving forward faster than I am pushing it—there is a primate hand on the impala's shoulder, pulling on it. The carcass flies away, is gone. Wild fighting and screaming outside as four males converge on it, playing steal the bacon. I'm terrified someone is going to try to hide in here with the carcass, but they all seem to remember that something strange is happening in this bush cave and they tear around outside instead. I huddle inside in terror, get my wits about me, and take blood from Uriah. Thirty minutes of tumult and yelling and snarling outside, shadows blowing past; hunker down there with the contentedly snoring Uriah until the carcass is done and everyone moves off. Uriah and I go and take a nap in the Jeep.

So went my worst darting ever. Kind of a silly way to spend one's time. But writing nearly two decades later, darting remains in my blood. The other night,

I was at the movies and watched some matron amble down the aisle past me, and my first thoughts were "85–90 kilos, .9 cc's of anesthetic. Go for her rump, lots of meat. Her husband will probably defend her when she goes down, but he has small canines." I am still delighted to be doing this for a living.

4

The Masai Fundamentalist
and My Debut as a Social Worker

Sure, it was great getting to hang out with a bunch of baboons, but the rest of the novel world I had flung myself into that first year was pretty interesting as well, and at the top of the list of amazing things for me to assimilate was having Masai as my neighbors. Most of Kenya never was a *National Geographic* special, and much of what still is is fast disappearing. Of the forty or so distinct tribes in the country, perhaps thirty of them are made up of agriculturalists, most of them ethnically Bantu—farmers eking out a living on the terraced slopes of their overpopulated mountains with one or two members of each extended family in the cash economy, trying to get the money for a first bicycle, watch, or pair of jeans, or to replace the traditional grass thatch roof with tin. These people are abundantly aware that there is an outside world and occasionally get enough of a glimmer of what that might mean so as to fervently want a piece of it for themselves and their kids.

But in the far corners of the country are the handful of tribes who are not trying to change, who have not yet become embarrassed by who they are. On the coast, by the Indian Ocean, are the Swahili Muslim tribes whose antiquity and culture and self-assurance put anything in the West to shame. Pushed into the remaining tracts of thick rain forests are the last hunter-gatherers, ethnically related to the Pygmies and Bushmen in other parts of Africa—silent, diminutive, graceful people whose ancient lifestyle predates the invention of agriculture, predates the dominating influx of the Bantu tribes.

And in the parts of the country often regarded as open, howling wastelands are the nomadic pastoralists. Wanderers, contemptuous of hunting, contemptuous of farming, those in the north living off the blood and milk of camels and goats, and in the more benign southern grasslands of my baboons, off of the blood and milk of their cows. It is a pattern repeated throughout Africa—the Watutsi of Rwanda, the Dinkas of Sudan, and, as the most likely to grace the cover of some Out of Africa coffee table book, the Masai of my neck of the woods. All of them ethnically and linguistically related; tall, angular Cushitic or Nilo-Hamitic people. Regal, aloof, intensely clannish, warlike as hell, raiding and plundering the agricultural tribes of whatever area they were passing through since time immemorial. I've always been intensely charmed by a theory that has floated around for years that way back when, a couple of millennia ago, the ancestors of all of these cow people were a garrison of Sudanese soldiers on the southern edge of the decaying Roman Empire—there is apparently some support for this idea in the clan and military organization of all of these tribes, as well as in the patterns of some of their military regalia. They happened to wander south a bit down the Nile, discovered that the agriculturalists were pushovers, and just kept wandering, until they had spread out all over the continent.

The Masai certainly fit that pattern. They had appeared on the Kenyan scene somewhere in the nineteenth century, wandering down from the northern deserts and wreaking havoc among everyone in their path. By the turn of the century, they had pretty much displaced the local Kikuyu farmers from the central highlands of Kenya, the lush heartland of the agricultural region. Today, a century later, the rivers and mountains of that region still bear Masai names.

Inconveniently, the Masai had usurped the Kikuyu just around the time that the Brits had started flexing their colonial muscles with plans to do the same. The Kikuyu seemed like altogether more reasonable people to steal land from than the Masai. Things might have turned nasty, requiring a bit of a dust-up, had not a jolly good pandemic intervened to help enforce Pax Britannia. In 1898, a staggering outbreak of a cattle disease called rinderpest occurred, killing about 80 percent of the cows and, as a result, a big chunk of the Masai as well. That took a bit of wind out of the sails of the famed warriors, making them altogether more docile negotiating adversaries. In 1906, the Brits concluded a treaty with the Masai. In exchange for giving up the plush central highlands, the Masai would get not one but two promised lands, one a desiccated track of grassland in the north, the other, my baboons' grassland of the south, plus a corridor linking the two to facilitate cattle drives. Swell deal; the Masai decamped. Within a few years, the Brits had taken away the northern land plus the now superfluous corridor, everyone squeezed into the southern grasslands, which turned out to have pretty substantial amounts of cattle sleeping sickness. Even though the Masai would continue to this day to be ferociously predatory toward their immediate neighbors, never again would they pose the threat of occupying some land that the Brits had measured out for a cricket pitch.

And so, the Masai have lived happily ever after. They have resolutely tried to hold back the twentieth century while much of the rest of the country leapt into its worst excesses, washed down with a bottle of Coke. Sure, in some corners of Masai land, change was coming. In the county seat, for example, fifty miles from my game park, one might spot some Masai guys hanging out and chewing the fat, half in business suits, holding briefcases, half in cloaks, holding spears. But in the relatively isolated corner I had settled in, nothing had shifted much. The nearest school was thirty miles away and perhaps one person per village spoke Swahili, every man still had to kill a lion with his spear in order to achieve warrior status, marriages were still polygamous, and wedding parties still always featured big tureens of coagulated cow's blood for dessert. It was not yet a world that was particularly open to new ideas.

I discovered this in a rather disconcerting way one morning during that first season in the troop. I had just pulled off a great darting, although a slightly unfair one. Solomon was in his first consortship with Devorah, the young daughter of highest-ranking Leah. They were mating in the bushes, mating in a tree, mating in the open field. She had a maximal swelling, probably ovulating, probably smelled like a dream, and ol' Solomon couldn't keep away from her. No, no, it's not what you think, I did not sneak up and dart Solomon in the back while he was mating. I have my professional standards. I darted Daniel. Squirrely little adolescent Daniel was sneaking around all day watching the two—couldn't take his eyes off them, spent the whole morning following at a not-so-discreet distance, trying to see the action, craning his neck, taking it all in, no doubt hoping to pick up some pointers from Solomon on how to meet female baboons.

So Daniel was more interested in voyeurism than keeping an eye on me, let his guard down, and I had zipped a dart into his keister. He had gone under fast, easy fun darting, and I was gamboling back. About a kilometer's walk to the Jeep, and he didn't weigh much. I was actually sort of skipping back, happy, with Daniel cradled in my arms. Great morning.

Marching over hill and dale with my sleepy boy, I encounter two Masai warriors, wrapped in their distinctive red cloaks and nothing else, guys from the village past the one where I was beginning to make some friends. They are quite interested in the baboon. I put him down for a rest, want to show him off. Lookihere, look at my baboon.

"Is he dead?" Atypically for these parts, one of them spoke some Swahili in addition to Maa, the language of the Masai. My Maa was nonexistent, but my Swahili was sort of serviceable.

"Nah, just sleeping."

"Why is he sleeping?"

"I have given him a special medicine to make him sleep."

"If you give that medicine to a man, will he sleep?"

"You betcha," I say. I go on, stating what seems to be an obvious truism. "That is because the body of a baboon is very much like the body of a man."

Both warriors seem utterly perplexed by this idea.

"No it is not," says the other Masai through his friend's translation. "A man is a man and a baboon is a wild animal."

"Yes, but we are very close, we are almost like relatives."

"No we are not," says the Masai, who is seeming a bit piqued.

I push my point. "But once we were even like baboons, we even had tails, we were close relatives."

"No way."

"Yes, yes, up north, in the desert, they have even found bones of people who are not really people, they are half people, with heads like baboons."

"No way."

"Yes, in my country, the doctors can even take the heart out of a man and give him the heart of a baboon, he will be fine, he will live to be an old man (okay, so I exaggerate medical progress a bit). I could take out *your* heart and give you a baboon heart and you would still be a warrior."

"You cannot. No way." He's getting a bit testy. The other Masai has been bending down, examining Daniel, picking through his fur, exposing the surprisingly white skin of a baboon.

"Look," I say, pointing to the white skin, "just like mine."

"No, you are a red man." I find this to be immensely pleasing, although no doubt he means I look like a white guy out in the sun on his way to a melanoma, rather than noting my natural resemblance to Crazy Horse.

"No, I am really a white man." I hitch up my shorts, expose my untanned rear. "Look. White, just like the baboon."

Suddenly, I get this giddy desire to shock these guys a little. I continue, "These baboons really are our relatives. In fact, this baboon is my cousin." And with that I lean over and give Daniel a loud messy kiss on his big ol' nose.

I get more of a response than I bargained for. The Masai freak and suddenly, they are waving their spears *real* close to my face, like they mean it. One is yelling, "He is not your cousin, he is not your cousin! A baboon cannot even cook ugali!" (Ugali is the ubiquitous and repulsive maize meal that everyone eats here. I almost respond that I don't really know how to cook the stuff either, but decide to show some prudence at last.) "He is not your cousin!"

He is pointing the spear right at me, and real slow and calm I say, Okay, okay, you're absolutely right, you know what? He's not really my cousin, he is not a relative, I've never even seen this guy before in my life, I just work here, etc. After many words of this sort, the Masai are finally mollified, put down their spears, and tell me in very broken Kenyan English that they are my friends very much.

End of incident, we go our separate ways swearing eternal brotherhood. How unlikely it would have been to be speared by a fundamentalist wearing no pants.

A short time later, I got another lesson as to how the Masai were dealing with new ideas. I had made my contacts with the nearest village, was beginning to make some acquaintances there, and had lucked out in finding an ideal person to introduce me to that world. My first friend was Rhoda, half Masai and half Kikuyu, the village's emissary to the outside world. Most probably, Rhoda's mother was taken by Masai warriors during a raid on a Kikuyu village, resulting in her forced marriage into Masaidom. Her mother had presumably been old enough to have learned much about her own tribe as well as the outside world that was just encroaching at the time, and Rhoda had been brought up as a complete anomaly—she speaks Swahili and some English in addition to her Maa and Kikuyu, can read a bit and handle money, can hitch a ride fifty miles to the county seat and negotiate the sale of some of the village's cattle and coordinate purchasing desired supplies in return. She has single-handedly brought driblets of the Western world into the village and, by inventing the middle class in the village, has also invented class lines in this "African socialist" society as well.

On some occasions, I was struck with how much of the outside world Rhoda could have gotten hints of, while still having an utterly Masai mindset. This I experienced the day I quizzed her about how to say "lion" in Maa. I had been leafing through my new Maa dictionary and had discovered that there are actually two names for lion. One, which I had been taught by Rhoda, turns out to be the fake name for lion. It is the one you say out in the open, and is not the real name. The real name, in contrast, is said only in the safety of your house at night. The dictionary explained that the Masai believe that if you say the real name of the lion out-of-doors, the lion will hear its name being called, will come and eat you.

Howsabout it, Rhoda, is that true? Yes, it is true, you should not say that name; she gets visibly itchy each time I do. Aw, come on, Rhoda, the lion isn't going to come. Yes, I have seen that many times, it will come and eat you. Aw, come on, really. Well, I have heard that that will happen.

I push harder. Come on, Rhoda, are you telling me that the lion will hear its name, you know that lions cannot understand that, they wouldn't come.

Yes, they will come.

The lion understands Masai language?

Finally, she gets irritated, and in one petulant paragraph, sums up the two worlds she knows about and how she balances them.

"The lion cannot understand its name. Anyone who has been to school knows that a lion cannot understand the language of people.... But if you say that word too many times outside, the lion will come and eat you."

The subject was closed, as far as she was concerned.

Now, I was about to discover just how much Rhoda was able to embrace outside ideas while still keeping one foot anchored in Masaidom. It had been a fabulous morning with the baboons. Young serene Joshua had been working his charm with skittish Ruth, consorting with her; some jerk adolescent male was hassling Job and had been mauled as a result by the righteous Rachel; Benjamin had sat next to me on a log. It didn't get better than that, so I'd decided to take off the rest of the day, to drop in on the village to visit Rhoda and her family. Rhoda looks completely Kikuyu: a little dumpling of a woman amid all the lanky ectomorphic Masai. Giggly, effusive, and motherly—more traits to set her apart from most of the villagers. Normally missing is her husband, who is a ranger in the park and is usually assigned to some distant outpost, patrolling for poachers. He is the tallest, gangliest, meanest, scariest-looking Masai I've ever known, especially when he is carrying an automatic weapon in his ranger's uniform. Actually, he is exceedingly gentle, especially when talking about the baby rhino under his guard, or when bending over double literally and figuratively to dote on small, pear-shaped Rhoda, whom he calls "mama." They make one of the odder-looking couples around, if one of the most endearing. Just to add some waves to the placid scene of a nuclear family are his second and third wives, both of whom are quite junior to Rhoda and are gently bossed around by her. The minute Rhoda's husband is off duty, he is out of uniform and back in his Masai cloak, cruising the village with his wives and many children. One child does not accompany him, however, as that one got some sort of fever and encephalitis during his first rainy season, so far as I can reconstruct, and was left a hydrocephalic monster with the neurological reflexes of a newborn. Rhoda and her husband spent god knows how many months' salary to buy an absurd, poignant British perambulator, circa 1940, that now sits in the mud and cow-dung house, the swaddled bug-eyed head of the kid peering out from it, moaning chronically.

Anyway, I stop in to say hello, and Rhoda takes advantage of the situation to commandeer my vehicle. Soon, we are driving the three kilometers to the trading post, instead of her having to walk. I find myself nostalgically reliving the irritation that all boys feel when forced to go shopping with Mom. We go into the store—also mud and dung and branches, run by the other half Masai, half Kikuyu, in the region, an old grizzled friend of Rhoda's. Rhoda inspects the twenty-odd items available in the store—two types of blankets, soap, soda, maize meal, eggs, sugar, tea, flashlights, batteries, bulbs, malaria medicine, snuff (a favorite of Masai). Then she goes to work comparative shopping. She has me stretch out the two types of blankets to compare their length and to estimate which would cover her children. This is academic—she is just window-shopping for blankets today, and besides, the same two models are the only ones that have ever existed here. She checks out the soap, hefts the individual flashlight bulbs, and finally settles on her choices for the day: an egg and two potatoes. She is happy with the half hour of shopping, and we return to the village, where I am invited for tea.

Trouble starts. Serere, the younger brother of her husband, is there and drunk. Serere is a fine man who, unfortunately, is hurtling toward the frequent accompaniment of Masai elderhood, namely being drunk half the time. Over the course of the traveling I would do throughout Africa in my free time in the years to come, it would become apparent that drunks were a major problem, but only if they were friendly drunks, as Serere always was. Angry drunks would be simple, because the same thing would always happen. Invariably, I would be hitching through some hamlet, waiting to catch a lift, and I would be accosted by an angry drunk who wanted to fight. Always an angry, incoherent character who in mixed English and Swahili would tell me that he wanted to fight, was going to fight *me,* and that he was an "A–number one Mr. Big [an idiom in Swahili—*bwana kubwa*] absolutely kung fu Muhammad Ali." I would be unafraid, not because I am capable of winning a fistfight with anyone except Mother Teresa, but because I would always be saved in the same way. I would stand there smiling moronically. A crowd would form and out of it would always burst an incredibly meek man, always in a white shirt and—here's the giveaway—pen in his shirt pocket. It would be the town schoolteacher, horrified at the insult to a visitor, the possibly literate and thus distinguished whitey. He would indignantly intervene with Mr. Kung Fu Muhammad Ali and, since, like all schoolteachers here, he would probably have been *the* schoolteacher since time began, the drunk was once his pupil and was under his magic sway. A veritable Norman Rockwell scene would ensue—"Schoolteacher admonishing his former pupil, the town drunk," drunk sheepish, incoherent apologies, looking at his feet, etc. Schoolteacher would then happily take me to his place for tea, where he would quiz me on the American presidents, attempt to discuss our lord Jesus Christ, and make me give him an example of my penmanship.

Thus, the mean drunks are easy, if you remember the order of the presidents. It's the friendly ones who are a problem. The minute they see you, they want to kill something for you. I once visited a friend at his family farm. His older brother George, drunkard, bully, black sheep, wife beater, child abandoner, etc., took a shine to me, and spent four days while I was there trying to slaughter his only cow, goat, so on, in my honor. The very last dinner, we're all sitting round the fire pit and gorging ourselves, all except George, who is missing. Suddenly, he bursts into the room, glowering in drunken concentration. In his hands he is holding a chicken. He marches up to me and in a spasm of alcoholic oration, sputters, You . . . are . . . my . . . *friend!*, and flings the chicken at me. Unfortunately, in his state, he has neglected to bind its legs and wings, and the bird goes scattering in terror, flying, squawking, crapping all over us and the food.

Now a similar menace, Serere immediately wants to slaughter one of his few goats in my honor (mind you, this is a village I constantly drop in on). I talk my way out of it, and he retreats to the corner, a bit sullen. Rhoda and I settle in for tea. As always, it is an interesting affair watching someone find anything in a Masai house. They are made of mud and dung, a labyrinth from the doorway so that no light penetrates except for holes here and there in the roof that let in shafts of light. Somewhere in there is a cow skin bed, somewhere some goats, maybe an old man sleeping off his boozing with Serere, somewhere the nightmare perambulator child.

We sit contentedly drinking tea. Rhoda goes to a secret cubbyhole where she has hidden more and, *disaster!,* she discovers someone has taken her stash of money. Rhoda, half Kikuyu, half Masai, the leading edge of all that is modern in this village, was among the first to introduce cash into the Masai world, and she is using every cent of hers and her husband's (one of the only men working a "job") to pay school fees for the kids. The money is gone. She knows the culprit—Serere has taken the money and used it for drink at the local tourist camp's staff canteen instead of drinking the home brew. Serere, proud arrogant Masai warrior and elder, admits his crime with a proud dismissive shrug, as if to say, Woman, this is my prerogative. Rhoda, with a howl, smashes him across the side with a firewood log.

All hell breaks loose. Serere regains his footing while Rhoda, wailing and shouting, chases him around the room. Once, he stands his ground shakily and reaches for his spear, as if to do her in, and Rhoda, outraged at his impertinence, decks him again with the log. More shouting and wailing, and the room quickly fills with villagers, excited and voyeuristic. Old grizzled elders take the corner, the young mamas stand behind Rhoda, everyone else crowds in to watch.

A scene out of a temperance play ensues. Rhoda and her female coterie wail and complain. Five years ago, the government would come to Masai country and demand one child per district per year to send to school, and parents hid their loved ones against the horror. By now, women like Rhoda in each village are agitating for the kids to be sent to schools—bookless, penless, paperless, nearly teacherless huts perhaps thirty miles away where school fees are demanded in exchange for a dubious education. The avant-garde in Masai land want their kids educated, and none more than Rhoda and her band. She and her supporters wail that the old men have got to stop drinking up all the school fees for the kids, the kids have to go to school. Rhoda takes the lead—she is articulate, she is the radical in the village, the new wave, Bolshie bra burner who, with her half-Kikuyu heritage, has brought all sorts of suspicious ideas into the village but is tolerated because of her smarts, her outside skills, her schemes for bringing cash into the village. And for what, to have it drunk up by you stinking old men! The accusation has generalized beyond Serere, now perhaps comatose on the floor, and has focused on all the old geezers. The goings-on are being translated from Maa into Swahili and English for me, and various individuals in the fray seem to be turning to me at various points in the argument, glancing at me expectantly. I begin to suspect with some horror that I am being viewed as an arbitrator.

Rhoda's women are certain that it's a swell idea to spend their money shipping the kids away to the empty schoolhouse with no books or paper or pencils before they are shipped back a few years later to tend the cows. "You old men have to stop drinking the school fees so that the children can go to school and wear school uniforms." The old men say, in effect, Schooling, a waste of time, stupid stuff, we old men work hard, we should be able to get blind stupid falling-down drunk whenever we want to (an old man here is anyone over twenty-five, an ex-warrior, and thus an elder likely to have recently married a thirteen-year-old. Contrary to the claims of these particular old men, old men do the least work in the village, the order of labor generally being women, children, dogs, donkeys, and only then the men). Amid continued yelling, the old men are adamant—"Ah, school, stupid stuff. What good is school anyway?" they demand.

The women fall back, a bit confused. In truth, Rhoda is the only one to have a clear idea of what a school really is, having gone to one for a bit. They regroup, confer, and start yelling, "Well, you old men have to stop drinking up all the money because there is no money to spend for food for the children." Aw, gowon, the old men say, we're Masai, there's plenty of food, there's cows, aren't there? There's always cow blood for the kids to drink, there's always milk, whataya dames complaining about anyway, Jeez Louise, etc. They're chortling and making fun of Rhoda and her band, which is shrinking in number by the minute. Aw, the kids look fine, the old men conclude (actually, protein mal-nutrition, malaria, tuberculosis, and every parasite ever known runs rampant in these kids). Rhoda, alarmingly, suddenly demands my judgment. I hem and haw, and come up with an attempt at a compromise:

"Look, if the kids are well fed and go to school now, they will learn *so* much and afterward get *such* good jobs and bring home *so* much money that you old men will be able to get drunk *all the time* on the really good stuff, the stuff they sell to the white people in the tourist lodge."

This is briefly acclaimed, but is lost in a sudden outburst of old men com-plaining about Rhoda—who is this Kikuyu woman anyway? She looks kind of short and round to me, not sure if we should trust her, blah blah.

Rhoda, in a fury, as her last supporters melt away, gives an impassioned tirade: "All of us women and Robert here agree that you old men must stop getting drunk and using money that should be for school and food for the children and all you dirty Masai should start washing the children's eyes so that they stop getting eye disease, my kids don't get eye disease, and all of you old men should start wearing pants and believe in our lord Jesus Christ."

Oh ho. The Christianized Kikuyu half of Rhoda has come out with a vengeance, and she goes on about the twin themes of all agricultural Kenyans when they complain about the Masai—too much bare buttocks and not enough Jesus. And I've been dragged in as a supposed member of the Cover Your Buns for Christ Party.

The meeting breaks up in a general confused hubbub as the old men filter out, chortling and victorious, off for a drink in the shade of a tree. Serere rouses himself from the dust long enough to announce the killing of a goat in my honor; he is ignored. I quickly make my escape.

5

The Coca-Cola Devil

$\mathcal{I}$t was a fitting day for my Jeep's engine, which had been sputtering ominously for a month, to give up the ghost, as that morning, I'd seen what had to have been one of the finales of old Isiah's life. He was the oldest male in the troop, by far, ancient, wild-eyed, arthritic, wasted. His personality seemed to consist mostly of his being old. He hobbled around, kvetched and clucked and groaned when he would sit down, repositioning himself repeatedly, swatting at the kids. He was not grandfatherly, charming, or going quietly into the night. I saw what I believe to have been his last mating that morning. Esther, a young kid coming into estrus who couldn't get any of the big guys interested, wound up being in a consortship with Isiah. He did a fairly credible job of keeping up with her, remembered the old moves about herding her away if any threatening males were around (in this case, young juveniles). Finally, he mounted her and, in the throes of the unaccustomed excitement, threw up on her head. Such was Isiah's farewell to the amorous life (as well as poor Esther's introduction). He disappeared forever shortly thereafter, probably picked off by a hyena or lion.

So with Isiah's tryst recorded in the archives, I turned my attention to the Jeep, which had clearly taken a turn for the worse that day. It expired some fifty yards from the mechanic's at the park headquarters, and his diagnosis was that some part or other had to be replaced. A few hours' worth of arduous radio calls to Nairobi brought the news that said part was not to be had anywhere in the country for a few weeks until some foreign exchange crisis could be resolved and a shipment of auto parts sitting on the docks in Mombassa on the Indian Ocean could be unloaded.

Faced with my work completely shutting down for a while, I did the only sensible thing, which was to grab my backpack, catch a ride with some tourists to Nairobi, just go travel somewhere, anywhere in East Africa that hitchhiking would take me.

I start off in Nairobi by going to the industrial area to find the petrol tankers doing the long-haul transcontinental trips. I hang out in the truck yard all day, finally find a tanker heading my way, weasel my way on. It is a cranky old Leyland, with a narrow bed jammed in the cab, bottles and cans of food everywhere, thousands of gears and widgets and tools and rags and oil cans—a soapbox racer that was somehow supposed to make it to Uganda. The drivers are two coastal Islamics—Mahmoud and Ismaeli, both wasted, sullen, sitting chewing on some mildly amphetamine-like plant from the coast. The lorry proves to be capable of nothing more than 15 miles an hour, so we creep off west of Nairobi into the sunset.

Dawn comes, we are still creeping along up a 9,000-foot escarpment. What an odd thing, moving at a steady walking speed in a lorry for hours on end, just sitting back and watching the scenery. We finally reach the top of the escarpment and the sorely tested lorry collapses utterly. Pile out, pore over the engine, and pronounce it near death. Mahmoud catches a bus going in the opposite direction, back to Nairobi for a mechanic. Ismaeli and I settle in for what turns out to be two days of sitting next to the lorry. My comprehension of his Swahili becomes more adept as he becomes less sullen. I am initially frustrated with the delay, but decide that this is absurd to worry about. So we sit. Soon Ismaeli disappears into the cartons of the cab, emerges with his prayer mat. A bit of cogitating upon the sky, he decides where east is, and goes about his praying. He soon is lecturing me about the Arabic roots of Swahili, enthusiastically assigning Swahili the status of a simple dialect. I delight him with examples of how close Hebrew is to Arabic. He ventures to place Hebrew as an Arabic dialect also, and when I fail to complain about that, he says I should bother no more with my food, I will eat along with him. His meals turn out to be, of all things, spaghetti. Ismaeli is from what was originally Italian Somaliland, and has picked up a passion for the stuff from the ex-colonials. He makes a huge pot of it on a kerosene stove, throws in some questionable camel's milk that he has brought along in a skin. We fall to eating, tremendous amounts, with our hands. He settles into praying and, bored, I pull out my alto recorder and begin to play a bit. This proves a revelation to him, and before long, Ismaeli has commandeered it away from me, tootling on it gingerly. He proves unable to get much out of it in the way of melody, but has a wicked Somali-Arabic sense of rhythm. He has soon incorporated the recorder into his praying. Sitting there, reedy and ascetic, noodling away with these sort of impatient rhythmic spasms, eyes closed, swaying back and forth. Suddenly, the moment is right, he drops the recorder and flings himself on the mat. So the time passes, I slowly become Arabic Italian, eating spaghetti and listening to Ismaeli chanting and ululating away.

The second morning another petrol lorry comes along, and it is decided that I will continue on that one. Ismaeli clearly covets the recorder, but settles for one of my sweaters, as he is dressed only in coastal casual and nearly freezes each night. The new petrol lorry seems equally senescent, but I jump in anyway. The driver is Jeremiah, a gigantic burly gruff older man. He has a stylishly shaved head, wears a rather natty embroidered fez, heavy square black-framed sunglasses, and has a marvelous upper incisor of gold. He has tremendous forearms, which impress me considerably. The assistant, in contrast, is Jonah, who is about thirty, with sunken eyes and scraggly beard, and reeking of undernourishment. His clothes are a shambles, covered with grease. He seems passably nice, in a thoroughly downtrodden way.

At a mountain village we stop for lunch. I reach for my food, but Jeremiah herds me along with him into a food kiosk. The normal procedure now would be to scan the menu painted on the wall and order something, but this seems to be other than Jeremiah's style. With a belligerence that initially shocks me, he bullies and threatens everyone in sight, and within minutes has the kiosk staff galvanized into uncertain action. Some run next door to buy fresh tomatoes and onions. Others get hot peppers from somewhere. A boy is dispatched to the meat shop to have some goat cooked, posthaste. Like a king in his court, Jeremiah clears off a table and, wielding a knife, begins slicing, dicing, and anything else imaginable with the utensil. Tomatoes in one bowl, spices off to one side. Peppers sequestered somewhere, meat arrives and is chopped. I attempt to help with my lowly pocketknife and am reprimanded and returned to the crowd of spectators that has gathered. Jeremiah continues to shout orders and pronounce judgment on each new item brought to him. His wrath is Olympian at the insufficient number of onions. Finally all is prepared, each item chopped and resting in its bowl. With manic grace, Jeremiah dumps everything onto the tabletop, mixes it by hand, and we all fall upon the food, grabbing great hunks of meat, wrapping it around tomatoes and onion. Jeremiah leads the way, holding on to a hot pepper in his right hand, taking a bite of it, then jamming in as much other food as quickly as possible to absorb the heat.

Toward the end of the meal, Jeremiah requisitions a share of it for Jonah, who has stayed on the lorry. Staggering out after the feast, I ask why Jonah has remained there. "He likes lorries." This proves to be a statement that does not begin to approach the magnitude of the truth. Jonah, indeed, does like lorries. His job is to sleep on the lorry at night as a watchman and to serve as the general handyman; whether his obsession brought him to this perfect occupation or whether it only bloomed and festered after he had begun his trade, Jonah has allowed his life to become inseparably intertwined with the lorry.

In short, he will not leave it. For days afterward, watching carefully, I never see him set foot on the ground. Whenever we eat, he instead scurries around on the trailers, checking petrol barrels, adjusting an infinity of bolts and latches, polishing the hood and doors of the cab meticulously, all without touching the ground, swinging from cab to trailer to cab to bumper. I conclude that his malnourished appearance is due to former head drivers who, unlike Jeremiah, failed to bring food to him at meals. He projects an air of subdued fervor, of his destiny with lorries as nothing less than a case of divine sentence passed upon him. He proves skilled at swinging out of the cab while we're moving, crawling to the second trailer, and urinating out the back of it.

We leave. Jeremiah is delighted with the meal, and soon falls into an odd song in his native Kikuyu. He has an undefined rumbly bass, which fills up the lower half of the cab. The song is generally lugubrious, but with occasional bouncy points at which he pats the top of his fez rhythmically.

Reaching the town of Eldoret in western Kenya one late afternoon, we also break down, seriously. I go off for a walk and return to discover that I've been traded to Pius, another driver heading for Rwanda. Thus began by far the worst nightmare of any of my travels in Africa. It started with a somewhat bizarre though innocuous evening. Pius, whose hometown is Eldoret, is the leader of a gang that is obviously the coolest collection of guys this side of the Rift Valley. He is young, quite tall, and thin. He wears skin-tight jeans, a sports shirt open to his pants, a flashy sports jacket, shades, a dangling cigarette, and, to top it off, an absolutely ludicrous pair of bright red six-inch platform shoes. I meet the guys, all similarly dressed. Everyone is chain-smoking and with the platform shoes all are at least 6 foot 14. Somehow I am introduced as "Peter," which quickly catches on despite my protests. Pius and the Boys go strutting out, as I hurry along after them. They are well armed with American slang.

"Man, Peter, we're gonna show you Eldoret tonight."

"Fuckin right, Peter."

We strut on. Hit the first bar, the crowd clears. I anticipate them getting into a fight with other patrons over an imagined insult.

"Gimme a fuckin beer."

"Gimme a fuckin beer."

"Gimme a fuckin beer."

"Gimme a fuckin beer."

"And one soda for me too, please." There are limits to one's transformations. Move to another bar. I seem to have captured their vague affections for no obvious reason.

"Yeah, man, Peter's okay."

"Yeah, Peter's okay."

"Yeah."

While this wasn't my textbook idea of fun, at least it seemed tolerable in the scheme of things. I would go along with Pius, we would hop in his vehicle tomorrow, bid the Boys good-bye, and go to Kampala. I had no premonition of the nightmarish quality that Pius would take on instead. In retrospect, I am not sure if he was truly malevolent, or just a rough bush Kenyan who didn't quite know how to go about being hospitable, or if I had somehow become a subject in some brainwashing experiment.

At dawn, I am awakened by Pius, fresh in clean new sports jacket, the rest of the outfit intact. "Today, Kampala, man, Peter, just stick with me." I rouse myself in hopes of actually going. "But first a drink." In we go. I am feeling mealy and diseased from lack of sleep and initially decline the Coke that Pius has delivered to go with his beer. I eventually drink it out of politeness, and he gets me another one, which I drink. We move to another bar, "And soon we leave," and soon to another. It is early afternoon. I am feeling hungry, because my every attempt at food is always jocularly shouted down by Pius and the Boys, with a Coke replacing the food. I protest about whether we are leaving, feeling a bit surly and unappreciative, as if I have somehow missed a subtle point in the conversation that would have explained why we were still here. Pius responds by looming over me menacingly and demanding I lend him 40 shillings. I numbly comply, he returns with another soda, which he makes me drink. My teeth take on a Coke fuzz. Pius is indefatigable, always moving on to new places. It has somehow evolved that I am being herded about by him and the Boys; midafternoon, I realize that they have not let me out of their sight since dawn. I am hungry and sick of Cokes and more arrive that I am expected to drink. He treats me with solicitous brotherly care that seems to barely mask the suggestion of wild violence. More moving around, more Cokes. I begin to look for ways out, but Jeremiah's lorry is still out of it, hood up, mechanics at work, Jonah peering from the trailer. I sink into carbonated oblivion, begin to feel disconnected from myself as if my body has somehow become that of this Peter, and I am stuck inside him. Exhaustion. More sodas. Pius borrows more money, returns some of the previous, begins an incoherent talk about taking me with him to Zaire to smuggle diamonds.

"Yeah, Peter's all right."

"Yeah, Peter's all right."

"Yeah, Peter's all right."

We push on, moving into a night similar to the previous. No one seems to require sleep except me, or else they sleep in shifts so that there are always a few of them there to keep me awake, keep me moving, keep me drinking Cokes. Four in the morning, finally asleep in one of the bars.

Dawn, two hours of sleep. As if I'm utterly incapable of learning, Pius is able to rouse me again with promises. "Ah, today, Kampala, man." Back to the bar, the guys there already, pushing me along when I get uncooperative: More sodas. Drinking into oblivion. I'll never get out, I'll die in Eldoret.

Around noon, like a savior, Jeremiah reappears. I rush to him for help, but he motions me away, as he is about to start preparations for another of his meals. He is dressed in a one-piece jumpsuit, which emphasizes his voluminous head in a way that would impress even the most jaded of observers. He has on a scarf and, of course, his fez, and has perhaps dressed up just for the meal. Pius and the Boys join in, herd me along, following Jeremiah. He obtains his tomatoes and onions without much difficulty, but the search for acceptable meat is Odyssean. Store after store, Jeremiah checking carcasses of cows, sniffing slabs of meat, rejecting here, chastising owners there, accepting a few choice offerings. He seems to be known everywhere and no money is ever visibly exchanged. A crowd has now gathered, following. Some get to carry the tomatoes or onions, but the meat is Jeremiah's domain. The selected samples go into various pockets of the jumpsuit. At one place he actually searches through his pockets, finds the right piece, and trades it in for a different one. Finally we all congregate at a table where the preparation rituals are repeated. We fall upon the food. I repeatedly broach the subject with Jeremiah of his saving me from Pius. "We talk after lunch." Lunch finished, Jeremiah disappears to wash his hands, Pius pulls me away and herds me to the other end of town for sodas. More money lent, endless Cokes, threats that I'm not even certain about.

Evening. We pass Jeremiah's lorry, where Pius wakes Jonah seemingly out of spite. Jonah asks me if I could bring him a soda sometime the next day, as he has become thirsty.

Morning, more of the same, no sleep, sinking deeper into hell. I decline my first offered Coke, at 7:00 in the morning, but then remember Jonah and say yes. Pius is suspicious. "What do you want it for, for Jonah?" I admit to it. He grabs me and tells me I'd better not try to get a soda to Jonah or else I'm in trouble. "Now do you want a soda?" I admit to no longer being in need of one. Good, he gets me a soda, which I'm forced to drink. I begin to make plans for my escape, my confrontation with him, and assume that he will knife me. Early afternoon, we are on the way to a new bar, I am just about to explode into a tirade about the whole situation, to tell him I'm leaving, when Pius suddenly brightens. "Ah, look who is here, Peter," as a car pulls up alongside us.

Great, now what. Of all people, it is his mother. "Peter, this is my mama." We drive to their house on the edge of town, she is impossibly sweet to me. "And what are you doing here in Kenya, Peter?" Pius has turned into a little boy, doting and giggly around his mama, shyly showing off family photos, drinking lemonade with me. To his credit, he even seems a bit embarrassed by his asinine shoes. Only this transformation keeps me from seeking help with his mother. "Madame, you're son is a Beelzebub and has made a captive of me" seems inappropriate, as if I've imagined the former Pius as he now rushes to help his mother carry in things from the car. We go, I shaking hands with her, Pius kissing her good-bye as we leave the car in town. We turn the corner, Pius savagely pushes me into a bar; back to business.

Early evening, in the bar. I go to the bathroom and Pius's toadies slip up—no one accompanies me. I see my chance to escape and decide to give up my backpack and possessions, trivial loss. I sprint out the back, into the street, and there's another lorry there, the engine revving, about to leave. I run over, begin to climb up the cab to ask the driver for a lift *anywhere,* when I am grabbed and pulled down. It is Pius. Forget it, I say, my name is Robert, I'm getting out of here, I've had it. No you're not, that man will cheat you, he is very bad. Don't give me that, I'm leaving. I begin climbing up again, when Pius wrenches me back, knocks me to the ground. It hurts, I feel a childish rush of tears, of feeling petulant instead of outraged or terrified. The Boys are out by now, I am hustled back in. Pius seems mildly uncomfortable about the whole scene, as if some social faux pas has been committed. "Aw come on, Peter, let's get you a soda."

Toward midnight as I sit drooping away over another Coke, Pius suddenly says, "Ah, Peter is tired, we have to get him to sleep." I am herded into a rooming house next door, where I am dumped into a bed and wished good night. Can this be true, this luck? I fall asleep and shortly afterward am awakened by hammering at my door. It is Pius, in sunglasses, cigarette, bikini underpants, and, of course, platform shoes. He is accompanied by what appear to be two prostitutes who are shoved into my room. "Yeah, Peter, all right!" The door slams. I politely explain that I am going to sleep, and the two women storm out and are soon engaged in some argument with Pius, tossing abuse upon him for reasons hopefully unrelated to me. Things are thrown, there is a beating, much yelling and crying; this goes on through much of the sleepless night.

Morning, back at the bar, over a Coke. I am desperate, and during the night, I have decided to poison Pius by slipping barbiturates into his beer. I have brought them along on the trip as emergency painkillers, and I am hoping to put him in a coma. Instead, luck is finally with me, and for no obvious reason, this is one beer too many for Pius at such a delicate time of day. He becomes violently ill, puking in the bar as he heaves toward the bathroom. His flunkies follow; one grabs me by the wrist and pulls me along. I am told to get a towel from the barroom. I run out and realize—I am alone. As a measure of the desperate extent to which I have been isolated, starved, exhausted, scared, confused, I pause for a second, worrying that I will be punished badly. Pius retches again in the bathroom, the Boys are arguing about what to do. I grab my pack and run out.

It is sunny, people are going about normal activities, on their way to work, maybe anticipating lunch. My luck is still with me. Miraculously, Jeremiah is there with his lorry, which is operable and seems ready to go. Jonah motions me on, I hide in the back. For an excruciating half hour, Jeremiah starts the engine, fumfers with things in the cab, gets out to polish the hood ornament, shakes hands, waves good-byes. I cower in the trailer, awaiting my recapture. And Pius and the Boys never emerge. We leave. I crawl to the cab while we are moving, with Eldoret safely out of sight, no sign of Pius. I swing into the cab using Jonah's technique.

"Mister Peter, you have left Pius. Very bad man."

By evening we have reached Kitale, home of Jeremiah's sister. We stop there for the night. I am still shaken with relief at my escape from the madman, readily fall into the maternal care of his sister and a number of her friends. The one-room house is filled with heavy maternal women who giggle at my every move. I am in ecstasy at the healthy family atmosphere. Children abound, Kikuyu music is on the radio, everyone is dancing and jiggling around. Jeremiah's brother-in-law is a doughy friendly man who seems useless at mechanical skills and has saved up an array of objects—lamps, kerosene stoves, flashlights—for Jeremiah to fix.

We sit down to eat, a communal bowl of stew. I continue to swoon in the safe atmosphere. Jeremiah's sister disappears for a while and emerges with the evening's prize—Jonah—whom she has either coaxed off the lorry with a bowl of food or caught by surprise and dragged off bodily. Her physical resemblance to Jeremiah makes the latter more plausible. Jeremiah, meanwhile, is engulfed with kids; he tries the ploy of being gruff, which doesn't work, and is soon singing his hat song, pounding away at his fez, the kids on his lap. Jonah nervously eats and is allowed to leave only on condition that he take some more of the food out with him.

It is evening, I get the rewards of survival—Jeremiah's sister is calling me Robert, there is a bed available for me, I will be allowed to sleep. After spending the previous four days cursing the continent for giving rise to a Pius, it turns out all I need is a good night's sleep to wake up in love with Africa again.

6

Teaching Old Men About Maps

The baboons were off inventing the wheel again, so I was passing the afternoon in camp. Sitting squat in the middle of the endless miles of open grassland and tree-lined streambeds that the baboons frequented for food each day was the great Impenetrable Thicket. It stretched for miles along a ridge top, thick scrub and endless thorn bushes, deep aardvark holes and jagged volcanic rock, teeming with animals you wouldn't want to meet. The previous grad students told me that the baboons couldn't be followed there. I tried once on foot and had nearly been flattened by a rhino. Then I tried by vehicle, promptly punctured two tires, nearly snapped an axle, and then came close to being flattened by a rhino. So I gave up. Inventing the wheel was what one of the grad students claimed the baboons must be up to when they thicketed us. They had just done it to me on a particularly interesting morning. Uriah was in the midst of his glacial campaign to wear down Solomon. They were having a pitched battle, Solomon likely to win but the number of times he was reversed becoming of critical importance. The two chased, fenced, and, at a moment of critical intensity . . . disappeared into the thicket, not to be seen again that day. Meanwhile, the older and rather dignified Aaron appeared to be paying an undue amount of attention to Boopsie, who was in estrus big time. That seemed an unlikely consort conquest for him, perhaps reflecting the preoccupation of Solomon and Uriah with the playing fields of Eton. Still, it didn't actually count in the data notebook until it was observed to be consummated, which appeared just about to happen when . . . they also disappeared into the thicket, not to be seen again that day. Miriam appeared with her newest child, who took its first, tentative, precious steps . . . into the thicket. It was like that all morning. Finally, even the newly awakened Benjamin bumbled out from beneath some bush, galloped off into the field on one side of the thicket, then the field on the other, looking for the rest of the troop, until he too plunged into wheel making.

I gave up and returned to camp. Ostensibly, it was to read, catch up on paperwork, but, as had evolved any afternoon that I was there, it was to play Albert Schweitzer. It was unavoidable. If you had watched *Marcus Welby, M.D.* once and possessed a box of Band-Aids, you were now the most knowledgeable and best-equipped practitioner for a hundred miles. And, most bizarre, all the Masai assumed precisely that.

By now, camp had the semblance of a regular clinic. The first kid has his foot slashed open, plus some open sores on his legs. Wash everything, give the mother a song and dance about washing him every day with clean water (from where?), put on bacitracin ointment and Band-Aids. The mother retrieves the throwaway pieces of the Band-Aids, puts them away in her pouch. I feel like a decadent wasteful Westerner. The next kid has diarrhea. Won't go near it; too hard to fix up, too easy to get blamed for. Mama with malaria; give her chloroquine. The woman accompanying her is sick as well. She coughs dramatically for me while I listen to her chest with a stethoscope. Sounds like air coming through a dirty air conditioner in an old institutional building. Probably tuberculosis, everybody has it, won't go near it.

Up the mountain comes an old old man. Maybe sixty. Perfect elderly Masai, archetype, a man with a look like nothing I ever see in my privileged world. He has a wool cap around his head, which he stopped shaving long ago. Little white tuft balls of hair, a wisp of a white beard. Taut jutting-edged face, like a Picasso goat, all angles. And wrinkles. Endless wrinkles, some of them even filled with dust, a hard landscape for the flies all over his face. His face has obviously played no role in his survival since it vaguely coaxed his mother to nurse him ages ago; since then, it has been free of contingencies, allowed to go to hell in every which way. One elongated ear—the Masai punch holes in their ears and spend their lives elongating them down to their shoulders. The other one ripped away, as if some vulture, taunting him, tried to fly off with him by his earlobe and just came away with a dried worm of sixty-year-old ear. The rest of him is burlap skin and dry branch bones except for his ass and upper thighs, which look like burlap stuffed with steel ball bearings.

He has a rotten eye. Conjunctivitis. Masai fly eye, as we call it—the flies walk in the cow dung, the flies walk on their eyes, good-bye eye. An amazing percentage of people missing eyes because of it. He's been around before, the eye is coming along, I'm giving him antibiotics to swallow and applying some as an ointment. The last time, trying to explain to him in my crappy Swahili that he takes the antibiotics four times a day for a week and should not eat food just before and after taking the pills, he came away with the impression that he was not supposed to eat for the week while taking the medicine. He apparently went a day with this mistake before remarking to his son that this white medicine was getting to be a drag. The son came and clarified, straightened it out.

The eye taken care of, he settles in to see if there is anything interesting in camp. I entertain him with the dry ice that I get shipped in weekly to keep the baboon blood samples frozen. I open the box of it, let the smoke pour out. "Hot," he says. I take a glass of water, throw some dry ice into the water, the smoke pours out. "Hot," he repeats, maybe a little bored. I take his hand, put it in the cup. *"Cold!"* I give him a small sliver of dry ice to hold. He does so very tentatively. "Hot cold." His voice has gotten very dry and crackly, almost fearful. He's not at all sure of the situation.

I let him listen to his heart with the stethoscope. I fit the earpieces in his ears, worrying about ear worts or something communicable. He looks trepidant, improbable with the earpieces, like some king of Swaziland listening to a simultranslated speech at the United Nations. I thump on his chest very tentatively and place the resonator on his heart. He listens and briefly nods his head to the beat of his heart. Mostly, he seems thoroughly disinterested in the whole thing.

"That is your heart," I say.

"I am an old man and I have many sons."

This strikes me as inordinately cryptic. Is he threatening me if I mess with his heart? Is he bragging? Is he stating his accomplishments and immortality in the face of a mere heartbeat?

On a whim, I pull out a detailed topographic map of the reserve. I spread it out, not quite knowing what I will show him or why. He squats, balancing on his thighs and balls of his feet, still. I guess, I'm sure correctly, that in his entire life he hasn't been more than thirty miles from here, knows the names of perhaps half a dozen places that might appear on this detailed map. I spread the map out. I point to a mountain cone near us, say its name slowly. Then I point to the map and point to the concentric circles of topo of the mountain, say the same. Next, I do the same tracing the river that runs behind camp, pointing to it, then to the map, saying the name once each time. Then I do the same for mountains to the east. He looks at me with utter blankness. Not impatience, not incomprehension, just blankness. I go through the whole procedure again, naming each solemnly, as if the powers of appellation are not trivial. Blankness. I decide to try once more. I point to the mountain cone, name it, and on the map. As I trace the river along the map, I hear him suddenly suck in his breath loudly. He is wild-eyed, breathing rapidly. In very rapid singsong, he repeats the name of the river, over and over, pointing at the actual one, then at the map. He teeters on his thighs, nearly loses his balance, and recovers. He is still hyperventilating. He points to the mountain, nearly shouts its name, smiling, and then allows me to take his hand, finger extended, and touch the equivalent spot on the map. He bursts into giggles. He traces the river again, very quietly, then the mountain range to the top, putting his hand out, waiting for me to lead his finger to it. He solemnly intones the name of the mountains. He returns to the first mountain cone and, inexplicably, breaks into giggles again at its spot on the map—a private joke. He suddenly becomes very sober, glances in all directions, and then carefully repositions the map so that it faces in the same direction as the real landmarks. Then he returns to his mountain cone, giggling again, shaking his head as if not believing that particular thing.

He abruptly grows quiet, pensive. I begin to think he is disturbed about something, thinking of something else. He tilts his head, cogitating. He stares at the map a while longer and then, very very tentatively, reaches out and turns the map over. I wonder if he is trying to find out what is contained below the ground. He seems either undisturbed, or even confirmed in some vague belief, when the underside is blank.

He stands, teeters a bit, maybe from suddenly getting up, maybe from the excitement of the unexpected day. He is getting ready to leave when another thought occurs to him. He looks at the map, looks at me awhile. Then he says, pointing to the map, "Where are your parents [where is your home]?"

I think of being a kid, going to the planetarium in New York, where, for the first time, the size of the solar system was brought home to me. You sit in a room, and above you, models of the planets rotate in concentric circles. The narrator says, Here is this planet, here is that one. Unfortunately, the voice continues, because of the scale of this model, Uranus cannot be contained here, as it would be across the street, in Central Park. And Pluto would not be contained here; it would be in . . . Cleveland. My god, you think, this is a big universe.

I point to his known places again. I walk three steps from the map (inaccurate) and say the name of the Masai county seat, which his son has probably visited. Then, I walk a half dozen steps and say, "Here is Nairobi," a place he has heard of. Then, I walk across the field, until I can no longer be certain of his one-eyed gaze but which, by the rest of his body's tension, is clearly trained straight on me. When I think I'm at the limits of his likely belief, I stop and shout, "My parents' house." He clucks to himself, disbelieving—maybe disbelieving that that's the truth, that the world is so big, that I would lie to an old man, that I would leave my parents so far away to come live in a tent. He continues clucking to himself and then taps his walking stick back on the map, at the center, where we are, and shouts, "My house," emphatically.

He is utterly content with the day, having not only seen these wonders but having been, perhaps, convinced that the future's inevitable inheritors, to the extent that I represent them, may not be such a mess. He shakes my hand, wanders off, mumbling to himself. "Good-bye, white man," he yells from the start of the trees. "Good-bye, Masai," I yell back, which strikes him as amusing. He goes clucking off into the bush.

7

Memories of Blood:
The East African Wars

OTHERS' FIGHTS

Toward the end of that first year, I visited the home of one of my acquaintances from the tourist lodge. Harun came from an agricultural tribe that lived near the Tanzanian border. I was charmed by the life there. Warm cheerful robust isolated backward mountain farmers, using every bit of land on the hills for producing endless quantities of food to feed endless numbers of children. Hearty strong large people who ate like hogs and worked like mad and filled their few leisure hours with hexes and witchcraft and clan feuds and revenge curses. Harun's own family had recently had their well poisoned through witchcraft, causing his sister to become quite ill. Or at least they were certain that the neighbors had to have contracted a shaman to poison something or other. They had had a dispute with them over a cow trampling some maize, and then the girl had become sick. Retributive cursing seemed the most plausible explanation.

The tribe's greatest fighting energies, however, were of course expended on their tribal neighbors, the Masai. Typically, the Masai bordering to the east and to the south would cause trouble with some cattle-rustling raid, and fighting would ensue. But in the last decades, independence had come to this part of the world, and everything had changed. Now, when Harun's tribe, the Kisii, fought with the Masai to the east, that was okay and everyone had a fine time. But when they fought with the Masai to the south, they were fighting with Tanzanians, and it was an international incident and the police would come and tell them to cut it out.

To the combatants, the whole thing seemed pretty bizarre and arbitrary. It reminded me that once, long ago, this border formed another strange arbitrary boundary. Once Kenya was British East Africa, Tanzania was German Tanganyika, and in 1914, the white colonists in each dutifully made uniforms, formed units, and conducted World War I. There were battles in Kisii land and even now, there were still legends about treasures buried in the hills by soldiers before battle.

Harun and I sat with the very old men who drank and chortled and belched and reminisced. I asked them about the time the German colonials and the British colonials fought each other. They remembered well.

"The white people had a fight among themselves for some reason, so they started fighting here. They would come in clothes like the policemen wear now, and they would shoot at each other. Dead white people, imagine. Once, an airplane came over. We did not know then what it was and we were terribly frightened; we ran to our mothers and hid ourselves.

"One day, the British came and said that we should go and fight also. We could not believe it—they would give us guns to shoot white people. They always said that guns had a magic so that an African man could not use it to shoot a white man, but they said that these Germans were different white men and the guns would work.

"Then they said a crazy thing. They said we should also go fight the Masai, that they would give us guns to do that. Yes, we said, we will fight them with your guns, but they said we could only fight the Masai to the south, the Masai to the east we must never fight. We thought that was crazy. So we refused. They beat some of us, but we still refused."

The old men thought it puzzling and basically funny. The Masai were delighted to fight, however. Units of British East African Masai from the east and Tanganyikan Masai from the south had several pitched battles in makeshift uniforms. No one remembered the outcome.

Harun's father had a different encounter with white men's wars, I learned during that visit. In 1930, at the age of twenty, he decided on the woman he wanted to marry. She was a young girl from the next mountain, whom he saw at the well when he went there with the cows. They had looked furtively at each other a few times, and once had said hello. When he asked her her name, she laughed and hid her face and ran back up the mountain with the goats, and thus he had decided to marry her.

He went to his father, Harun's grandfather, to inform him that there was a girl on the next mountain he wanted to marry. Could he now receive his inheritance of cows so that he could purchase the girl from her parents, pay their bride price? Harun's grandfather told him he would have to wait a year because he, the grandfather, then in his forties, was going to use the cows to purchase a third wife for himself that year. Somewhat disgruntled but obedient he waited, only to discover a week later that the third wife had been purchased and she was . . . the girl from the well.

Distraught, Harun's father, for the first time in his life, fled down the mountain with all his colonial money, went to the bar at the trading post, and drank himself into a stupor. Staggering out drunk, lamenting and yelling in Kisii, he was arrested by the colonial police. Who shipped him off to military service in India. For fifteen years. Harun's father disappeared, spending fifteen years fighting for the British in India and Burma, fighting in World War II, fighting the Japanese alongside conscripts from Sudan, Nigeria, Gambia, Rhodesia, the whole empire of natives. He returned in 1945, age thirty-five, and married the girl who was to become Harun's mother, then fifteen. And, according to Harun, he never said a word again to the grandfather, or to the third wife of the grandfather, and never mentioned his fifteen years fighting, except to say that he didn't like the food.

When I met him that visit, he was near seventy and, I think, more than a bit demented. He sat in a chair in the corner, peering about and mumbling, while Harun's mother hurried about preparing food and tea. When Harun introduced me, his father pulled back anxiously. He stared at me for the rest of the afternoon and would not join us eating. Eventually, he called Harun over and, gesturing to me, said in Kisii, "If that white man is from the army, tell him I'm not going again."

DREADLOCKS

It was during this time that I was also able to piece together this tale of East Africa's next war:

Wilson Kipkoi was probably the only person in the bush for a hundred miles in any direction who was angry about Hitler. Or angry about the role of the Arabs in the slave trade, or the American genocide of Indians, or Israeli treatment of Palestinians. He was probably the only person around who had even heard of any of that, let alone developed a simmering, bitter anger over the injustices. And his anger was not just limited to history and politics afar. He was angry that his own country was a one-party state, that the press was muzzled, that people disappeared, that the army was bribed with half the budget to stay in their barracks and not take over the government. And he said so, a very dangerous thing to do.

Wilson Kipkoi was raised in the bush, got next to no schooling. Somewhere along the way, he developed a feverish need to learn. He taught himself excellent English, spent every shilling and moment on books. And found that everything he learned made his anger grow. He didn't yell, never even spoke loudly, and he wasn't the type that brawled in an explosion of self-depleting anger. His anger simmered and grew, barely fit in his lanky, taut frame, his triangular head. It powered the constant rhythmic throbbing of the vein in the side of his jaw. When the rangers or police came around to shake down people for some of their salaries, Wilson would confront them and tell them they were worse than the white South Africans. And get beaten. When whites would call some black a "boy," Wilson would call them colonial pigs. And often lose his job. He talked in a dispassionate way about killing people, something occasionally done but never spoken about with pensive premeditation. His friends regarded him with awe and fear, and mostly worried for him.

Perhaps the greatest measure of Wilson's oddity, the uniqueness of where his twenty years had brought him, was an activity he kept secret—in the evenings, when alone, Wilson wrote short stories and poetry, in English, in Swahili, in the language of his tribe, the Kipsigi. They were in the style of the pulp spy adventure novels popular with the Kenyan intelligentsia; tales of betrayal and political repression and of the right side losing. None of his friends knew he wrote them; he certainly never mentioned them to his wife. She was an uneducated Masai, the traditional enemy of Wilson's people. He had gotten her pregnant and refused to do the simple act expected of him, which was to pay the father off with a nominal sum. Instead, he married her without hesitation, and thereafter paid her less attention than if she were a zebra.

The person who most dominated Wilson's anger and mutterings, his jaw-throbbing threats of murder, was his father. Wilson's father went by the old-style name Kipkoi wa Kimutai—Kipkoi, son of Kimutai—and was known to all as Kipkoi. He wore his ears in the old tribal manner—with holes in them, the earlobes elongated down to his shoulders. He had a battered face, looked and dressed like hell, and couldn't care less what anyone thought. Unlike Wilson, with his angry talk, Kipkoi had actually killed people, dozens of them. He worked for the game department and headed the antipoaching unit that patrolled that part of Kenya. Long before independence, as a young man, he had been trained to be a "boy," to assist a British "bwana," one of the great white hunters. He accompanied the hunter on his commercial safaris, or when elephants were destroying crops and had to be shot, and when near-toothless, starving old lions were desperate enough to pick off villagers. He was the boy who oiled the rifles, held them over his head when the rivers were waded, stood by the bwana's side and never flinched when a buffalo came straight at them—handing the proper gun at the proper instant. He learned to stalk, he learned to track; he could remember a path through bush country years after he had last been there, could smell when a rhino had last brushed by a tree. And he learned how to shoot exceedingly well, although he had had to learn furtively; the boy never did the shooting, so there was no need to teach him.

Around the time of independence in 1963, the game was thinning out—the human population was booming, more and more bush and forest was being burned for agriculture. And unexpectedly, the rich whites were no longer coming to hunt, but to watch the animals, to take pictures. Just at the time that they gained back their own country, Africans were being told that their animals should not be shot anymore, instead should be maintained. And Kipkoi became part of the new trend, this strange concept of watching, protecting the animals, establishing and preserving parks. The old British bwanas became wardens for a while; then as the last of the hunting was phased out, it also became politically untenable to have white faces running African parks, and the first black wardens emerged. By all logic, Kipkoi should have been one of them. He was the right age, he had been in the game service from the beginning. But his heart was not in organizing animal counts or assuring that the rangers at park gates didn't pocket too much of the entrance fee or making sure the campsites had proper garbage pits. He still wanted to hunt. So he hunted humans. He rose up in the antipoaching wing of the department, serving on every frontier where people would slip over the border to machine-gun a rhino or elephant and slip away with the horn or tusk. When he patrolled near the Somali border, he filled his unit with tough, near-criminal southern Bantu Kenyans who wanted nothing more than to kill a Somali, the traditional desert raider from the north. When he was assigned to the southern Tanzanian border, he formed a patrol of nothing but cold, silent Somali Kenyans, who itched to ambush the round, water-soft Bantu poachers. He had an explosive anger, raged at his men, knocked them over and beat them if they failed to follow his instructions, was loud and abusive and supremely competent. He was long past the point of being eligible to retire, but in his late fifties, Kipkoi led every skirmish, every trap, every gun battle, with poachers. More and more, he was fighting Tanzanian army units, as the hunger south of the border got worse and the ones with the arms thought of zebra meat. Kipkoi wouldn't retire. He liked to hunt, he was afraid to go home to his farm to sit and age and die. And most bizarre of all, he had a desire that no African ever had, something absolutely inexplicable and alien to the traditional life of battling with the difficult, demanding world. He had bought the nonsense that the whites had started spouting around independence: Kipkoi had come to love the animals and really wanted to protect them.

Kipkoi had fourteen children; he would typically depart from each leave home with one of his three wives pregnant. Of the fourteen, he could barely recognize or be recognized by thirteen. But Wilson, the first son, was raised with him. Wilson had grown up in his father's camps, in the northern desert, in the western rain forest where the Ugandan forest people would slip over to snare bush buck, at the isolated, besieged outposts along the Tanzanian border. As a boy, he would hear the gun battles at night, see the men, including his father, come back wounded. Or, with some of them, not come back at all. He grew up frightened and isolated, bush-wise, bush-crazy, tense, vigilant. Life seemed like an ambush, and half the time it was Kipkoi who seemed to be the one to ambush Wilson. He kept him by his side, taught him what he knew about the bush (although he never taught him to use a gun). The cutthroat men in Kipkoi's units would find the boy's presence puzzling, but they'd leave him alone. Later, when Wilson was old enough to start to work in the tourist camps, when Kipkoi and his unit were assigned to the part of the country that encompassed that camp, no local ranger would dare come and try a shakedown of Wilson on payday. Kipkoi and his unit were too well known, and too feared. What no one knew, what Wilson would never mention to anyone out of shame, was that on those same paydays, Kipkoi himself would show up to beat Wilson and take much of his pay.

The taking of the pay was a mere formality. Kipkoi had been beating Wilson since he was a boy. First he would beat him in a rage, and then lecture him in a rage. On how the whites had taken the country and demeaned the people and killed the animals. On how the whites would set tribe against tribe so that Africans would always fight. On how the whites kept the place poor so that soldiers had to shoot pregnant animals for food. On how Wilson must become tough and ready and mean and angry so that no one would ever rule him, so that he would always make his father proud of his first son. And then Kipkoi would beat him again.

Faced with these contradictions and humiliations, the cyclonic ragings and danger of Kipkoi, Wilson responded with the only way open to someone smaller, less well armed in every respect. He became the antithesis of rage, his anger was ice. He was silent, taut, watchful. He developed traits very rare among bushmen—causticness, irony, cynicism, bitterness. Against Kipkoi, he used the best weapon that had evolved in his mind—open contempt. Contempt for Kipkoi's bush ways and bush education, bush values. Wilson began to read voraciously, in order to hold himself up to the mirror of Kipkoi's near illiteracy. He learned about the world and history, to show how small Kipkoi and his men were within it. He developed strong political opinions that highlighted the repressiveness of men who wore uniforms and carried guns, men who were trained only to hunt other men. He began to think of Kipkoi, and eventually to speak of him, in odd colonial pejoratives—my father, the bush monkey; my father, the bush nigger.

That was around the time that Wilson went to work for Palmer. Wilson had just been fired from yet another tourist lodge job, was back in Kipkoi's camp, his corner of the tent crammed with incongruous books and papers. One day, Palmer roared into camp in his old Land Rover for a periodic inspection.

"Where is Kipkoi!?" he hollered at the shocked Somalis. "Where is he, off drunk someplace? I'm going to eat Kipkoi today, roast him up, good bush monkey meat. Where the bloody hell is Kipkoi?"

Kipkoi would eventually emerge from his tent.

"Hello, white man. I've been cleaning my gun to shoot you with, you colonial piece of shit."

Palmer beamed at this.

"Save your bullets and what aim you have left in you for the Tanzanians, bush boy. You need all the help you can get."

And in front of the gasping Somali men, they would go into Kipkoi's tent to talk.

Palmer was one of the white men in Kenya with no official position, yet with power that defies definition. In that strange financial netherworld of poor African governments with many animals, and wealthy whites who cared about the animals, Palmer paid for a large percentage of the salaries, uniforms, petrol, and bullets for Kipkoi and his men. He was a Brit, raised in Kenya, who had come into a large inheritance and owned an immense wheat farm on the edge of the southern grasslands. But mere wheat profits and charitable acts did not earn Palmer the right to inspect Kipkoi's unit. Long before, Palmer had been one of the last British wardens, and a ferociously effective one with a penchant for antipoaching operations. When his white face had to be retired, he took it well, recognized it as the political necessity it was, and urged that the antipoaching duties be made a separate division, with Kipkoi as his replacement. Palmer knew Kipkoi and his skills well, because before he was a warden, before independence, Palmer was one of the white hunters. And from the time they were both in their early twenties, Kipkoi was Palmer's boy.

Once inside the tent, Kipkoi and Palmer would drop the chest-thumping that each reflexively fell into when the two were in front of others. Instead, they discussed the unit's situation. Which men Kipkoi thought were in with the poachers. Where the Tanzanians were likely to hit next. What could be done about the powerful member of Parliament who was running most of the ivory smuggling north of there. And more and more frequently in the conversations, what to do about money. According to the agreement Palmer had worked out with the government, the ministry funded half the unit, and Palmer half. But with each month, as the economic crisis worsened, the government's half shrank, and the men were getting hungry. Palmer would complain and threaten in response to Kipkoi's demand for more money for his unit. He would curse the government people, insist that Kipkoi's men were embezzling funds, insist that Kipkoi himself was doing so. But it would all be show. Because at the end, Kipkoi would cite a truism that he and Palmer had learned and that haunted them both. Kipkoi would say, "A hungry man makes mistakes," and Palmer would come up with more money, more than even he could really afford.

Such was the gist of one of those conversations, which Wilson sat and listened to while pretending to read. They ignored him. Afterward, in front of the men, Kipkoi and Palmer insulted and pretended to aggress each other again. As Palmer was about to leave, Kipkoi asked him the question he had been preparing all visit.

"Palmer, you farmer, why don't you give my son a job? He is a piece of shit who cannot even keep a job in a camp for tourists, but it should be easy for even him to do farmer's work."

"Sure, Kipkoi. And if he's anything like you, I'll probably have him back here in a month."

"Just watch your cash box. He'll steal it first chance."

Thus, Wilson went to work for Palmer. He got trained in a variety of jobs. He worked on the machinery, learned to tally the books. He supervised the workers, negotiated with the local Masai about curtailing raiding, acted as a liaison between Kipkoi's unit and Palmer. He excelled at all of it, but he never got to do one of the things that secretly excited him. Palmer never taught him to shoot. Palmer, ex–great white hunter, ex-warden, ex-antipoaching commando, was an anomaly to begin with, having wound up with the contemptible profession of farmer. But not only that, he was one of the only farmers who didn't shoot wild game that came to eat his crops. He would put up miles of ineffectual electric fences, hire game beaters, even tried experiments with taste aversion conditioning to get the animals to avoid the crops. But he would not shoot the animals. Palmer, as incongruously as Kipkoi, had come to really love the animals—the reason why he funded the antipoaching unit—and he even loved the animals that ate his crops.

But other than that disappointment of not learning to use a gun, Wilson liked the work and the life there. Palmer fell naturally into treating him as he had treated Kipkoi years before—teaching him, berating him, mocking him, promoting him. Wilson, already accustomed to the shifts of mood from his own father, fell naturally into his role: anger at Palmer, condemnations of his colonial ways, all the while coupled with superb, loyal work. Together, they would argue constantly. Wilson, dispassionately, would accuse Palmer and all his ilk of ruining the Kenyan lands by introducing cash cropping, of assuring the Indian-Pakistani wars by exploiting the religious differences there during the Raj, of suppressing Northern Ireland, the whole gamut of his Anglo angers. Palmer would rail against Wilson's politics, his economic ideas, warn him, more explicitly, that Wilson was spouting Bolshevik crap and he'd better not start trying to organize the workers on the farm. And Palmer would promote Wilson, give him more responsibility, and leave more books of all persuasions for him to read. And Wilson began to take on many of Palmer's rough assertive mannerisms, even while telling his friends how he was going to kill that old colonial.

The problem began when the government cut back even more on the money to Kipkoi's unit. Eventually, even Kipkoi's veiled haunted line to Palmer about how a hungry man makes mistakes could not get more money from Palmer; he was giving all he could. The months went by with the government salaries late or nonexistent. There were not enough bullets, not enough petrol to operate the vehicles. There was not enough food. They began to be as hungry as the unpaid Tanzanian army units across the border, and to think the same thoughts. The Somali men had few compunctions about anything, but they feared Kipkoi, even had a grudging respect for him, knew his opinions and did him the honor of confronting him. They were hungry. They could start shakedowns of the local people. That wouldn't bother them, these were Kipkoi's tribesmen, not theirs. Or they could shoot something, something with meat. We are hungry, Kipkoi, this is bullshit, not getting paid. Get us some food, or we will get it ourselves.

Kipkoi, who was just as hungry as they, who had been foreseeing this crisis emerging for months, already knew what he had decided. They would start shooting animals for meat. Adult males, zebras or giraffes or wildebeests, something with meat, something not endangered. Somewhere quiet. And he, Kipkoi, would do the shooting. His men had to eat.

That night he didn't sleep, the same fitfulness that had not been there since the night before the first hunt with the bwana, forty years earlier. Kipkoi used an old .458, a huge elephant gun, instead of the automatic weapons they used in the battles with the poachers. And at the first shot, he trembled, something he never did. And missed the giraffe. One of the younger Somali men snickered, continued to do so even after Kipkoi took down another giraffe while it was further away and running. That night, the men, satisfied with the meat and the promise of an animal a week from Kipkoi, indulged themselves in mockery behind his back—"The old man is finally slowing down, did you see him tremble?"

A week later, when Wilson came to deliver some money and instructions from Palmer to Kipkoi, his father was out on patrol. Wilson lounged with the men, although he had never been particularly comfortable with them. The men, who still regarded Wilson as an anomaly, a coolly off-putting kid, nevertheless recognized his growing status at Palmer's and knew Palmer's power over them. It occurred to them to try to curry favor with Wilson, or at least try to get on friendlier terms. The youngest ranger, the one who had snickered and could recognize Wilson's smoldering anger at Kipkoi, told Wilson the story about how Kipkoi trembled when he shot at a giraffe at only 100 meters. Wilson, your old man's losing it.

Wilson didn't respond to the ranger, left shortly after that, without waiting for his father. That evening, he was unusually quiet around Palmer and could not even be drawn into an argument about the recent shutting of the university and the government beating of students. Instead, Wilson surprised Palmer with a rare request—a few days off. He wanted to go see his wife for a bit. Palmer found this odd, given Wilson's usual apathy about her. He agreed readily, since Wilson rarely took any time off.

Wilson departed the next morning. But instead of heading toward the small plot of land in the hamlet straddling Masai and Kipsigi country where his wife lived forgotten, he went to Nairobi. In the streets of Nairobi, where every sort of illegal or illicit thing could be obtained, Wilson paid for a service that shamed him. He had come this far, although he could have obtained the same in the town near Palmer's farm, for fear of being recognized. He went to a writer, one of the educated men who sat at a booth and wrote letters for the illiterate, read important documents for them. Wilson was, of course, anything but illiterate, and was shamed at being mistaken for some wild bush kid. But he needed a letter written in a handwriting that was not his own. Carefully dictating to the ex-student, a few years older than he, he detailed the poaching activities of one Kipkoi wa Kimutai, the places and dates, the rangers who could verify the facts. He mailed it, unsigned, from the general post office in Nairobi to Palmer. And Palmer, who knew and could prove that half the game park men in the country were poaching, who could do the same concerning the poaching activities by government ministers, who accepted it as part of the rot in the system and did not bother to do anything about it, Palmer decided to go after Kipkoi.

It did not take him long. The young rangers, scared for their hides, were more than happy to cooperate, even with something as unorthodox as being interrogated by a white man with no government connections, while their guns sat at their feet, unconsidered. Whether Palmer understood that Kipkoi poached in order to feed his hungry men is not clear, as he did not care to pursue that part of the story. Instead, he went to confront Kipkoi in his tent.

On the wall of Kipkoi's tent was a picture that he took with him everywhere. It was a famous photograph, shown in the National Museum, known to schoolchildren, one of the few images that were part of the hagiography of Kenya's history, part of its fragile, just-emerging sense of national identity. It was a photograph of the dead General Lenin.

In the late 1940s and early 1950s, the Kikuyus rose up in a peasant rebellion against the British colonial rule. It was motivated by the British seizing of the Kikuyu traditional lands and by the disenfranchisement and second-class citizenship in their ancestral homes. Most immediately, it was motivated by the British attempts to outlaw some of the more alien elements of Kikuyu customs, such as female circumcision or infanticide. The Kikuyu rose up, and the world learned of it as the Mau Mau rebellion. Young men took to the forests to fight, raid, plunder, sabotage. To the extent that there was any driving ideology beyond tribal outrage, the orientation was vaguely leftist, and many of the Mau Mau fighters took noms de guerre reflecting this. General Lenin was the name taken by one young man who emerged as a charismatic leader and moderately effective fighter. He led a large band that roamed through the thick Aberdare mountains of Kikuyuland, and he was among the most wanted by the British army trying to suppress the rebellion.

On September 23, 1954, General Lenin was caught in an ambush on the lower slopes of the Aberdares, while he was attempting to shoot a forest buck with a bow and arrow. He was killed by a single bullet to the chest. The famed photograph shows him a few minutes after his death, with his beard and Mau Mau dreadlocks and traditional clothing made of animal skins. He is on his side, the chest wound visible. Standing, with his foot perched on General Lenin's rib cage, is the British soldier who tracked and shot him. He is a young man, with a jutting beard and a tough bush-hardened face, but not a displeased one. He has affected the traditional hunter's pose upon a downed lion, and his face, intelligent and wry, shows how aware he is of the statement he is making. At the time, its cynical, reassuring message to the British public for which it was meant was "Just another prey, just another day's work." To the Kenyan public, when it is reprinted in the papers each Independence Day, it still says, "Look how they treated us, look at what they considered us." The soldier in the picture, of course, was Palmer.

It was an accomplishment that the young Captain Palmer was proud of, although, to his credit, the pride did not last for long. Palmer aged with his shame, lost his hair, shaved his beard, lost the cocky wryness, until he was no longer recognizable. There were endless Palmers in the vestiges of the empire and of British East Africa who would claim to be that Palmer over a drink, but the real Palmer spent less time with the other Brits and never drank with them. He was delighted for someone else to take the credit, and he disappeared into the new nation. The British soldier who seconded Palmer, Arden, the one whose shooting reflexes were far slower, was pensioned off somewhere in the UK, a forgotten drunk. Arden's hunting boy had been killed in a road accident sometime after independence. And Palmer's boy was Kipkoi.

In the photograph of the keen Captain Palmer and the deceased General Lenin, there is a shadow on the leftmost field of vision. Naturally, Kipkoi was not allowed to share in the photographic moment of glory of his bwana, but he stood just off-camera. The strategy of the hunt had been his, as Palmer readily admitted. "A hungry man makes mistakes," Kipkoi had said, and they had deployed men to find and destroy the traditional Kikuyu snares in the forest, depriving the Mau Mau fighters of meat. It had been hard tedious work, spotting snares that were not meant to be spotted. But it awakened in both Kipkoi and Palmer an appetite for the strategies needed to fight poachers. They had destroyed enough of the snares, controlled enough of the farms below that might smuggle maize up to the fighters, that the Mau Mau began to starve. And spent their time going after forest buck with bows and arrows, instead of fighting the British.

On that cold September morning, when the rainy season had come early and made the forest paths difficult but telltale, Kipkoi had lead the way and picked up General Lenin's track. They had taken an unorthodox strategy, climbing high, into the near moor lands, and then dropping down, until Kipkoi found the tracks. Lenin, as he had guessed, was moving downward, despite the British proximity below, in order to hunt for the plentiful game on the lower slopes. Kipkoi led, Palmer followed, and the other two covered the rear. They were tense with excitement and caution, although no more so than on any other hunt. Kipkoi spotted him first, Palmer shot merely the one time that was necessary. Kipkoi felt the same pride that Palmer did, appreciated the extra pay for

Mau Mau patrol. And as a Kipsigi, the Kikuyu grievances made little sense, and he welcomed the chance to set back the fortunes of the other tribe.

The first time Palmer came into Kipkoi's tent in one of the antipoaching camps and saw the photograph pinned up, he asked Kipkoi in some annoyance why that was up there. "Someday, I will receive a great deal of money from the newspapers to tell where that captain is now, and then I will drive a car like yours," answered Kipkoi, sardonically. He was a bit surprised, hurt, that Palmer would even ask. He thought the answer was obvious as to why he commemorated that moment. Because in their long years together, that September morning was the time that Kipkoi's feelings of respect, rage, gratitude, fear, and emulation for Palmer converged into something resembling love.

It is not clear what transpired in Kipkoi's tent when Palmer came to confront him about the poaching. Perhaps Kipkoi made threats about the photograph, or perhaps he would have died of shame before doing such a thing. Perhaps he explained himself, perhaps Palmer relented, perhaps Palmer got exactly the punishment for Kipkoi that he wanted. Kipkoi was not charged, but took retirement. He returned to his home, the two surviving wives and nine remaining children. Palmer returned to his farm work and soon told the government that he could no longer afford his disproportionate half of the antipoaching unit, which was disbanded soon after that. And in that period, Wilson's angers at Palmer were finally realized. It was in fury at Palmer for attacking his father, and for doing an incomplete job of it. Wilson became more withdrawn, inconsistent in his work, eventually dangerous. He drank for the first time, began to smoke bhang. He fought with the workers and, one day, even assaulted Palmer, who gave him one more chance. And shortly after that, Wilson disappeared with the farm's cash box (although conspicuously leaving the cash behind). He lives now in the shantytowns of Nairobi, with the other young men who flock from the bush to the city to look for nonexistent jobs. Drinking, occasionally stealing, wearing his hair in dreadlocks.

AT THE KIOSK

The Mau Mau lost. East Africa was going to have to be given its independence; even British statesmen were making noises about winds of change. But they were certainly not going to turn the colony over to forest fighters in dreadlocks and monkey skins who took names like General China. The Mau Mau were rather effectively crushed, and when the British made it clear that they were in charge and could damn well hold on to the colony as long as they wished, they turned it over to the Kenyans. But to the Kenyans who had been hand-groomed and coached—British-educated, latent Anglophiles who, decades later, would still have their Kenyan judges wear powdered wigs.

But the new government had the problem of what to do with the ex–Mau Mau. During that first year as I pieced together the story of Wilson and Kip-koi and Palmer, I also learned the unexpected fate of the fighters. It was con-venient for the national mythology to claim that the Mau Mau had won, that independence was a direct outgrowth of their rebellion. It was convenient to say that Jomo Kenyatta had led the Mau Mau. Kenyatta, a consummately urbane man, an author who had traveled the world, had been accused by the British in the early '50s of being the mastermind behind Mau Mau as a means to put him away. Most evidence suggested that this was a frame-up. Now, it was convenient for the new nation to say it was really true. Mau Mau led the rebellion, won the war, and their leader now sat in the president's office.

The problem, of course, was what to do with the real Mau Mau fighters. Some were trotted out for public ceremonies. Dazed men in matted dread-locks and animal skins soon bound for the Independence Museum, looking more than a little bit suspicious of the new government Kikuyus in their pin-stripes and ties and government Mercedeses. But after that, what to do with them? The new pinstripe guys were more scared of them than the Brits were; angry, uneducated guerrillas named Commander Moscow. No thank you.

In a surprising success for the new government, the fighters were quietly dispersed into the national mythology. A few did wind up in the government, one notably running special security forces for Kenyatta. By some quirk, many of them were given licenses to operate food kiosks in town, a plum of a reward. The kiosks are all over the place in Nairobi, on the outskirts. Large, airy wooden shacks, with wood benches and tables. A booth for the proprietor, huge cooking cauldrons sitting on fires that have probably burned continu-ously for years. Smoky Kenyan tea, bowls of maize and beans (a traditional Kikuyu dish), occasionally a goat or chicken stew. Ubiquitous, cheap, con-venient, good food. It was apparently decided that the kiosks would be the reward for the fighters.

I learned of this during that first season. Whenever I was in Nairobi, I fre-quented the same kiosk. Maize and beans each day, loud, raucous Kikuyu dance music, men sitting and eating and shouting, cats and chickens under-foot. It was run by Kimani, an older middle-aged Kikuyu who dripped avun-cularity. Big, round, battered Kikuyu face, patches of white stubble on his face and head, a habitual heavy greatcoat and wool cap, as he stood behind the counter, shouted, made change, handed out tea, joshed the regulars. I, happily, had become one myself, and he would greet me each day with handshakes and bows and tea. I practiced my Swahili with him, and he seemed to consider my every gesture to be amusing and commendable.

One day I asked him if it was true that many of the kiosk guys were Mau Mau. Yes, of course, he said, even me. You, Kimani? Aw, come on. He roared with laughter and delight at my surprise. Yes, I was Mau Mau, I ran away to the forest and fought, after they took my father's land. We were fierce, we wore long hair and did not wear the clothes of Europeans. Did you kill anyone, Kimani? Oh yes, many times. Really? Well, once we were in a battle with the British and I shot an arrow at someone, but I missed.

He seemed so jolly, the whole story sounded rather implausible. I wondered if claiming you were ex–Mau Mau was a pleasing innocent scam for Kikuyu men that age. But then he said, Aii, we had a terrible battle with those British, and they captured us, and they sent me to the desert for eight years in prison. And look—holding up his hands—those British pulled out my fingernails. He found this uproarious and seemed to melt with nostalgia. I had never noticed his fingers before. There was something on the end of each finger that might have been a fingernail or some distorted remnant of a fingernail; his fingers had the definition of turnips.

But, Kimani, aren't you angry at the British, don't you hate them? This he found even more amusing—"No, no, because we won!"

He chuckled awhile, but then quieted and considered his fingers. He said, Well, I did not like them when they pulled out my fingernails, and I did not like that prison in the desert. I do not hate the British, but I do not like those people either. They are not good people.

Suddenly, he remembered his manners and felt vulnerable in the way that Kenyans feel in not being able to discern the nationality of white English speakers. "Uh, you are not British, are you?" he asked.

No, American.

He was delighted, roared, Then what am I telling you for? You Americans have fought the British also, you know about those people.

He served up more tea, this graceful man with no fingernails.

THE SOURCE OF THE NILE

The transition from the reign of Solomon to that of Uriah had come and passed. Joshua was learning how to take care of young Obadiah, and crazy tense Ruthie was even calming down a bit in Joshua's presence. It had been a few weeks since Benjamin had stumbled into a beehive, and Rachel and her family seemed to have things under control with poor, beleaguered Job.

My first year was drawing to a close, and I was due back in the lab soon. To celebrate a successful and safe period, I decided to do the most impetuous thing in my life. I went to Uganda.

Now, I had been hoping to go to Uganda for some time, to fulfill a dream of sitting at a particular crossroads that I had spotted on the map. It was a perfect crossroads—to the north, the only road ran to the desert and on to Sudan. To the west, Zaire and the Congo. To the south, on to Rwanda and Burundi and the mountain gorillas. I could visualize it—a dusty empty crossroads, with, perhaps, a rusted laconic sign—"Sahara, bear right, mountain gorillas, left, Congo, straight. Buckle up for safety." I dreamt of sitting underneath that sign as a hitchhiking tabula rasa, to go in whichever direction a ride presented itself—a mosquito net in case my ride took me to the Congo, a thin shawl to wrap around my head in case it was the desert, a sweater for the mountain gorillas.

But now I went to Uganda to see the overthrow of Idi Amin. You remember Idi Amin, I'm sure, two decades after his ouster. While probably no more savage or brutal than most dictatorial murderers, he managed to combine it with such a boyish demeanor, such a joie de vivre, that he was irresistible to the Western press. He did sordid mundane things like kill his people and terrorize his country and loot its wealth. But he also had a certain loony panache about it all. He was, as the Western press often said, a buffoon. He declared himself the king of Scotland and serenaded his guests with Scottish accordion music, dressed in kilts. He sent silly outrageous telegrams to other world leaders, reminiscent of a king of Uganda a century earlier, who sent love letters to Queen Victoria and invited her to come to his royal village as his umpteenth wife. He threatened the British expatriate community in Kampala and was mollified when prominent British businessmen carried him around in a sedan chair. Oh, the buffoonery. And he became just one of a number of Africa's postindependence leaders, if the rather solid documentation is to be believed, to kill his opponents and then eat them. How could the West resist? Amin could not have been invented more satisfyingly by Westerners who got the heebie-jeebies at the idea of independent Third World nations—he declares himself the king of Scotland *and* is a cannibal.

He destroyed his country while most of Africa's other leaders looked the other way, a point of considerable bitterness among Ugandans to this day. His only consistent critic was Tanzania's Julius Nyerere, an intensely dignified principled man who was, on some visceral level, probably as upset by the buffoonery as by the terror. Nyerere campaigned incessantly for Amin's ouster, supported the many rebel groups that had sprung up in Uganda's misery. In a grandiose miscalculation, in 1979, Amin declared that Nyerere was just an impotent old hen and seized a piece of Tanzania. In African circles, these were fighting words indeed, and Tanzania counterattacked. And, oddly, bowled over Amin's army. Nyerere was then faced with the difficult decision of following the Organization of African Unity's cherished rule about respecting the sovereignty of other African leaders (i.e., the colonials gerrymandered the hell out of the continent's borders out of capricious European interests, but it was now in everyone's best interests not to touch those sacred demarcations) or pushing on and ousting the murderer. He went for the latter, and within a few weeks of relatively fierce fighting in which Tanzania's troops were aided by a wellspring of local support, Amin and his people were driven out of the capital.

Everyone went bonkers in Kampala. Dancing in the streets, the radio said. A new government, and end of fear, emptying of the jails and the torture chambers.

The Tanzanian army had swept up the western side of Lake Victoria and looped east to Kampala. The north of the country was still in control of Amin's people, as was the whole eastern side bordering Kenya. The Tanzanians concentrated on the eastern front and managed to open up a narrow corridor to the Kenyan border. That was the day I entered Uganda from Kenya.

I had wanted to travel at the end of this stretch with the baboons. I was feeling, atypically for me, a journalistic reflex, a desire to see history being made, and I was moved by this particular history—dancing in the streets, a freed people. I spent my years at college flirting with the Quakers and, intellectually, thought that it would be important for me to test the ideals of pacifism that I was toying with by observing an undeniably just war.

Ah, this is nonsense. I was twenty-one and wanted an adventure. I wanted to scare the shit out of myself and see amazing things and talk about it afterward. And for the previous month, I had been missing someone badly, and I thought that going to a war would make me feel better about it. I was behaving like a late-adolescent male primate.

So I went, hitching on the petrol tankers that were the only vehicles being allowed to pass through the border from Kenya. I made it to the capital of Kampala, spent some time there, hitched further west toward the mountains that border Zaire, at which point I felt too deep into scary unknown territory and turned around, starting to hitch back east to Kenya again. A day into the country, in that eastern corridor, a petrol tanker about thirty minutes in front of us was blown up by Amin's soldiers. A few days later in Kampala, where there were still corpses everywhere and swarms of vultures in the sky, our district was shelled and the lorry driver and I huddled for the night underneath the vehicle. That was it for my war stories, all the proverbial action that I saw, and that was quite enough. But the main thing was not the war. In a weird way, it was cleansing to have those moments of sheer absolute terror and, when the shelling stopped, to feel the relief. What weighed so much more, what could never abate, was the sickness of the previous decade of Amin.

The euphoria, the release of the looting, had spent itself by the time I got there, and the sense of poison had returned. During the day after Amin fled Kampala, a huge percentage of the stores in the capital were looted by crowds. There was a vague tone in the Western press of "*those* people running amok once again, destroying their own communities." It was anything but that. Amin, the repression, and the looting were the logical outcomes of yet another residue of colonialism. At the turn of the century, when the British smashed the Sudanese uprising, they decided to roll on further south, mop up Uganda while they were at it, and bring Nubian troops as their backups. And the Nubians—tribes like the Acholi—stayed, northern Muslim tribes amid a country of southern Bugandan Christians. When the Brits allowed Uganda its independence, they left the Nubian firmly in control of the military. Amin had been a general from the northern tribe, and when he took over, he systematically seized the stores of Kampala and turned them over to his tribal compatriots. Thus, the orgy of looting and revenge against the northerners.

But that felt good for only so long, and now the poison was back. So many years of fear could not be forgotten. Anyone who was educated, who was political, who was a religious leader, who had money, paid for it in some way. I sat one evening with one man, a Bugandan businessman who recited the vehicles that had been taken from him over the years, as if they were his lost children. "First they took UGH365. It was our car. That was a good vehicle. Then they took UFK213. That was the lorry. Then they took UFW891. That was the pickup truck. I used to see the Acholi man driving it around town for years afterward. He was army." One old man, who helped run the bombed remnants of the YMCA I stayed in, sat and recited the children he had lost. All taken. Two confirmed dead, one who disappeared somewhere down the drainage troughs of Amin's torture chambers.

The teachers had suffered among the most. Uganda had spectacular education. Churchill, at the time of Victoria's jubilee, began the British tradition of viewing Uganda as its pearl in Africa, and it developed its education as in no other African colony. By the time of Amin's coup, its university was unmatched on the continent, its public schools superb. Predictably, the teachers were targeted early. One day in the border town of Tororo, I walked down the street and was seized by an excited trim middle-aged man in a white shirt. "Ah, you are a foreigner, god bless you for coming, this means we are free now, Christ has delivered us through the sons of Tanzania, I used to be a schoolteacher, the school is gone, they burned it, I was in a jail, they tortured me, look where they beat me." He forced me to sit with him as, more and more manically, he told me his story. In that mad day in Tororo, four different teachers accosted me with their similar stories, all just released, broken, from the jails.

The papers that had just resumed publishing had a phrase already—they referred to the need now for "psychological rehabilitation of the country." Every gesture, every encounter, every smell, was wrong, was tense, was watchful, was inappropriate. A subliminal sense of wrongness. Too many people ready to seize you and tell you, a stranger, their story. Too many people ready to laugh and kick at some body in the street in Kampala. Too many people pulling away from me in a xenophobic panic on the sidewalk.

One day, I walked in downtown Kampala, near the palace of the new president (a professor, appointed by the tribunal of Ugandan rebels and Tanzanians. He was destined to rule for only two weeks before being replaced, a pattern to be repeated with spasms of coups and countercoups for the next decade until the memories of Amin took on a nostalgic tinge). A busy crowd of people, going about their business. Something subtle happened, and it triggered the gears of fright in everyone's head. I would guess that three or four people, independently, just happened to stop on the same block at the same time—to remember where they had put the key, to decide which errand to do next, to sneeze. Some psychological critical mass had been reached, enough people were standing still. Everyone stopped dead. It spread, until in the whole downtown, everyone was standing still. We all stared at the presidential palace, everyone breathed tensely, families huddled together. Oh my god, what is about to happen? everyone was thinking. We all stood there in silence, waiting for the next trouble for maybe five minutes, until Tanzanian soldiers came and yelled at everyone to start moving again.

By all logic, the most emotionally persistent moment should have been when I got into big trouble in Kampala. I did something truly stupid, something that someone who had been in Africa merely a day would probably have had the smarts to avoid. I am too embarrassed even to say what I did, but as a result of it, a pair of Tanzanian soldiers decided that I was an ex-mercenary for Amin's army. There had been plenty of white guys willing to serve that role, and the soldiers' thinking was not outrageous. A seething, vengeful Ugandan crowd developed, the soldiers vacillated, I was made to lie facedown on the concrete with a gun pointed at me. It was certainly the most frightening moment of my life. The Kenyan lorry driver I was traveling with argued heroically and convinced them to release me.

The most intense moment, unexpectedly, came later. I had finally felt frightened and disoriented enough that I had to flee, had to get out of that impossible place. I started hitching back east to safe, familiar Kenya again. Despite my near panic to be gone, there was something I very much needed to do, against all logic. I made a detour in the town of Jinja, in order to see the source of the Nile. It is here that Lake Victoria spills over its edge and begins the White Nile. It was here that Burton had dreamt of, that Speke, slipping off on his own, had finally reached, over which one of the great debates of Victorian science raged. I had grown up on all of these men as my heroes, had read Burton's journals and biographies, had traced their journeys on maps. I wanted to see the point where the Nile began.

It was not hard to find. There was a bridge over it now, a concrete wall below that formed some sort of hydroelectric dam, with a torrent of water bursting through an opening. Oddly, there was even a plaque commemorating Speke's "discovery" of this spot. Standing at the very center of the bridge, you could see, just below, a staircase coming down the concrete wall, down to a platform right at the water level with a hole in the wall. No doubt related to the workings of this dam. I stood there and looked down, seeing something extraordinary. A soldier had been marched down the stairs, his hands tied behind his back. A rope had been put around his throat and tied to some piece of machinery inside that hole, such that as the river rose, the man had eventually been swept off his feet, so that he had drowned or choked. He was dead, the body bloated and stiff, floating straight out in the rushing water. I thought, Was he Ugandan or Tanzanian? There was too little uniform left to tell. I thought, If he was with Amin, he deserved it. I thought, But no one deserves to die that way. I thought, But how many civilians did he kill? I thought, But maybe he was just a forced conscript, forced to do it. I thought, Yeah, I know what I think of Nazis who said they were just following orders. I thought, I bet the current is too strong there for the crocs to get to his body. I thought, I wonder if he was alive as the waters rose on him, how did that feel? I thought, I wonder if I can get closer, to see, I must remember every detail, so I can tell people about this. I thought, I want to forget this, I want to get the hell out of here, to be home, to be safe. And I stood there, transfixed, unable to move from that spot.

•   •   •

Decades later, in the neurobiology classes I teach, I always spend some lectures on the physiology of aggression. The hormonal modulation of it, the areas of the brain having some influence over it, the genetic components of it. Somehow, each year, it takes more and more lectures to cover the material. There aren't a whole lot more facts known than about the neurobiology of schizophrenia or language use or parental behavior, just to name a few of the other topics I cover. But somehow, almost embarrassingly, I spend more and more time talking about aggression. I think each year I lecture longer because of that man with his head tied to the dam and because of how long I stood there looking at him, unable to leave. I think it is because of the ambiguity of aggression. It is the most confusing emotion to me, and with the defenses of an academician, I clearly believe that if I lecture at it enough, it will give up and go away quietly, its simultaneous attraction and repulsion will stop being so frightening to me. Parental behavior, sexual behavior, those are usually pretty unassailable positives. Schizophrenia, depression, dementia—definitely bad. But aggression. The same motor pattern, the same burst of viscera and neurotransmitters holding razors, and sometimes we are rewarded as with few other behaviors, and sometimes we have been unspeakably harmful. A just war, a nation freed, and a head jammed in the hole in the concrete. I stood watching for hours, mesmerized, as if to see how long it would take for this man to be washed away, bit by bit, into the Nile.

Part 2

The Subadult Years

8

The Baboons:
Saul in the Wilderness

*Y*ou never want to be an ex–alpha male baboon in the troop where you were once alpha. By the early 1980s, Solomon sank, but into anything but obscurity. Uriah, not a particularly vicious kid, was not overly cruel to his ex-nemesis after he had unseated him. But everyone else couldn't get enough of the change. Solomon did not merely trade places with Uriah, becoming number two in the hierarchy. He had held on to the alpha position long past the point when he had the physical means to do so, holding on purely by dint of the status quo and intimidation. Once everyone saw that Uriah had successfully challenged that status quo, everyone else tried it, and by 1980, Solomon had plummeted to ninth rank, solidly middle. And a pattern emerged that has grown familiar to me over the years. When you look at the frequencies of dominance interactions, the typical pattern you see is that, for example, number 4 is having his most interactions with 3 and 5, losing to the former, defeating the latter. Number 17 mostly interacts with 16 and 18. But, as an exception to that nearest-neighbor pattern, you'll suddenly note that ranks 1–5 are having an extraordinary number of interactions with the lowly number 11. Why are they so intent on rubbing Mister 11's nose in it all the time? He, invariably, turns out to be the ex–number 1 who used to dominate 1–5. The tables are turned, and baboons are endowed with long, vengeful memories. Solomon got no end of grief. Isaac, Aaron, both in the top six positions in the hierarchy, even Benjamin, who by then was about number 8 or so, got their licks in. Solomon lost his austere minimalist style and became craven and obsequious around those higher ranking and pretty vicious to those lower. He harassed poor, weird Job endlessly, to the point where his probable family of Naomi, Rachel, and Sarah once chased Solomon across two fields. He lunged at me a few times, sending me cowering back inside the Jeep. And, finding the resolution that many ex-alphas come to, he upped and left one day, joining the troop to the south, where, if of a mediocre and declining rank, he would at least be anonymous. He would be seen occasionally when the troops met and hollered at each other from across the river.

There were some changes in the troop on other fronts. Joshua was hitting prime age, and Boopsie and Afghan went wild over him. Devorah had her first child, a daughter who appeared to have been Solomon's child, since he was the only male to spend time with Devorah during her conception estrus. This had been his last consortship as the alpha male, while he was in the final throes of Uriah's harassment. Thus the rape of Devorah by Solomon must have occurred when she was a few weeks pregnant. Had Solomon not been toppled by Uriah, this infant would have been growing up now with the troop's alpha male being reasonably certain that he was her father. Despite the change in the political winds, she was hardly an abandoned child. Between Devorah and her dominating mother, Leah, the kid grew quickly and with no lack of confidence. By chance, the low-ranking Miriam had a daughter the same week, and the differences between the two were striking. Devorah's daughter was larger, held her head upright first, walked first, sat on her mother's back first. Devorah could sit and feed while her child was able to wander off; lower-ranking females would cluster around and groom Devorah, for a chance to examine the kid. Miriam's daughter, in contrast, could go only a few steps before Miriam would nervously retrieve her—the world was full of endless individuals who would be delighted to maul the kid. Miriam had to feed with both hands full, had to frequently scamper away from a fight with the child barely clinging to her belly. Various studies had shown that having the good fortune to be born to a high-ranking mom like Devorah, rather than a Miriam, made for faster, healthier development, and a greater chance of surviving during the tough times. On a day that each of the babies was about a week old, they interacted with each other for the first time. Devorah's kid scampered toward Miriam's, who scampered away and ran back to Miriam. A first dominance interaction had just occurred, and it shocked me to think that I could go away that instant, go live decades of my life and return middle-aged, and that asymmetry would probably still be in place.

Meanwhile, on other fronts, Jonathan, a young guy who had recently joined the troop, was barreling into adolescence and had developed a bad crush on Rebecca. She was the prepubescent daughter of beautiful, bound-for-tragedy Bathsheeba. She lacked the classic looks of her mother but had a fresh baboon-next-door quality to her. This appalling anthropomorphism was aided by the fact that I had recently darted her and given her a pair of yellow numbered ear tags that stuck out like barrettes for her nonexistent pigtails. She was cute and bouncy and played with her many friends, including her closest pal, Sarah, of the Naomi-Rachel-Sarah clan. And naturally, she had no idea that Jonathan existed. He, a shy young beast, was unable to pull off the suave worldly strategy that had worked so well for Joshua in wooing Ruth back in 1978 (i.e., patiently following her each time she sprinted off in one of her nervous states). Instead, Jonathan just sat and moped, face on his arms, gazing at Rebecca from a distance.

There were also changes with David and Daniel, the two kids who'd transferred in together a few years before and had become inseparable buddies. Daniel happened to reach his growth spurt about a year before David, and the former soon was absurdly decked out in shoulder muscles, a cape of hair, an expanded chest. He looked like a junior high school kid in football gear to me, but the whole thing was impressive enough that he was beginning to make some waves in the hierarchy. Perhaps most impressed by the change was Daniel himself, and suddenly he had no time for wrestling and chasing up and down trees with David. He was too busy with important stuff.

This was also the season when Isaac, a heretofore obscure young adult, became friends with Rachel. Naturally, I applauded this, given my feeling that Rachel was the nicest baboon in the troop. Now, a male and female baboon might best be defined as friends if they hang out together and don't happen to be having sex. Barbara Smuts, a primatologist at the University of Michigan, wrote a wonderful book a few years ago on the subject—who are the rare baboons that manage to establish friendships, what traits does it take, what are the rewards and heartaches (the heartache for the male mostly being that he has to restrain himself from beating up on the female anytime he has a frustrating day, the reward being that she would actually choose to have something to do with him)? So Rachel and Isaac became friends. Isaac was someone who, in the last year, had emerged as one of the most unique animals I ever knew. At first glance, at the first two years of glances, he seemed to be somewhat of an underachiever and had a silly flat forehead to boot. Prime-aged, perfect health, he shoulda been a contender. Instead, he kept walking away from fights, showdowns, provocations. In your less charitable moments words like "coward," "sissy," "mama's boy," would flash, but you'd realize he wasn't running away with a tail flag and fear bark. He was walking, disinterested, unruffled. He wasn't losing fights—he simply was choosing not to be part of them. If it took giving someone a subordinance gesture, crouching on his belly, for example, he'd do it and then remove himself from the unpleasant situation.

He had an interesting sex life. A very attractive female would come into estrus. "Very attractive" to a male baboon usually means she's had a few kids already who've survived (proving that she's fertile and a competent mother), but not so old that her fertility is declining. In the case of such a female, the high-ranking males compete ferociously, and number 1 is likely to be with her on her most likely day of ovulation, number 2 for a day on either side of that, number 3 for a day on either side of that, and so on. Very young females, like Ruth and Esther, having their first few estrus cycles, were probably not yet fertile, and of little interest to the high-ranking males. Instead, they would wind up with an earnest young Joshua or an ancient Isiah. Or, as was beginning to be the pattern, the canny Isaac. Isaac would have nothing to do with the crazed, canine-slashing competition for the prime females. Instead, he'd be willing to shove aside a very young or very old male and thus spent an extraordinary percentage of his time in consortship with young females in their first cycles. Sure, they would almost never conceive, but if they did, he would be 100 percent certain of fatherhood, instead of the "I was with her for eleven hours the day after her peak swelling, so there's a 17 percent chance he's my kid" calculations. If Isaac had had that strategy sorted out in 1978 when Ruth was having her first nervous cycles, Obadiah would probably have looked like him instead of like Joshua. But it wasn't until late 1980 that Isaac hit his stride with that style.

So Isaac passed his days in tremendous numbers of uninteresting (in most other males' view) consortships. When he wasn't consorting, he hung out with Rachel, his friend. Oh, lascivious gutter-minded reader, you're probably wondering if they ever got it on. He consorted with her a few times. Never on peak days, as he would relinquish the consortship at any sign of interest from a more dominant male. Mostly, they were friends. They sat together, fed together, groomed endlessly. Idyllic. Just Rachel and Isaac and all the peripubescent young things he was screwing around with. The strategy paid off in many ways. Yes, only a few of the young females conceived, but as the years passed, Isaac, still in fine shape, would be surrounded by their occasional offspring, eventually hordes of kids with flat foreheads, to whom he would be abundantly paternal. And by then, almost all of his peers were dead or decrepit, burned out by their more competitive lifestyle. And he just kept going. An impressive individual.

Benjamin, ah, my Benjamin, had not improved his lot much by 1980. His hair was, if anything, more disheveled, and his jaw didn't fit any better. We had one moment of rather unsuccessful cross-species communication. A male baboon, when faced with a formidable adversary, will occasionally be able to coax another male into forming a cooperative coalition. And when such pairings prove stable, they constitute a force to be reckoned with. There's a whole series of gestures and facial expressions that a male gives to get a potential coalitional partner to join him in the glory of the fray. One day, Benjamin was about to be trounced by some bruiser, who was bearing down on him with a look that meant business. Benjamin, in a growing panic, glanced around every which way for a coalitional partner and saw nothing but infants, zebras, and bushes. In a moment of desperate inspiration, he turned to me and solicited my partnership. In the name of all my professional training and objectivity, but to my perpetual shame, I had to pretend that I didn't speak the language and had no idea what he was talking about. Another drubbing for Benjamin when, no doubt, he was hoping I'd run the guy down with my Jeep.

This was also the period when I discovered why the baboons napped so much during the day. It was Benjamin's fault. He kept everyone awake at night. When baboons are lost, they give this two-syllable "wa-hoo" call. "Where is everyone?" in effect. This was the call that Benjamin gave the day in 1978 when he and I both lost the troop together. I had recently begun to camp out occasionally in the forest beneath the trees the baboons slept in. It turned out that on an amazing percentage of the nights, with everything peaceful and quiet, Benjamin would suddenly start bellowing wa-hoos at the top of his lungs. "*Wa*-hoo! . . . *Wa*-hoo! . . . *Wa*-hoo! *Wa*-hoo! *Wa*-hoo!!" Eventually, Daniel would give some cranky, half-asleep wa-hoo back from the next tree, then Joshua, Bathsheeba, so on, until everyone would be out of control, wa-hooing their heads off for half an hour in the middle of the night. My theory was that Benjamin would have a bad dream, suddenly get the willies, and want to know that everyone else was still there.

It was in the early 1980s that Nebuchanezzar really hit his stride. He was mean, stupid, and untalented. He had only one eye and a disturbing rotty socket. He had a flinty face. And he had bad posture. He spent years in the troop, never made a friend. He just bullied everyone. Actually, he was no fool—he didn't threaten higher-ranking males, he didn't push, never went anywhere in the hierarchy. But as a prime-aged male, there were still a lot of occasions where he could throw his weight around, and he invariably did.

He excelled at kidnapping. This is one of those behaviors that provoke endless debates among primatologists as to what they mean, whether human terms should be used. A male is about to get trounced by someone. The high-ranking male approaches, and the impending victim, in a panic, suddenly grabs a terrified resistant infant from its mother, clutches it conspicuously. Miraculously, he then is not beaten. An old, starry-eyed ethological explanation for this was that infants are so cute and vulnerable, and everyone knows this so innately, that clutching the kid inhibits aggression. Who would want to hit a guy holding some kid? Any abused child can tell you that it is nonsense that kids automatically inhibit aggression. Careful field study showed that to be nonsense as well—in some circumstances, males will systematically murder infants. So much for the "kids make adults gentle" explanation. Sometime later, the sociobiologists came up with a far more Machiavellian scenario. The alpha male is about to pound you. You don't grab just any kid, you grab someone who he thinks is *his* kid. Mess with me and your kid gets it. Kidnapping, hostage taking. Pretty clever. The idea generated all sorts of predictions. The kid grabbed should be the most likely offspring of the attacker. A terrifying, high-ranking male who only recently joined the troop should never be kidnapped against—he hasn't been there long enough to have fathered (or to believe that he's fathered) anyone. You'll note that all of this depends on the actors being able to remember who mated with whom back when, what your species' gestation period is, and so on. Not recommended for beginners or small-brained species. The sociobiological model has been supported only to some extent by the data. Appendices have been added on to the theory. Sometimes it's Machiavellian kidnapping, sometimes the guy is grabbing the kid for comfort in his frightened moment, sometimes he's grabbing his *own* kid, to get it out of the dangerous situation.

The debate rages on, keeping primatologists off the dole. Whatever the reasons, Nebuchanezzar was an inveterate kidnapper. He'd be off raising hell, and some higher-ranking male would come by, and Nebuchanezzar would instantly set upon and chase and pummel some screaming female until he'd wrested her infant away. Oh, you can bet he never tried that with the high-ranking Devorah's child. But lowly Miriam was a different story, and her daughter was always getting wrestled away from the screaming Miriam. And, as was inevitable, one day Nebuchanezzar broke the infant's arm while flailing for her. The whole troop mobbed him, chased him around the field for a bit, maybe, although unlikely, taught him a lesson. But the damage was done, and she has limped ever since.

In retrospect, the thing I'm least willing to forgive Nebuchanezzar for was what he did to Bathsheeba. Oh, I had a crush on her, if that's not obvious by now. The tip of her tail was wondrous, snowy white, unlike any baboon I've ever seen. She was elegant and understated, like Ingrid Bergman. She was not an especially attentive mother to Rebecca, mostly hung out with Devorah, had a particular fondness for euphorbia fruit, always trying to lead the troop to such trees. Okay, so she didn't have a particularly striking personality, but there was the tail tip. Her downfall was in a classic baboon social interaction. Among baboons, when the going gets tough, the first thought is to find someone else to pay for it. A male loses a fight and spins around and chases some subadult who, cheesed off, lunges at an adult female who swats an adolescent kid who knocks an infant over. All in about fifteen seconds. "Displaced aggression" is the term for it, and an incredible percentage of baboon aggression consists of someone in a bad mood taking it out on an innocent bystander. Just ask the endlessly put-upon Job or Benjamin. So this time, Nebuchanezzar was hassling Ruth and her kid Obadiah; Joshua, Obadiah's likely father, came to their rescue. He and Nebuchanezzar fenced a bit, lunging at each other with their canines, and the fast maturing Joshua trounced him. Nebuchanezzar sprinted off, badly in need of someone weaker to take his defeat out on. He lunged at the screaming Job, chased some kid, and then bit Bathsheeba on the flank as she leapt to get out of his way. Typical displaced aggression, if on the somewhat escalated side, but what else would you expect from Nebuchanezzar? Except this time, the bite went septic. Maybe Bathsheeba had a crummy immune system. More likely, Nebuchanezzar had a particularly fetid mouth. But she went septic and died, horribly, two weeks later.

Sociobiology is often faulted for the Machiavellian explanations it gives for some of the most disturbing of social behaviors. And for the suggestion that some of those horrendous behaviors are highly rewarding to their skillful practitioners. Less noticed is that it also generates just as valid (or invalid) explanations for some of the most selfless, altruistic, caring of behaviors and shows the circumstances under which those are highly rewarding behavioral strategies to follow. Yet, nothing about that science at this stage can begin to explain the individual differences—why did Isaac take the strategy that we recognize as being such a "nice" one, while Nebuchanezzar behaved in a manner that was vicious and rotten? At this stage, as a trained scientist, all I can conclude is that Nebuchanezzar was a shit on some fundamental level. And during 1980, the troop would have agreed heartily.

And what happened to Uriah, young behemoth, inheritor of the throne of Solomon, vanquisher of the invincible? The kid never had it in him, couldn't possibly last. After Solomon went, Uriah hung around for a while, but he just didn't have what it takes. He didn't stand a chance when Saul came in from the wilderness.

Saul had been in the troop since 1977. His entry was worth noting. He had been in the neighboring troop, a subadult there, when the two troops met by the river. As usual, everyone hollered and craned their necks and looked at each other and got bored and went back to what they were doing. But there was magic in the air that day. Boopsie spotted the striking Saul; Saul spotted the slinky Boopsie and flashed his eyebrows at her, meaning roughly the same thing that it does among primates like us. She ran over to the riverbank and presented her rear end to him. Delighted, Saul crossed over and approached her. Boopsie ran about ten meters and presented again. Saul approached again. And Boopsie ran again and slowly reeled Saul into the troop. He never left, although I might add that he never had a particularly sustained relationship with Boopsie.

Within about six months, though, Saul became a hermit; he simply stayed by himself. He slept with the troop, but in the farthest branch of the last tree. I'd never seen anything like it. He was the first one down in the morning, first one out, way out on the edge. If anyone approached, he moved away. He was not frightened, he was not low-ranking. When he did interact, he was a fairly forceful, high-ranking male. He simply wanted to be by himself most of the time. I had two years of behavioral observations of him that consisted of his sitting alone. My belief is that from early 1978 until late 1980, he principally passed his time watching and thinking. He watched Solomon in his prime and in his downfall, the pairing of Joshua and Ruth, Isaac's benevolent strategizing, Nebuchanezzar wreaking havoc. He would do his day's eating in a frenzy while everyone else was just yawning at the base of the trees and spend the rest of the day on the edge, sitting and watching. Eventually, he must have decided it was his time, because he came in from the periphery of the troop and deposed Uriah in one day.

That first afternoon, he beat Isaac in a contest that the latter had little stomach for, demolished Nebuchanezzar in a sustained fight, dispatched the aging Aaron. Joshua, Benjamin, Daniel, a few others all stood around nervously. By sunset, he had threatened Uriah, and they had had a series of ambiguous interactions, showing that neither was quite sure where things stood. And by dawn, with everyone looking kind of frazzled and sleep-deprived, Saul descended from the trees as the alpha male, and Uriah descended with two deep canine slashes, one splitting his nose down the middle. He spent the day moping alone on a mound.

So ushered in the reign of Saul. He had an astounding proclivity for extremes. He could be explosively violent. Alpha males, especially early in their tenure, will occasionally be challenged by other high-ranking males. The response could be to ignore the guy, to make a threatening facial expression, maybe lunge, even chase the individual halfheartedly. But it quickly became apparent that even the most trivial of provocations would be answered by Saul with an attack of the highest intensity—ferocious chases with canines bared, slashing at the flanks of the fleeing male. It was not long before no one challenged Saul about anything, and everyone got out of his way instantly. Yet, on a certain level, he was not really a very aggressive individual. He did not start fights, he did not seem to hold grudges or harass animals pointlessly. Most strikingly, he never attacked females with displaced aggression, never chased them when he was feeling cranky. For a male baboon, this was extraordinary behavior, akin to the lunatic fringe forms of pacifism where the loinclothed adherent abstains from eating certain fruits for fear of inadvertently killing the flies festering therein. There was a yin-yang quality to Saul, an imperturbable serenity about him, a mandarin-like calm, until someone messed with him in the slightest and he became insanely retributive. It was as if, in his meditative isolation for two years, Saul had developed this amazing capacity to generate behavioral extremes and never to do something pointlessly. If everything about Isaac's uniqueness led him to reject typical male baboon values, walking away from every possible conflict and spending his time in undesirable consortships and in friendship with Rachel, everything about Saul's uniqueness made him succeed at those values brilliantly. Saul was what most males aspired to, if only they had a stitch of smarts or discipline or energy.

Peace descended on the troop, and the trains ran on time. Saul fathered many kids, dominating reproduction to as great an extent as any alpha male I've seen, although he was not especially paternal. He had good affiliative relations with almost all the females in the troop, although he was never particularly close with anyone. Years passed, and no doubt Saul was beginning to contemplate the building of grand commemorative cathedrals and endowing of monastic orders in perpetuity with florins. For other males in the troop, watching their prime years come and maybe go amid Saul's stranglehold, it must have been a trying time indeed. As it turned out, it took extraordinary measures to topple this extraordinary individual.

Usually, there is an heir apparent or two, waiting for a bit more nerve, for the alpha's reflexes to slow a bit. Uriah breathed down Solomon's neck in 1978, as had Solomon and Aaron down the mythic 203's in 1975. Now there was no obvious number 2, just a bunch of young males in their prime, none of whom would dream of messing with Saul. Finally, they did the logical, if rare, thing; they formed a cooperative coalition.

Joshua and Menasseh, another big male, soon bound to be enemies, teamed up first. They spent a morning making coalitional appeasement gestures to each other, cementing a partnership, and finally worked up the nerve to challenge Saul, who promptly kicked their asses, slashed Menasseh's haunch, sent them both running. By most predictions, that should have settled that. Instead, the next day, Joshua and Menasseh formed a coalition with Levi, a fireplug of a young male who had been around for a few years. Saul dispatched the trio in seconds. And they came back the next day with the vile Nebuchanezzar in tow. Nebuchanezzar and Menasseh managed to hold their own for a few seconds fencing against Saul before he scattered them.

The next day they were joined by Daniel and, as a measure of how much they just needed cannon fodder for this grand enterprise, Benjamin. Six against one. I was betting on Saul. He emerged at the edge of the forest, and they surrounded him. I was on top of the Jeep, trying to follow everyone at once. It seemed like the assassination of Caesar.

I'm sure the six were wetting their pants. I suspect Saul was not, despite the fact that all the males were conspicuously grinding and displaying their canines, half-lunging forward and slapping at the ground, things baboons do when they try to ruffle you big time. Saul seemed markedly unruffled and still. I can't conceive that the six had it together enough to have a strategy. Baboons are simply not up to that. They must have happened on their strategy by accident. Levi and Menasseh were the two most physically likely to be able to inflict damage, and they wound up on opposite sides of the circle. Saul couldn't face one without putting his back to the other.

Saul made his decision, launched himself at Levi and Joshua. I'm sure he would have gotten away with it, scattered the six, but Menasseh got in a lucky shot from behind. He lunged at Saul's back as the latter leapt, managed to hit Saul's haunches. It knocked him off balance, and he missed Levi and Joshua, landing on his side. And everyone was on him in an instant.

For three days afterward, he lay on the forest floor. Why he wasn't killed by hyenas then, I'll never know. When I darted him a few weeks later, he was covered with half-healed canine punctures. He'd lost a quarter of his weight, his shoulder was dislocated and his upper arm broken, and his stress hormone levels were soaring.

He recovered, although it was iffy for a while. He learned how to walk with three limbs, could eventually run for short stretches, looking like a fullback in a three-point stance, his useless arm at his chest. He was never in another fight, never mated again, disappeared to the bottom of the hierarchy. And he returned from whence he came, back to the wilderness. Unlike in years before, he was no longer the first one out, rushing ahead to keep a distance between himself and the others. Now, in his crippled state, he was the last one out. He kept to himself, moved away if anyone approached, sat and watched from the same distance as in the past.

9

Samwelly Versus the Elephants

I returned to Kenya for the reign of Saul, feeling altogether more weathered and worldly than the quivery kid who'd started out there a few years earlier. I now had a passport full of visa stamps plus a persistent fungal problem from Uganda that made me a perennial teaching tool for dermatology grand rounds at the medical school. I had come to own two ties and had recently been forced by circumstances to eat dinner in a Manhattan restaurant that required the wearing of one. I was making some progress with my research—I was starting to accumulate data suggesting that the bodies of low-ranking baboons chronically activated stress responses, the sort of profile that would predispose you to stress-related disease. And I had even survived my first scientific conference as a graduate student, giving a petrified fifteen-minute talk about that work. By the standards of my scientific tribe, or even by those of the baboon troop, I was becoming a somewhat credible subadult.

I celebrated by betraying the political principles of my union label family. I joined management. The baboon work was booming, and I was limited in how much time I could spend in the bush each year, ignoring my lab studies and the polite inquiries of my academic adviser as to whether I was ever going to finish my thesis. I needed the baboons to be monitored in my absence, and I hired two Kenyans to collect behavioral data on them year-round. Neither had degrees in zoology or primatology. Neither had degrees of any sort. Each had had a few years of schooling before their families had run out of money for school fees, and at roughly the same age as I, they had washed up in the army of hangers-on at the tourist lodges of the park, distant cousins of some waiter or pot-washer, sleeping on the floor in the staff quarters, hoping for any kind of job. I should congratulate myself for my astuteness in choosing them among the endless office-seekers, but it was dumb, random luck that I found these two who have become, I anticipate, my friends for life.

Richard was from an agricultural tribe north of the Masai, Hudson from one to the west. Both had the initial task of coming to terms with working in the territory of their traditional tribal enemy, living there, with their wives and families long distances away in their tribal farmlands. But beyond that, they were veritable opposites. Richard was bubbly, emotional, triumphant at a successful darting and inconsolable at a bad one, constantly trying out new personas, sopping up the mannerisms of every Westerner he encountered and brilliantly mimicking them. Hudson, in contrast, was reserved, pensive, steady as a rock, frugal and ascetic while supporting endless distant relatives through school, a man who would very rarely give you a hint of his depths of feelings and judgments and sly caustic humor. They settled into rooms at the staff quarters in the lodge, since, unlike me, they had no desire to live in a tent. Richard would spend a dozen years on the project before deciding he wanted to move back home to be with his family. Hudson would soon spend much of that same period working at a baboon site at the other end of the country, only to return to work with me in the 1990s.

My decline into capitalist depravity went even further. I hired someone to stay in camp with me. During the early years, my campsite was up on the remote mountain at the far corner of the park, and Masai and other visitors might wander up only once every few weeks. Because of some shifts in the movement of the baboons, it made sense now to move my camp to the open plains below. This was hotter, drier, and, unfortunately, far closer to the growing number of villages on the park's boundary. My possessions started to get pilfered while I was away during the day, and it became obvious that I needed someone to watch camp while I was out.

Finding someone was easy—every acquaintance at any lodge or ranger post had some relative looking for work. The trouble was that the camp guys kept going to pieces on me. There was a long-standing tradition of such individuals turning out not to fare very well in the bush. I had recently observed a rather dramatic case of that in the camp of Laurence of the Hyenas, the Berkeley scientist who had started his research on the other side of the mountain around the same time I did.

Laurence had been short on research funds and had thus set up a campsite for an organization called Earthwatch, which sends ecotourists out to work at actual field sites. It had succeeded handsomely, and soon he had hired guys to cook for the guests. He first landed Thomas, a brilliant camp cook, famous with safari companies throughout the land, a man with many skills, some of which were useful. He made a rather dramatic first impression: short, squat, cackly, filthy, wheezy, bristly, leering, unapologetically soused all the time. At every opportunity, Thomas would scoot off to the Masai village nearby for a bottle of home-brewed Masai hootch, come back smashed, wiggling and leering and dancing and singing in a raspy chortle.

Whenever he had spare time, Thomas would roar up and down the river, drunkenly carrying on. This was where two of his truly unique traits shone. In a drunken reel, Thomas would sit down by a narrow side-trickle of the river, a streamlet a few feet wide and barely inches deep, and begin to fish. And he would instantly pull out fish by the score, big meaty honkers that had appeared out of nowhere, as if Thomas was not only the secret god of grapes, but of fish spawning as well. Unfortunately, few would ever get to see these fish because of Thomas's other miraculous trait, which was to attract buffalo. Over the years, Thomas had been charged, chased, thrown, gored, catapulted, and stomped by endless buffalo. He would start home, cackling and wheezing and singing, bent under the weight of the fish, pausing to polish off the bottle, and like clockwork, like the flow and ebb of the seasons, a buffalo would inevitably leap out of the bush to get him. Buffalo would scamper in from miles away to nail Thomas, toss him over their shoulders, and send his fish sailing into mudholes, thorn bushes, high into trees. His attraction for buffalo was a miracle. Game Department officials, if concerned about diminishing wildlife, could repopulate entire lifeless provinces with surly buffalo merely by driving through with the singing, snarfling Thomas tied to the front of the Jeep, like some hood ornament out of Hogarth. Put Thomas in a gardening section of a Sears in Winnetka, Illinois, and I guarantee that within minutes an African cape buffalo would leap out from behind the snowplows to toss him into the ventilation ducts. Endlessly, we would go out searching for Thomas, only to find him cursing and spitting and cackling at some buffalo, threatening it with his trademark, an astounding pelvic grind, as the monster approached. Most amazing of all, he was only partially crippled by his numerous buffalo encounters, his femur shattered once and incorrectly set.

In stark contrast to Thomas was the number two cook, the saintly Julius, a meek, giggly, thoroughly delightful man, heavily influenced by the missionaries who'd gotten hold of him at an early age. As the older of the two, Thomas naturally took on the role of elder of their microvillage and soon, in magisterial fashion, was relieving Julius of half his salary on a regular basis. This was apparently not too much of a problem, as Julius had already reached a turn-the-other-cheek accommodation with the Masai warriors who were also ripping off chunks of his salary in some sort of protection racket. The major problems ensued whenever Thomas had time off and would come storming back into camp particularly soused. Even in this state, he noted that this pained Julius, and he thus doubled his efforts around him. Thomas would dance and cackle, make kissy noises at Julius, and torture the poor man with his wildly grinding pelvis. This was an affront to all that Julius held to be holy and tasteful, and soon he was spending most of his days in his tent, singing hymns.

One would have thought that Julius was the one likely to succumb in this unlikely conflict, but one day he inadvertently managed to turn the tables, once and for all. We had entered camp to find the denouement in progress; it was unclear what drunken outrage Thomas had committed, but instead of retreating to his tent for religious solace, Julius had grabbed his Bible and was orating *at* Thomas, hurtling fire and brimstone at the sinner. Unexpectedly, the meek had indeed inherited this patch of the grassland: Later that day, an angry, sobered Thomas informed Laurence that his job description did not include being subjected to this sort of shit, and he quit. The whole incident appeared to rob him permanently of his enthusiasm for life in the bush. To this day, Thomas wanders the streets of Nairobi, blasted on big-city moonshine, ignoring the frequent pilgrimages of tour operators who arrive, scraping and bowing, to beg him to come and cook for their outfits. He has found a new, more remunerative niche. A man with an astonishing memory, he somehow knows every colonial white living in Nairobi, rushes up whenever he spots one of them, with an obsequious "Memsab" or "Sahib." Then he regales the old Brit with the latest chortly libelous gossip about all the other old colonials in town. Brawls, adultery, fallen soufflés, murders, fabulous inventions; no one quite knows how he gets his information, but nothing slips by him. He relays it all with such a gleeful malicious insincerity, such an air of improvisatory fraud, most of it so transparently false, that all are delighted to rush off immediately and repeat the slander. But not before Thomas invariably cadges a "loan." So he grows rich and more dissipated, although buffalo have yet to regain a foothold in town in their pursuit of him.

So, surprisingly, it was Thomas who proved to have the less stamina for the unlikely demands of the bush, and Julius settled into a long, august career in Laurence's employ.

It was around the time of Thomas's departure that I realized I needed to have someone stay in camp with me. Thus began the series of camp guys cracking up on me. In retrospect, I think this was because of the Taiwanese mackerel in tomato sauce. I was making the same impatient culinary mistake each year. I'd be sitting in my laboratory in the States, getting itchy as hell to get to Kenya. Finally, reach Nairobi, a mere day away from finally getting to the bush, rearing to go. Rush to the market to get three months of supplies so I don't have to go near Nairobi again, tear through the store, get some food, don't even think about it, just hit the road. Grab a sack of rice, one of beans, some vegetables that will rot after the first week in the bush, some chili sauce to hide the taste of the rot, some cans of plums in thick sugar syrup for days when I'm celebrating something. Then, search for some stable protein source. Cheese turns to an alarming liquid after the first two days in the bush heat. Meat I was still trying to avoid. Cans of American-style tuna fish are expensive beyond the dreams of mere field biologists and are probably reserved for the American diplomatic corps anyway. Then, each year, I spot the cans of the Taiwanese mackerel in tomato sauce. Cheap, plentiful, teeming with protein and bones and gristle and nameless fish parts that make me queasy to contemplate. Each year, for an instant, I stop and think, Don't do it, get a few different things, take the time to look around a bit first. But then there's this impatient rush, Let's get going, already, food is food. Grab a case of the stuff, gun the engine, and before you know it, I'm at my beloved campsite with nothing to eat for three months but rice and beans and goddamn Taiwanese mackerel in tomato sauce with the bones that keep jabbing your gums with each bite.

After three days of this, you're hallucinating about strawberry Pop-Tarts and Velveeta cheese food and Yoo-Hoo chocolate drink. But at least it was my decision, I keep telling myself. For the poor bastard hired to live out here, it slowly dawns on him that this is the grub for the duration. With the exception of people from the coast or the lakes regions, most Africans I've met seem a bit alarmed by fish to begin with, and rice and beans are definitely novel, since the local starch is a tasteless white maize paste that solidifies your bowels. So, each meal goes by, the man sitting and watching with Bantu stoicism as yet another can of mackerel is opened, the distressing *shploooog* of tomato sauce spraying out, the sickening sucking noise of the fish plopping out of the can, the glint of cartilage. Slowly, the guy begins to go to pieces.

Well, maybe this is unfair, blaming too much on the mackerel. The camp guys probably also went mad because it was a crummy job. You're a Kenyan farm kid, trying to get some cash, and suddenly you have to live in the middle of nowhere with some white guy. It's basically pretty scary. I eat weird stuff, have strange habits, talk marginal Swahili. My skin changes color in the sun, and then big chunks of it come peeling off. Richard admitted after endless questioning from me that we white guys smell kinda peculiar. To add to the problems, I have a large beard and a lot of bushy hair, which definitely gives the heebie-jeebies to Africans. And the goings-on in camp do not help, with half-awake baboons lurching around and crates of dry ice and liquid nitrogen belching smoke and everything covered with baboon piss and baboon blood and baboon shit.

But that was only part of the problems for the camp guy. A stoic person in a tough situation might try to take solace from interesting surroundings. But the guys were from some upcountry agricultural village, and the nearest such village was eighty miles away. And the bush is not much solace to a farm kid. From his perspective, the place was teeming with lions to maul you and buffalo to toss you in the river and crocodiles to grab you from there, and, if there's anything left, swarms of hissing army ants to eat your eyelids. And worst of all, the neighbors were Masai, the nightmare of every Kenyan farm boy.

All in all, not their idea of fun, and soon after the start of each season, they would go to pieces. One guy, following the path pioneered by Thomas but without his verve or gifts, declined into a shapeless alcoholism after having reached enough of a rapprochement with the Masai to buy moonshine from them. Another festered in the same sort of religiousness as Julius and soon found objections to me; the president of the country had spoken out against beards as a moral blight, and in the classic merging of patriotism and religious piety that holds sway here, the camp guy made it clear that he'd be damned if he was going to hell in my bearded camp. One was mute with terror at the animals and Masai, and slept with a shovel. Another had a full-blown psychotic break, screaming in his tent at night about the lights paralyzing him. One went not so much mad as pointlessly larcenous, pilfering all sorts of minor objects and disappearing for days on end without explanation. I reached that strange maturational stage of having to fire someone for the first time and spent days obsessively planning it, alternating between guilt, sufficient anger that I wanted to machete him to pieces, and sufficient paranoia to be convinced that he was about to do the same to me. I gave him a prepared speech in Swahili invoking the Puritan work ethic, the golden rule, Vince Lombardi, made-up tales of similar misdeeds from my own misguided youth (i.e., trying to impress upon him that if he pulled himself together, he could still rise to become a professor like me), and, speech completed, I sacked him. He took it like a man, and to this day, I am convinced that every murmur, every crackling of a twig, at night in my camp is he, rising out of the riverbank to chop me into little pieces and feed me to the willingly cooperative hyenas (for this is how a surprising number of bush murders are carried out here).

But the most extravagantly Byzantine case of bush crazies I had ever seen came with Samwelly. I still wonder to what sordid end it would have led to had he not been saved by the elephants.

Samwelly was the brother of Richard, my research assistant. As I mentioned, Richard lived in the staff quarters of one of the tourist camps, five miles away. That year, Richard had brought Samwelly out from the farm to take care of my camp. We started off auspiciously enough. The first day was brutal work—putting up tents, digging garbage and latrine holes, collecting firewood. Late in the afternoon, fire going, we were getting hungry. I said I would dig the drainage lines for the tents if Samwelly would get supper going. Here, I said, cook up some rice and beans and, when they are ready, toss in this fish— handing him a can of the mackerel delight. I went back to work until, periph- erally, I noted that he was standing, lost in consternation. Uh-oh, some sort of cultural snafu has occurred. One gets used to that—you don't quite know what you have taken for granted and not explained, but something has occurred. For example, when I began to teach Richard how to drive, we lurched and jerked into camp, he, a pleased, excited mess. I leapt out to run to the toilet and returned to find that I had neglected to teach Richard a basic—how to open a car door. He was inside, clawing at the window to get out. Now, I had neglected something else basic with Samwelly, but I did not know what. Finally, he made it clear that while he was plenty familiar with canned food, he had never actu- ally operated a can opener before. This was easily remedied (far more easily than with one prior camp guy, for whom the canned food concept was itself novel—lookathis, we white folks hide food inside metal). We opened up a can of plums in sugar syrup—after all, this was a special occasion—and we were on our way to becoming friends. The next day, while I was out with the baboons, Samwelly displayed his new skills in opening three months of cans of mackerel and plums. We ate like hogs that night and distributed the rest, and things were corrected after an extra resupply trip to Nairobi.

From there, things with Samwelly got even better. Very soon, it became apparent that he had a genius for constructing things, jury-rigging contraptions out in the bush. Camp was soon boiling with projects. The rainy season was still continuing when I first got there, and Samwelly went to work. Marching off into a grove of trees with a machete one afternoon, he had soon cut off four large branches, trimmed and straightened them into posts; he dug little holes, poured water into them until they were soft mud, and soon had the posts solidly upright. More chopping and hacking, and a bunch of leafy branches were being roped together with vine—vimblix, we had a nifty lean-to to stand under dur- ing the rain. A few days later, I returned to find a back wall made of branches and leaves. Then another wall, and then a third. A window appeared for the back wall. Projects began to pop up everywhere. Samwelly dug cisterns for the water barrels—one day, I returned to camp, stinking hot, and Samwelly was sit- ting there drinking *cold* water. One evening in the lean-to, which now had a hearth, Samwelly suddenly asked, "Why don't you go down to the river to wash?" I headed down, on the lookout for buffalo in the fading light, and dis- covered that he had diverted the river into a series of bathing pools.

The center of all the activity was the lean-to, fast becoming a more and more complex house. All four sides were enclosed. A door was put in, a vestibule, a second room. Around the hearth there were soon benches. A table. Everything made of mud and sticks and leaves and vines and rocks, seemingly defying gravity. Samwelly waterproofed the house with flattened tin cans still smelling of mackerel. One of my baboon cages was soon commandeered to form an animal-proof pantry. Every cup and bowl in camp disappeared, ferreted into little secret hiding holes in the wall, angled so as to fill with water in the rain. Shelves for the utensils, a picture of the president on the wall, cunning little platforms in the walls to display cans of mackerel. It got to the point where, each day, I would come back to camp anticipating what new wonder he would have constructed—a mud and dung calliope, perhaps, hand-carved busts of famous zoologists, or a perfect 1:10 replica of the palace at Versailles made out of cans of Taiwanese mackerel.

Then, one day, something must have snapped. I blame it on myself. I had had engine trouble, been stuck out overnight, sleeping in the vehicle, and anxiety or relief or whatever at not having me there must have thrown Samwelly into a frenzy of activity. I returned the next day and found him with an excited gleam about him. He suggested I go wash in the river.

"Samwelly, you have done something very big to the river, haven't you?" Yes. Yes.

I went down, Samwelly following excitedly, to discover that . . . the river was gone. Puzzled, alarmed, I walked up the riverbed a bit, came around a bend, and found that Samwelly had presumably labored nonstop for two days in a maddened outburst of work and had managed to dam up the entire river. Stopped cold. Our pathetic pissant six-inch-deep, three-foot-wide trickle of a river was now forming Lake Samwelly behind a five-foot wall of sand and rocks.

Samwelly beamed with pleasure—this was his proudest accomplishment. Hey, Samwelly, what's going on? I stopped the river, he said. Yeah, I can see that, but why? Now it will not run away, it will not dry up now that the rains have stopped.

In theory, the dam was wonderful; for years I had fantasized about damming the river. The river fed into the Mara River, which fed into Lake Victoria, which fed the Nile, and I figured that if I blocked our river, eventually Cairo would be reeling, the Suez Canal disrupted, the Indian raj isolated, and Queen Victoria and the whole empire under my control. But despite the attraction of that, there were some insurmountable drawbacks to blocking the river, and the dam had to go. I tried to explain that in about two weeks of sitting here, this water was going to be completely stagnant and full of mosquitoes and wildebeest shit and bilharzia and infectious snails and more malaria than had ever been dreamed of. Samwelly was adamant—he did not want the lake to go. We will always have water, we can go swimming, we can grow fish here, even mackerel, he argued. Naw, the dam has to go. Samwelly wasn't budging: I will build a boat out of branches so that we can go sailing, we can put crocodiles there to protect us, the tourists will come and pay us to take pictures. Finally, I had to remind him of the biggest problem with the dam. Yeah, but Samwelly, I said, you have cut off the water supply of the Masai in the village and tonight the warriors are going to come and spear you.

This turned the trick. Obviously unhappy, he conceded, and we spent the rest of the afternoon breaking down the wall.

The disappointment seemed to break his spirit as well. He withdrew to his tent for the rest of the day. The funk continued the next day and the next. Work stopped on Samwelly's house after merely three mud and leaf rooms. The wine cellar, the gingerbread trim, the captain's walk—none materialized. Samwelly stopped talking, would sit and stare at the fire all evening. He no longer jumped up to open tin cans; his mackerel went uneaten.

Samwelly was depressed, he was becoming unhinged. The river dam debacle had taken the wind out of him, his illusions of building Xanadu out of mud and sticks and leaves had crumbled, he was stuck out here in the howling back of beyond with some white guy and a bunch of drugged baboons. Richard and I consulted, and he was at a loss as to how to reenergize his brother. Another faithful camp guy was about to go over the edge.

It was not a good time for it to happen. The dry season was in full swing by then, and anyone, even in the best state of mind, would have been teetering under the circumstances. Every day, it became hotter and hotter, stinking hot, and soon Lake Samwelly would have been academic anyway, as the water evaporated before our eyes. The river became mud, the air full of dust and dry crackling tension, and all your moments were spent thinking of sno-cones and bathtubs. It was the time of year of the fires and the wildebeests.

Each year, the Serengeti, the great plain that the park was a part of, has a cyclical pattern of rain, so that at any given time of year, the grass is lush and five feet high somewhere, and throughout the year, a massive, teeming migratory herd of two million grunting wildebeests follow in the wake of the rains, racing the dry brush fires for the oceans of high grass. Following them is every hungry carnivore in the county.

Every year it was the same. The rains would stop, and a bush pilot, flying in, would report that the herd was fifty miles down the border in Tanzania. A week later, reports of them on the border. Then, the next afternoon, you'd stand on the roof of the Jeep and with your binoculars, spot a trickle of them coming over the slope of the far mountain. Then, the next morning, you'd awake with a start, because in every direction you could look, there'd be crowds, herds, thousands and thousands of rank, galloping wildebeests, belching and running and hemming and hawing and crapping over every inch of the front lawn.

It's a parched frenzied maddening time of year. No water, no nothing, just dust and the fires, the whole Serengeti burning up, five-foot-high dry dry grass just exploding with lightning fires, huge waves of flame sweeping through— drive up to a mountain at night and watch the wall of flames below, the clouds reflecting orange, and amid it all, the mad wildebeests racing the flames, mowing down the grass, tangles of panicked, disoriented masses of bovid hyperkinetics dashing hysterical amid the fields, carnivores trailing them and giving us the willies at night, wildebeests screaming in the bushes amid packs of hyenas, somebody's carcass scattered over an acre behind the tents in the morning, but, no problem, don't worry, there are another hundred thousand wildebeests in the front yard, all of them running around hysterical without a care in the world or a thought in their heads except to maybe finally run stupidly and randomly enough, to paraphrase Peter Mathiessen, to fall over and dash their skulls open on rocks, as if to stop the itching in their mindless bovid brains. So the wildebeests and the fires, spires of flame and smoke and dust and heat, and Samwelly growing more sullen by the hour.

But, good luck, the elephants came and ate his house at night.

Elephants at night in camp are quite a spectacle, enough to speed up anyone's heart. You wake up in a panic—chaos around the tent, crackling, a tree has fallen just missing the tent, someone is eating a bush just by the door, the tent lines have been torn loose. You peer out the window, and the tree trunk that wasn't there when you went to sleep lifts up and comes down—an elephant leg! Now for certain you'll be crushed to death by some oaf elephant dropping a tree on you. And each time, as you lie there in absolute terror waiting for your end at the feet of the elephants, there is this bizarre countercurrent of feeling, this amazement you feel at hearing . . . their stomach sounds. The elephants make monstrous amounts of noise with their stomachs. It's the most perfect sound on earth: low bass rumbles like the core of the earth, like you're a child again and you have the most perfect ancient white-bearded enormous loving grandpa who, just because he loves you, is going to lift you in his gnarled hands and put you in his lap and put your ear to his belly and just for *you* he's going to *belch* loudly and so slow and deep that it will last and make you tingle happily until the next ice age comes, that's what it sounds like, you're lying there in your tent prepared for death and you're surrounded by this wonderful lulling aura of stomach noise that makes you want to curl up and sleep like a puppy, but you *can't* because there are fucking *elephants* outside that are going to kill you, and invariably, you suddenly find yourself having to go outside the tent and take a crap. Once I really had to at such a time. Even I had become crazed with the rice and mackerel and had been taken to lunch at the lodge by tourists I had pulled out of the mud. I made up answers to their questions about animal behavior and mostly ate like a pig, finishing it all with mountains of the hideous lugubrious tasteless puddings that the British adore and have left as their most lasting legacy to Kenyan hoteliers. Chicken gumbo, meat loaf à la Kikuyu, curries, Spam loaf with pineapple slices, all topped with brown thickened murk pudding with crystallized sugar doodads and filigrees on top. I was up all night with the runs and regretted nothing until the elephants came. During one wave, I suddenly found myself cramped over in front of my tent, stark naked, painful, liquid acidic craps, and, the *humiliation* of it all, surrounded by six elephants, silent, quizzical, polite, murmuring, almost solicitous, their trunks waving in the air investigating my actions and moans. They watched my agonized shitting as if it were an engrossing, silent Shakespearean tragedy performed in the round.

That's how it would be when the elephants came at night. And, good fortune, one night they came to eat Samwelly's house. Samwelly turned out to be a natural-born elephant fighter. He and Richard came from the farmlands, where an elephant hadn't been seen in generations. Yet, somewhere back in time, I knew some ancestor of theirs must have been in Arab elephant parties, as Samwelly had a natural fearlessness in battling them. A bunch of elephants were suddenly there, in the middle of the night, munching on the roof and back wall, destroying the waterproofing cans that Samwelly had so carefully placed. Samwelly, who had not uttered a word in days, Samwelly, who had been sinking into catatonia—suddenly, Samwelly was out there, roaring out of his tent. Silent Samwelly was yelling, flailing, hoo-ha-ing, throwing stones at the elephants, trying to get them away from his house. At first, I just cowered in my tent, charmed in terror at my impending death at the feet of the pachyderms. But Samwelly was out there fighting for his house. I finally went out to try to stop him before he was flattened, just as he was about to set fire to their tails. They looked more puzzled than angry, waved their trunks with the same patience as the ones (perhaps the same ones) who watched my Shakespearean craps a mere kilometer upriver some years earlier. Samwelly and I argued, grappled, yelled, and debated while they ate. I finally convinced him to return to his tent—he could not stop the elephants from their meal.

And they saved him from what seemed to be inevitable decline into the bush craziness. The next morning he was out surveying the damage—half the roof, one wall, gone, many of the tinned mackerel knickknacks upset, general disarray. By the second evening, amid more energy and smiles than I had seen in weeks, the damage was repaired. That night, the elephants returned again and ate the back wall and vestibule. And by the next nightfall, it was repaired, along with the construction of a clever vine-pulley system for hauling water out of the nonexistent river.

And thus it ran for the rest of the season. Samwelly would fix the house, the elephants would return to feast on his architecture, and each dawn, with renewed vigor, with renewed schemes, with vengeance and architectural soundness at the center of his soul, he would repair the damage. And for years to come, Samwelly and I would always stay in camp together, and elephants would always be welcome for dinner.

10

The First Masai

$\mathcal{I}$n camp, late afternoon, alone, Samwelly off visiting Richard in the tourist camp. I had spent much of the day collecting behavioral data on poor Jonathan, who really was an innocuous soul, pathetically stuck in the throes of this futile crush on Rebecca. It had left me in a sour, brooding mood. For what seemed like the zillionth time in a row, my behavioral sampling of him consisted almost entirely of his hopelessly following after her. She'd sit and groom with her friends; he'd sit at a stoic distance. She'd walk along, foraging on flowers and roots, and he'd agitatedly keep a perfect ten feet behind her, forgetting to eat in the process. She'd go and present to one of the big, prime-aged males, and Jonathan would sit and frantically pick at the fur on his knees and ankles. And then, when she'd finally settle down, sitting by herself, he'd quickly seize the opportunity and approach her . . . and she'd quickly scamper away without so much as a glance at him.

Let him sit near you, I thought with irritation. Talk to him a little, go out for a soda with him. And you could do worse for a prom date than him. I was angry with her. Look, the poor guy isn't asking for you to groom him, *he* wants to groom *you*, it should kill you to let him groom you a little? Come on, Rebecca, it would make his day. No doubt the core of the problem was that I was badly in need of someone grooming *me*, if you know what I mean.

So I had a touch of bush crazies and was stewing in it. Thus, it is a good thing when some of the Masai guys stop by camp. They are led by Soirowa, a relative of Rhoda's husband, a terrific guy who is fast becoming my friend. They're up to something and very excited, gleaming with conspiratorial glee. It's a goat roast.

The Masai actually do live almost entirely on cow's blood and milk, just like the legends have it. More than a little bit repulsive to contemplate (or to drink, as I did once), but fairly logical from the standpoint of a nomadic pastoralist. So most of the time blood and milk, with a little maize meal thrown in for the modern ones, honey when you can get some sucker kid to brave the bees. And meat. On fancy occasions a goat is slaughtered. Certain wild animals are deemed to be "wild goats" or "wild cows" that have run away, and thus are suitable for hunting without spoiling the Masai's reputation for never killing wildlife. Along with the occasional goat eating is a strong cultural prohibition: it is very bad luck, very bad luck, indeed, for men to be seen by women to be eating meat. How convenient—thus, only the guys get to eat meat in this protein-starved culture.

So a bunch of the guys are off for a goat roast. They've told their wives that they're taking a nice little walk, when instead, they're off to the bush to be men, eating goat! The old men burble and tee-hee with pleasure when telling about their subterfuge. They've ostensibly come to borrow some salt and an onion from me but are mostly wondering if I want to tag along. Sure.

Get to a clearing. The goat has been strolling with us, as if one of the guys. We stand around; the Masai spit on each other's feet, as a gesture of pleasure with each other, while a spot is cleared. The oldest three come forward, hold the goat's head carefully, as if blessing it or performing a phrenological examination. They nod, a young guy steps forward, slits the goat's throat. Everyone, including the goat, is silent. Its blood is drained into a calabash, which is passed around for drinking. I take a polite sip through gritted teeth, trying not to think of the anthrax or parasites or god knows what in its bloodstream. Their job completed, the old men retreat to the viewing stands. They take off their blankets, spread them out, and lounge naked, as if at the beach, propped up on elbows, spindly muscled gnarled legs and slight potbellies and shriveled penises, looking like the doctored cheesecake photo of the naked reclining Henry Kissinger that popped up as a poster in college dorms during the early '70s. The rest go to work making a fire faster than I can usually light a stove. The goat is butchered, bits put on plates made of leaves, which the Masai dog sniffs at. Things cook, the first small pieces are done, salt and my onion are added, we all begin to eat. It is time to kibitz about things.

They want to know about "Merica." I describe New York as being like Nairobi. Crowded, awful, and, if you can believe it, a whole village will live in a house and then, *on top of them,* another village lives—multistory buildings. No one believes this except the worldly Soirowa, who has been to Nairobi once and assures them that such things exist. They ask me about the animals in Merica, and I say there are very few wild animals. Because they have been hunted? they ask. Somewhat, but mostly to make room for the farms. This is playing to the deep-seated contempt that Masai have for farming and farmers, their traditional prey. "Stupid maize," one of them says.

They ask me why, of all the animals here, I come to study baboons. I explain how much they are like people, how their diseases are similar. No, they are not so much like people, they retort.

I try the paleontology number on them. "You know, up in the desert, up north, there are scientists there finding amazing things."

"The scientists from the museum," says Soirowa. How does he know that?

"Yes, they have found bones of men, but they are not really from men."

People want to know what I mean by this.

"Well, they are like half men, but they are also like half baboons. The head bone [I don't know the Swahili word for skull] is not as big as a person's, but it is bigger than a baboon's. And the face, the face is not so long like a baboon's, but longer than a person's. And they can tell from the bone here [pointing to the pelvis] that these people did not walk up like this, but not like a baboon either. Halfway."

"These are baboon-men," one of the elders says. Exactly, I confirm emphatically.

"But where are these people?" someone asks.

"That's the thing—these bones are very very old. So old, from before the Europeans, from before there were tribes, from before people were speaking languages. The scientists think that these baboon-men are the great-great-great-grandfathers of people and of baboons."

Everyone sits and digests this for a while. The old men pick at the goat gristle in their teeth. Someone shoos away the dog. Someone else spits.

Aw, go on, you're full of it, one of the old men in effect says.

"No, no, really."

"Did they have spears?" Soirowa asks.

"No, but they had little rocks that they would use to dig at things and hit things." (Okay, so I'm cleaning up the paleontological record a bit.)

"Did they have tails?" No.

"Did they wear clothes?" No one knows—clothes would not last that long, but the scientists think that they did not wear clothes.

Everyone sits and thinks about this for a while.

"Did they wear shoes or watches?" asks a young guy. The old men snicker, and he realizes he has asked a ridiculous question and gets embarrassed. (Shoes and watches are hot stuff in the region this year. Shoes are worn on the hip, tied around the waist, to keep odds and ends in; watches are worn without regard for time.)

Everyone mulls some more. Finally, Soirowa asks what is probably the question they were all wondering: "Were they Masai?" I tell him maybe, but no one knows.

More mulling. More goat passed around. The high point of the meal, the coagulated blood pudding, is passed. I decline. I wonder what anyone thinks. Finally, Soirowa, after some brooding, says:

"You know, these days, I can tell time and I can speak Swahili and I know about money, and my grandfather could not do any of these things. People are always learning new things. Maybe, once, a long long time ago, these were the first Masai, and they did not even know how to be people yet."

Everyone seems satisfied with that answer, and soon people are quizzing Soirowa and me about two-story houses in Nairobi and Merica—when the cows in the upper village pee, will it go on the heads of the people below?

11

Zoology and National Security:
A Shaggy Hyena Story

One highlight of my subadult years in the troop was becoming friends with Richard and Hudson. Another was my finally connecting with Laurence of the Hyenas. As a general rule, field biologists tend toward the unwashed and unhousebroken; Laurence was the most feral example of these trends that I'd ever seen. Laurence of the Hyenas spent his childhood amid the lizards and snakes in the California deserts. He spent years alone studying foxes in the Aleutians, and then a stretch chasing after some kind of bird across the wastelands of northern Scotland before coming to Kenya to be Laurence of the Hyenas. My first year with the baboons, I had given him a wide berth, as I was terrified of him. He was a large hulking man with a tendency to sequester himself in his tent at length to bellow hideous stark Scottish folk dirges. Even more unsettling, when perturbed or irritated, he had the unconscious habit of thrusting his chin and heavy dark beard at bothersome males in a manner that any primatologist instantly recognizes as a very legit dominance display.

That first year, he chin-thrusted at me frequently. The next year, we each moved down to the plains below, and we slowly got to know each other. I think the real turning point was a day when Laurence made an important discovery. It was a stifling hot day in the middle of the wildebeest migration during the reign of Saul. I was sitting in camp, staring at my toes, shaking the flies off my face, surrounded by a zillion snorting, noisy wildebeests, snuffling about and crapping all over the place, probably the thousandth day of being surrounded by snorting, snuffling, crapping wildebeests. Suddenly, Laurence's Land Rover barreled into camp. He emerged, strode up to me purposefully. "Hey," he said. "Did you realize that 'gnu dung' is a palindrome?" In fact, I had not. The ice was broken. In the twenty years since, he has taught me to bellow Scottish folk songs, made futile attempts to chip away at my ignorance about car engines, tended me during times of malarial attacks and failed experiments and homesickness. He's the nearest thing I have to a big brother, and he's been damn good at it.

In addition to all of this, Laurence has taught me to be very fond of hyenas. Laurence passionately loves these beasts, which is good, since they need all the supporters they can get.

Hyenas are neither canines nor felines and have doleful beautiful eyes, wet noses, and jaws that can snap off your arm in a second. They also have gotten an utterly bum rap in the media. We know all about hyenas: it's dawn on the savanna, there's something big and dead with a lion feeding on it, and Marlin Perkins is up to his elbows in the gore, filming the scene. You know the score. Ol' Marlin is waxing poetic about the noble lion and his predatory skills, said king of the jungle, covered with his usual array of flies, is munching away at somebody's innards, and the camera will occasionally tear itself away from this tableau of carnivory to pan the edges. And there they are: skulky, cowardly, dirty, snively, skeevy, no-account hyenas lurking at the periphery, trying to grab a piece of the vittles. Marlin practically invites us to heap our contempt on the hyenas: scavengers. Now, it's not entirely clear to me why we laud the predators so much and so disdain the scavengers, since most of us are hardening our arteries wolfing down carcasses that someone else killed, but that is our bias. Lions get lionized, while hyenas never get to vocalize at the beginning of MGM movies.

Oh, but a revolution occurred in carnivorology a while back. As part of our national defense, it is vital to be able to shoot people at any time of day or night, so the military developed all these nifty night-viewing goggles, with photon enhancers and infrared viewing scopes. The army was up to their umpteenth-generation model and decided to unload some of their old ones on zoologists, and suddenly, a revolution!—people could watch animals at night.

Redemption of the hyenas. It turns out that they are fabulous hunters, working cooperatively, taking down beasties ten times their size. They have one of the highest percentages of successful hunts of any big carnivore. And you know who has one of the worst? Lions. They're big, conspicuous, relatively slow. It's much easier for them just to key in on cheetahs and hyenas and rip them off. That's why all those hyenas are lurking around at dawn, looking mealy and unphotogenic—they just spent the whole night hunting the damn thing and who's eating breakfast now?

So Laurence was in the thick of this revisionism concerning hyena public relations. It was no doubt all this hubbub about the suddenly much-vaunted hunting skills of these beasts that led to an unlikely phone call to Laurence one day during a trip back to the States. It was from the U.S. Army. A colonel wanted him to come to a conference and talk about his work. Are you kidding, I watch hyenas mate, he replied. We know, we know, the colonel replied, we know all about you, and proved it to Laurence. Come on, come to our conference, all your carnivore biologist friends are going to be there and it'll be great and we'll pay you, it's all courtesy of the U.S. Army. Puzzled, Laurence finally agreed.

The day came, and as promised, Laurence found himself at a plush hotel with a confused collection of America's carnivore biologists. Lion people, wolf people, wild-dog people, hyena people, the works. Plus some silent army guys in shades. The biologists initially fell into their reflexive behavior at conferences—giving their formal talks about their work, bragging about their animals or study sites, pumping each other for unpublished information. All the while the army guys sat silently in the back taking notes, and the biologists finally got the willies. They conferred together at the bar that night and resolved to demand to know why the army was interested in them. They presented a unified front after breakfast the next day, and the colonel relented. He would explain what was up.

You fellas have all seen the *Star Wars* movies, haven't you? Nearly everyone. Well, remember in that second installment, there are those Imperial Walker things? Those big transporters that kinda looked like elephants and went walking through the snow and over everything and stomped down on the rebels? Sure, everyone has probably played with their nephew's toy version of one. Well, the U.S. Army is designing something like an Imperial Walker. We've spent a bundle on a prototype, working like crazy on it, and it still has problems.

It seemed that the best the army had could walk only a few miles an hour, and only on really smooth surfaces, and still it fell over all the time. So they needed help, and someone had the bright idea of getting the carnivore biologists—after all, carnivores run after things while they're hunting, why not consult with them on how to design things that move? And, gentlemen, the colonel concluded, ignoring the ladies present, that's why you are here—tell us about how your animals move when they do things like hunting. He smiled sunnily.

Field biologists are a fairly unruly lot They spend most of their time living alone, and they wind up pretty ill-mannered. They take on a lot of the traits of their animals. They're reflexively suspicious of guys in uniforms, since they pass a lot of their time being lied to by park wardens. And, given the fairly narrow age window during which field biologists are actually active, most of the current generation came of age in the '60s and definitely retain some opinions about things. The colonel smiled sunnily again, and everyone smelled a rat.

Bullshit, pal, they said collectively. No, really, said the colonel, we just want to hear about how your animals run around when they are hunting.

No one was buying that. You want to learn about locomotion, you buy yourself some locomotion experts. There are people out there who design prosthetic devices and build robotic limbs. If you really want to find out how animals do it, you get bioengineers and biophysicists. There are lunatics out there who make X-ray films of animals running to see how they locomote. You hire them, not social behavior experts. Bullshit, Colonel Scheisskopf, something is not right here. The biologists caucused and announced they weren't talking anymore. They were ready to start chanting about Ho Chi Minh and the NLF.

Everything broke up. The colonel sequestered himself with a telephone, talking to his superiors. The army guys descended on the trays of little croissant sandwiches. The biologists converged on the bar in thirsty, self-righteous excitement. This was turning out to be fun after all, instead of being just some dumb scientific meeting.

Finally, later in the day, Scheisskopf returned. Gentlemen, he said, I have good news for you. I've been given special permission to let you in on the whole scoop, since you're all my special pals.

It turned out there was a hidden agenda after all. The army had been building some new tank for years. It was grotesquely expensive—one carburetor cost more than America's entire ecology budget. It had had endless cost overruns, and some poor sacrificial general would be tossed up to Congress annually to explain the obscene costs in order for Congress to dutifully approve more bucks down the sink for it. And the army loved it, because it was the best tank ever! The colonel glowed with pleasure in the telling. Getaloadathis. It could withstand direct missile hits. There were no exposed windows or portals on it—instead, it had video cameras mounted on the body, transmitting to the death-troll soldiers crammed inside. It was insanely maneuverable—it could tear along at 60 miles an hour and still fire a missile with pinpoint accuracy while bouncing in midair—it was one big gyroscope. Best feature of all, it came with these gas chromatograph air samplers that would let you know when you could safely open the top and breathe your postnuclear air. The perfect family car for the end of the world.

The colonel was pulling out all the stops now for his biology buddies. They brought in a film, a training demonstrator for the tank, filmed from the inside, outside, underneath as it blasted over you. Everyone got to wear daddy-o 3-D glasses and clutched their stomachs queasily as the film tank did some full gainer into a computer-simulated Grand Canyon and still was able to shell the refugee camp accurately. It was fabulous.

So this is our tank, and we're damn proud of it, the colonel said—he came just shy of passing around baby pictures of it. But there were these problems. Apparently, in traditional tank warfare with traditional tanks, the strategy is to use the unstoppable force of the tank to bash to the top of the highest thing around, sit there, and shoot anything that moves. Now, with this new tank, tank crews would be able to dart all over the landscape with this mad-assassin abandon. The trouble was, whenever they put their best tank crews in them, the guys would bash to the top of the highest thing around and just sit there, waiting to shoot whatever moved. And another problem—the tank was planned for use in fighting Russkies on the "Central Front" (the area that the rest of us sentimentalists typically call Europe). All indications were that the Central Front Armageddon was not only going to involve this miasma of nerve gas and radiation but tons of electronic jamming as well, and no one would be able to communicate with one another. Thus, the difficulty: nobody knew how to use the tank properly, no one was thinking in this mobile predatory way, or knew how to do it while out of touch with the other tanks. And some bright lad in the Pentagon had had this idea of calling the carnivore biologists, and here we are, gentlemen, and, well, teach us to think like predators. How do your hyenas figure out in a high-speed chase who is going to cut the corners on the prey, how do wolves communicate once they get going, what do they do if they lose each other? Teach our tank crews to hunt like your animals.

Jeezus, thought America's carnivore biologists. No one had bargained for this. It wasn't clear if all this was a measure of how godawful stupid the army was, spending zillions on a weapon no one could use, or a measure of how terrifyingly smart they were to try to get their tank crews trained to act like predators. Suddenly ol' Colonel Scheisskopf seemed more like a mix between Darth Vader and Machiavelli.

The biologists tried to stall. These are very difficult questions, very difficult, these will take some time to answer, they intoned. All right, gentlemen, said the colonel, seeing through their ploy, we are more than willing to fund your research. Now there was some moral reckoning to do.

One bunch decided they wanted nothing to do with this kind of thing and left the conference. Another bunch decided to screw this hippie stance and sell out but big; soon they were falling over themselves to sign on the dotted line with Beelzebub and teach tank crews.

Laurence spearheaded the middle-of-the-road pragmatists. They reasoned that these people are going to build their tanks regardless. Anything we have to tell them they can just look up in our papers anyway. This may divert a trickle of money that could help conservation. And besides, these colonels are greatly misinformed about cooperative hunting species—there are actually very few of them, most of the hunts are just uncoordinated free-for-alls, and we could happily do research on their bucks for years before telling them, sorry, they're not very good hunters after all. Yeah, help conservation research and work undercover to drain dollars from the war machine, leave the Pentagon too destitute to afford to paint racing stripes on their tanks. Where do we sign up?

So the remaining biologists settled on down and resumed their meeting. More croissants were brought in, talks went on, everyone had their usual fine time arguing over minutiae concerning optimal foraging strategies or reproductive fitness equations, remembering to bow and scrape in the direction of the army guys now and then, citing some facile connection between what they were talking about and hunting techniques. The colonel turned out to be named Chuck, and soon he was drinking at the bar with them, and he turned out to be a good storyteller and a damn good guy, but really. Everyone had a swell time, posed for a group picture at the end. The army sent them their checks for coming to the meeting, and everyone dashed off their army grant proposals to cash in on the action. Laurence wrote for some new night-viewing goggles, and some walkie-talkies, and a good field computer with solar panels, and, well, as long as he was at it, seven research assistants and a flame thrower and a satellite and some death-ray guns and a million zillion dollars. Everyone wrote in, no one got a cent, no one even heard from Colonel Chuck or anyone in the army again. And to this day, whenever the carnivore biologists get together, they shake their hoary heads and ask suspiciously, What did those guys really manage to find out from us?*

---

*Obvious possibilities as to the true story of what went on:
   a) The carnivore biologists are just saying they never heard from Colonel Chuck again and are actually in cahoots with him up to their ears, sworn to secrecy.
   b) The whole meeting was an exercise for Colonel Chuck and his pals in order to learn how to bribe, bully, cajole, and manipulate scientists. The carnivore biologists were just for practice, and they are now pulling this off on rocket scientists.
   c) Colonel Chuck and his army pals were actually herbivores in disguise, trying to gain information about carnivore hunting strategies.

12

The Coup

The details changed, but the theme was the same for each dream. It was certainly not nightly, but still occurred with surprising frequency, given how long it had been since I was getting beaten up in junior high school. In the dream, I might be traveling on the subway. A gang of thugs confronts me, planning to rob me. Or I may be walking down a street, and a dangerous murderer is about to make me the victim of a random act of savagery. Or perhaps I am sitting quietly in my room, and a frenzied mob bursts in, intent on some act of incoherent political revenge. In any case, I am about to be hurt badly, and I am frightened. And here the dream was always the same. Somehow, I talk my way out of it. Sometimes, I talk in a way to show that I am even tougher, more street-smart, than they, and they back off. Sometimes, in a premeditated way meant (literally) to be disarming, I am buffoonish, so amusing and entertaining and unthreatening that soon I am considered one of the guys, long enough to make my escape. Sometimes, I try an unorthodox, straightforward approach. I say, "Look, there's just me and a whole bunch of you; you can obviously beat the crap out of me, but what is it going to accomplish?" Somehow, that gets to them, and they leave me alone. Sometimes, there is a bizarrely psychotherapeutic flavor to the dream; I am able to empathize, perceive the thug's very core of hurt and resentment and troubles and speak to it, an almost Quakerly centering on him as a person, and soon he is no longer a threat.

When in Africa, the dream even took on an appropriate, colorful local flavor: I am a gnu, surrounded by hyenas, and I beat them into submission with a lecture on predator-prey ratios. I am a hartebeest, pursued by a leopard that I manage to convince of the wisdom of vegetarianism.

Always talking my way out. It was perfect—if I ever finished grad school, I might even get a job where the only weapon of the trade was lecturing people into submission. But then there was the day in Kenya when it didn't work.

It was 1982, during the reign of Saul, and Kenya was in the news, always a bad sign. When the Third World makes it into our Western awareness, it's usually because of some tragedy, some drought, pandemic, or something explosively violent and abrupt to jostle our consciousness. This time it was a truly messy coup attempt. The whole thing was both amateurish and suitably sordid—a planned coup that apparently encompassed key elements of all branches of the military, university, and government opposition, all screwed up by a group of air force officers who decided to jump the gun and do it on their own weeks early. A key moment when the president could have been grabbed that was lost in drunken revelry, an army that vacillated half a day deciding whether to back their erstwhile air force coup colleagues who had proven unreliable or to come out against the air force. The university students who made a grand, romantic suicidal miscalculation in terms of showing their enthusiasm for the air force revolutionaries just as the latter were getting their asses kicked.

The army rolled in and quickly routed the air force rebels. The students emerged for their rally in support of the new revolutionary junta just in time to be bazookaed by the army. The government regained the radio station and, in order to instill confidence in the populace, ordered everyone to go downtown and start shopping immediately, just as a major tank battle began there. The civilian casualties were numerous and unacknowledged.

The beaten air force took to the hills, forests, and back alleys, fell into guerrilla attacks, frantic attempts at sprints for safety, and just plain old-time banditry. A group of them held on to the main air force base to the north, threatening to bomb and strafe Nairobi if they were not given amnesty. With the general military action quieting down in Nairobi, the populace exploded into an orgy of civil unrest, sometimes over the protest of the controlling army, sometimes with its instigation. This mostly consisted of devastation of the Indians.

At the start of the British adventure in East Africa, coolie laborers had been imported from India to build the railroads and gradually to provide the comfortable colonial infrastructure familiar from the raj. And, taking advantage of the superior education of the Indians as compared to the Africans, the Brits had ensured that the former filled a necessary niche—just as with the Jews of medieval Europe, it was next to impossible for the Indians to own land and to farm, or to serve in the government. Instead, just as with the Jews, they had no choice but to evolve into the mercantile class, the shopkeepers, the moneylenders, and for close to a century, the Africans' hatred of them had been building. In colonial times, a peasant in the bush might never in his life have seen one of the white overlords, the people controlling the economy of the colony, yet it would be the Indian shopkeeper, running the remote trading post in the hamlet, who demanded that peasant's money. And now in spanking, modern Nairobi, in which the tiny Indian minority constituted the bulk of the middle class, little had changed—it would now be some Bantu government official in a pinstripe suit setting economic policy, often based on how much of the economy he could stuff in his pocket, but this was a mere abstraction for the average African; it was still the Hindu shopkeeper ringing up the cash register.

So the anger at them simmered. In recent years, it was no longer just for the Indians' wealth, but also for their refusal to become "real Africans" (a complaint, usually between the lines but sometimes in the lines themselves, that centered on the fact that Indian women never married or slept with African men). And any demagogue could unite disparate and hostile tribes by attacking the Indians—Idi Amin was never more popular in Uganda than when he summarily stripped the Indians of their citizenship and property and threw them out of Uganda; "wealth for all" was the official slogan for the persecution.

The situation for the Indians in Kenya always felt to me like Berlin in the 1930s. And the aftermath of the coup became their Kristallnacht. They were subjected to a ferocious pogrom of looting and plundering, and the hospitals were overflowing with the Hindu victims of beatings and gang rapes.

The tumult went on for days, until the government visibly regained control. Whatever was to be looted had been, and the glaziers were going into action; the air force rebels were gradually rooted out from their lairs, and the national anthem was played repeatedly over the government radio station.

In the aftermath came a long stretch of trials officiated by bewigged magistrates. The government had a slight problem, in that it couldn't readily admit that the coup was a case of the air force guys jumping the gun on a massive planned revolt that permeated numerous branches of society. Instead, the coup had to be presented in the most minute, concrete ways as resulting from the actions of this handful of unconnected madmen. The newspapers screamed with details about the senior private who first started shooting, about the enlisted man who drove the private's vehicle for him, about the revolutionary musicologist who chose the celebratory records to be played over the air after the radio station had been seized by rebels. Eventually, everyone appropriate was duly hanged or locked away forever. But then the government had to get all the folks who were obviously in on planning the big coup that never came off, without admitting that an event indicating such widespread dissatisfaction could have been contemplated. A series of flimsy purges of the coup's obvious godfathers was carried out, highlighted by the show trial of the attorney general, where the official charges were something on the order of his being a smart aleck and having a Caucasian wife and foreign friends.

Soon everything was back in order, and the tourist industry resumed, unruffled.

I reached Kenya on the first commercial flight into the country after the start of the coup. I had been itching to go and decided not to defer. I pooh-poohed the Western reports of the violence, planned to scoot out of Nairobi as quickly as possible and get to the quiet countryside. I was depressed about some personal events back in the States and figured some civil unrest would clear up the neurotransmitter problems in my head. And besides, if anything hairy came up, I would talk my way out of it.

The last leg of the Pan Am flight went from Lagos to Nairobi. There were three other passengers in the 747, which was an experience in terms of personal service from the twenty or so flight attendants. There was one frantic Hindu businessman rushing home to his family whose safety was unconfirmed, and a tourist couple who seemed only marginally aware of the fighting. I took them under my wing and regaled them with useless hints about black-marketing and getting fraudulent visa stamps. We were met at the airport by an automaton of a functionary who welcomed us to Kenya and told us what a happy place it was, and we were loaded into an army troop carrier. Nighttime, soldiers everywhere, grim-faced. We were told exasperating news—because of the shoot-to-kill curfew in effect, we were being taken to the main hotel in the center of town, where we would have to stay until the next morning. This was fine with the tourist couple, as they had reservations there anyway. The businessman was frantic, as this meant another twelve hours until finding his family. And I was cheesed off, as this was a hotel that I had previously entered only in order to steal toilet paper, and the one night was going to wipe out my budget. Nevertheless, it did seem a bit unreasonable to ask the army to drop us off at various places. At the hotel, I was escorted to my room by the unruffled assistant manager, who, in a voice as if he said this nightly, advised me to sleep on the floor and keep the window shades drawn. Throughout the night, I heard gunfire on the street.

The next day brought some feeling of the devastation. Soldiers were everywhere, nests of machine guns set up on every corner. There was still active looting and fighting in one corner of town, but elsewhere, everyone had basically been ordered to go back to normal. The citizenry had adopted the interesting accommodation of walking to work with their hands up in the air and identity cards in their mouths; when in Rome, etc., and soon I was salivating inelegantly on my passport.

I stopped in at the various places in town, both to check on acquaintances and to try to pull together the necessary supplies to get out to the bush. One shop I knew was in a shambles, the Hindu shopkeeper hospitalized from a skull fracture suffered while defending the place. Another man was missing, in hiding, his store trashed. Another had resumed anxious, wary business, and seemed near tears as he recounted events. I made the rounds and everyone was a mess.

Around noon, I discovered the current disadvantages of being a naked man in Nairobi. The place had always had a disproportionate share of naked people in its streets—it had always struck me that when people in Nairobi who were not that many generations (or even years) removed from the bush had their occasional psychotic breaks, the first addled thing they would do was toss off all their Western clothes. (Years later, my clinical psychologist wife, in her conversations with Kenyan colleagues, would confirm my impression that this was indeed a common event.) So Nairobi had always had more than its share of ranting and raving naked men and had treated them with a certain aplomb. Now it meant trouble. Many of the air force rebels had taken refuge in Nairobi buildings and alleyways, when their triumph had come up short. The lucky ones would find someone to waylay—kill the guy, steal his civilian clothes, and slip into the crowd with his identity card in their teeth. Those not so fortunate were all independently reaching the same odd conclusion—dump the air force clothes and make a run for it naked. Every few hours an air force desperado would make his nude run and be gunned down by an army unit, and it was around noon that I got to see my first street execution. Army flatbed trucks intermittently rumbled through with naked corpses. They stopped for traffic lights in a way that was both incongruous and calming, leading to an odd air of normalcy.

By late afternoon, I had made my way to Mrs. R's boardinghouse, the place on the edge of town where I stayed, the house of the old Polish woman who would rent beds or floor space or tent space to overlanders passing through. I had not seen Mrs. R for a year, which would normally make for an excited return. Now I felt as if I were the first person to successfully smuggle supplies into the Warsaw Ghetto. There had not been a new face since the coup; everyone had been huddling inside for days, sleeping on the floor to avoid flying bullets, coping with the enforced blackout. Coming in from the outside world, I was able to bring information about what was going on a mile away, in contrast to the state-controlled radio station, which, now back in the hands of the state, was spouting every type of gibberish—old quiz shows, country-western music—but no reliable news. Everyone was tired and frazzled and hungry from the food shortages, which were acute by now. I brought in cookies that my mother had baked for me. Mrs. R, Stefan and Bogdan, the two Polish boys who had been regulars there for years, and I huddled in the corner of her room. I split up the cookies, Mrs. R produced a bottle of soda she had hidden, the brothers came up with something. They were euphoric with the food, and thus so was I; there was something excitingly stoic about sharing the bits of food amid candlelight and distant gunfire.

Going to sleep that night, it all seemed a fine adventure. The upsetting things I could explain away—it was horrifying that the Hindus had been trashed but inevitable given the scapegoat role they had been maneuvered into in the country. The two Swiss overlanders at Mrs. R's who had been beaten up by soldiers the day before had simply done things the wrong way. One was big and stocky and seemed, at least to me, inordinately white, and he had to have seemed provoking to the army men. Both had unfriendly, scowly faces, and that couldn't have helped. And neither spoke Swahili or English—they didn't have a hope of talking their way out of whatever they had blundered into. I was not worried.

The next day, I was ready to clear town except for a few last chores. I had my vehicle, had bought enough food to get me through the next few weeks, had retrieved my camp supplies out of storage. I went over to the Game Department to check in. It was about ten miles out of town, at the entrance to Nairobi National Park. The park was closed because of the troubles. The main air force base bordered the park, and when the army had attacked, many of the air force men went over the fence and were running loose in the park, armed and panicked. They had shot animals, perhaps for food, perhaps in a displacement frenzy. They had also waylaid a group of rangers and escaped with their clothes—the naked bodies had been found. The park staff was reasonably freaked out, and I commiserated.

Returning, I passed through a number of army checkpoints. They were ostensibly checking to see if anyone was air force trying to escape, if anyone was taking advantage of the situation to hoard supplies. They were clearly also roughing up people, hassling, robbing, seeking private vengeances. I was waved through the first two checkpoints and managed shit-eating howdy grins for the soldiers as I passed.

At the third one, on a remote bend in the road, the three soldiers motioned with their guns for me to pull over. I got my passport and research permit ready. I got a smile ready. I had planned that the best approach for dealing with any checkpoints would be to say hello exuberantly in Swahili, howsitgoing's, all the usual blandishments that occupy the first five minutes of encountering anyone here, to ask lots of questions about their exploits, to congratulate the soldiers on their difficult and important task of saving the country, to be smiley and starry-eyed and unfazed, and to just keep talking.

I got out smiling as the three soldiers approached.

"Bwana, you have a problem, this is very bad, you have a problem, bwana, a big problem," the first one was chanting.

I was going to say "Howsitgoing, guys? There's no problem" in my best Swahili slang. I said, "Howsitgoing" as the first soldier pushed me against the door of my car. Again, I said, "Howsitgoing?" He slammed me against the door again, harder. All three were around me now. There was an odor of alcohol.

I was somewhat breathless by then, but still began, in an airy voice, to say "There's no problem." At the first syllable, they slammed me repeatedly against the door. The first soldier had been pushing against my chest. By now, a second one had me by the collar and was hitting my head against the glass. I suddenly noticed my head hurting.

The one with his hands on my neck was curling his lips back, displaying his teeth with the effort he was extending. It occurred to me that he was smiling, and, in an instant's stupidity, I thought, Oh, he's the one I should be talking to.

While collecting my thoughts as to what to say, I turned my head and smiled sunnily at him. I think I even chuckled, to show him that I was relaxed and that they could relax too. Still showing his teeth, the soldier punched me hard in the stomach.

Something was odd about my perception. My stomach was hurting terribly, but the pain seemed to be inside my head as well. My head seemed thick, stuffed, imploded. There was a taste of vomit, and I could not catch my breath. They were punching me in the stomach again. Or maybe it was still the first punch I was feeling. I seemed to be having trouble paying attention.

Suddenly, I was paying attention. One of them was holding a knife to my throat. Again, there was a chant of "You have a problem, bwana, this is very bad, you have a big problem."

A thought repeated through my head—Be careful with that thing. Be careful with it. It was close to my throat. I didn't speak, just looked from face to face. They had grown still as well.

Someone yanked off my watch; I felt the band break in the process. A voice boomed, real close, "Now you have no problem, bwana." Abruptly, they began laughing as the knife was lowered. And then one of them struck me on the side of the head, knocking me to the ground. They were already walking away, examining my watch among them.

I stood up, uncertain, wondering if I should run. One of them gestured angrily at me, at the car—"Go on, get out of here."

I left as they hooted. Never since that time has it occurred to me that I can talk my way out of anything.

13

Hearing Voices at the Wrong Time

*N*ow, part of the fascination in hanging around with folks from an utterly different world is seeing things that were unprecedented back home—someone's particularly flamboyant scarification pattern, the nice fresh tureen of cow's blood all set for the drinking, the brash kid carried back from the bush after being mangled by a lion but with the lion in even worse shape than he.

But sometimes, what I was seeing was something *just* like back in my world. And what was fascinating was the completely novel explanation given for it.

I'd seen one version of that when Hudson, my on-again, off-again research assistant, had passed through on his way back from the other baboon site where he now worked, and we had decided that I'd go on with him for the half day's trip west of the park to visit his village. We were sitting around, chewing the fat with the old men, when into our afternoon kaffeeklatsch came a sudden apparition from out of the bush. He was late-middle-aged, dazed. Unshaven scraggle face, vacant. Barefoot, pigeon-toed, mildewed blanket wrapped around him, balls hanging out the bottom. Drooly face, seemingly not a thought in his head. The others regarded him with the accepting indifference that village idiots are always accorded here. Conversation resumed, and after mumbling now and then, he wandered back from whence he came.

So what's with that fella? I asked Hudson.

"You see how handsome he is, terribly handsome."

"Yes, I noted how handsome he was," I said. Actually, he looked like a half-drowned squirrel, but I was being agreeable.

"That man has two wives, and he is so terribly handsome that they were always fighting, fighting to see which one he would be staying with at night. He favored one wife, and the other one got angry and went to the witch doctor and put a curse on him, and now he cannot even remember his name."

"If you have two wives, it can be dangerous to be too handsome," one of the old men concluded, chortling.

Early onset Alzheimer's, I decided. But a few months later, I saw something similar in Rhoda's village. It had been a wonderfully calm day with the baboons. Nebuchanezzar hadn't been giving anyone any grief, Job hadn't been getting any. Benjamin had sat for a while on the roof of my vehicle, peering in through the windshield now and then, his face upside-down. Joshua seemed closer to grasping the concept of play, watching his son, the now juvenile Obadiah, wrestling with the other kids, Joshua only occasionally making a threatening face at the others. And Isaac was up to the usual. He had nonchalantly relinquished a consortship with a young female the second Menasseh had shown any interest in her, and had instead spent the rest of the morning grooming with Rachel. So that was the day, when, back at camp, I got to see some of the Masai dirty laundry being aired. I don't think it reflected any particular intimacy that was emerging between the Masai and me. It was that I was convenient. I had a vehicle.

That day Rhoda and some women from the village came running into camp in a panic. Now, to see Masai in a panic is a sufficiently rare event that it really does quicken one's heart. They needed my help, there was no time to explain, I had to drive to the village immediately, we had to get rid of her!, there was no time to lose, imagine, killing a goat. It was all an unexplained jumble, but it was clear that I was not going to get out of driving to the village with them.

Once we were under way, they were able to calm a bit and tell me what was happening. There was a woman in the village who had gone mad, done some terrible things, and she had to go. They wanted me to drive her to the government clinic, many kilometers away, at the other end of the reserve. I tried to protest, to no avail. They were desperate. As they gave me details, it sounded like a classic psychotic break. The clues were there, as they described her. In my many visits to the village, I had never seen her—she was either kept hidden away or kept herself that way. She had done dreadfully inappropriate things—disrupted ceremonies, disobeyed the elders, and, today, the final straw, she had run amok and killed a goat with her bare hands. She had to go.

We approached the village, and I braced myself for a scene: perhaps a tearful departure as her family clustered around, telling her to get well soon and hurry back. Perhaps the woman, frightened, begging not to be taken away. Maybe a sullen cooperation. Instead, as we got out of the car, we were attacked by an apparition of frenzied, terrifying energy. The woman came sprinting toward us, howling god knows what war cries in Masai. She was huge. She was naked. She was covered with goat shit, goat blood, goat innards, the bulk of which was smeared downward from her mouth. She still had part of the dead goat in her hand as she barreled into us, knocking us down. The goat was flung free, and, instead, she seemed intent on strangling me.

You know, I have as healthy and varied a fantasy life as the next guy, but being strangled by a huge naked banshee smeared with goat bowels has never even once infested the darkest corners of my musings. I thought I was about to die and wondered if my parents would bear some scar of shame for my having gone in such a bizarre, embarrassing way.

While I pondered my mortality, Rhoda and the women fell upon her and managed to wrestle her away. Goat guts spraying everywhere, they pushed her into the back of the Jeep, into the back of *my* Jeep for god's sake, and piled in on top of her. Go, go, they shouted, and we roared off.

It was as awful a ride as one might expect. A Jeepful of Masai is quite an olfactory experience, under the best of circumstances, given their paucity of water, and the effect is positively sickening when everyone is frantic, sweaty, and frightened because at their epicenter is the equivalent of a water buffalo roaring on angel dust. And that doesn't even mention the by now sun-warmed goat innards. Throughout the trip, she bellowed, rolled about, and made repeated efforts to grab me from behind and pull me into her goat shit lair; Rhoda and crew, thank god, continued their wrestling and kept her at bay. We bounced along for a good forty-five minutes that seemed interminable, crossed a river, went through the gate of the park headquarters past sullen rangers who seemed to consider the tumult commonplace. Once, as if to calm her, imbue an air that all was well and we were merely tourists on a game drive, I pointed out some giraffes, but she continued to bellow.

Finally, we came to the government dispensary—a ramshackle building with a single nurse who had a tendency to treat all illnesses as malaria and dispense chloroquine. This time, the man did not appear to make that diagnosis. He told us no way was she staying there unless the women got her in the back room themselves—he wasn't going to touch her. More wrestling, pushing, bellowing, and Rhoda and the women eventually got her in the room, which was locked and barricaded.

We could hear her yelling from the room. The nurse shook our hands nervously. We stretched and yawned in the sun. So what do we do next? I asked. Wait till she feels better, talk to her through the door, discuss her case with the nurse? Let's get outa here, said Rhoda, and they propelled me back to the village.

I had just gotten my first taste of cross-cultural psychiatry. The Masai, living a life as different from us as anyone can manage, appear to have about the same tolerance for mental illness that we have. Push her in the room, lock that door, let's scram. As we drove back and calm returned and the opened Jeep windows began to air things out to a tolerable level, I recognized a wonderful opportunity to learn more about their view of mental illness, do some nifty medical anthropology, see how something like schizophrenia seems in such a different culture.

"So, Rhoda," I began laconically, "what do you suppose was wrong with that woman?"

She looked at me as if *I* was mad.

"She is crazy."

"But how can you tell?"

"She's crazy. Can't you just see from how she acts?"

"But how do you decide that she is crazy? What did she do?"

"She killed that goat."

"Oh," I said with anthropological detachment, "but Masai kill goats all the time."

She looked at me as if I were an idiot. "Only the men kill goats," she said.

"Well, how else do you know that she is crazy?"

"She hears voices."

Again, I made a pain of myself. "Oh, but the Masai hear voices sometimes." (At ceremonies before long cattle drives, the Masai trance-dance and claim to hear voices.) And in one sentence, Rhoda summed up half of what anyone needs to know about cross-cultural psychiatry.

"But she hears voices at the wrong time."

Postscript: a year after the naked goatwoman launched herself at me, I returned to my field site for my annual season. I soon encountered Rhoda. What ever happened to that woman?

"Oh, they locked her up, and then she died. Masai do not like to stay inside like that, so she died," she said, dismissing the dull subject.

14

Sudan

My first evening in Sudan and I couldn't find a toilet anywhere. Up until then, my luck had been good. I had flown into Khartoum that morning— Sudan Airways had had enough fuel to do that week's flight. I had immediately caught a ride coming out of the airport. Dropped off at a ramshackle hamlet on the edge of nowhere, the desert rubbing up behind each hut on the single street. Reported to the police, as required. "The police" turned out to be a lone man in tattered uniform. Friendly guy, quizzed me at length about my last name, seemed amused and taken with it. "You are not from here," he concluded. I confessed he was right, and he invited me to put my tent up in the yard at the police station, amid the half-dead rows of corn and chickens and obscure debris. Everything was turning out hunky-dory, except that I had had to go to the bathroom all day, and by now, evening, it was becoming critical. There wasn't an obvious outhouse, and I figured I shouldn't take a crap in his yard, didn't want to make some horrendous faux pas my first evening. I wandered up to him, he lost in twilight thoughts.

Do you have a bathroom? His English is good, but he isn't familiar with the term.

A toilet? He nods assertively, assuringly, disappears in the back and returns with more hot tea, which he thinks I am asking for. I am getting antsy and desperate.

An outhouse? Huh?

A men's room? A loo? Befuddlement.

A water closet? The little boy's room? The john? No dice.

Frantically, I squat and pantomime defecating. He suddenly roars in happy comprehension.

"Oh, you mean the *latrine*! Here in Sudan we call it a *latrine*! Do you know the word '*latrine*'?"

Yes, yes, I know the word "latrine," please, do you have one close by?

"No, here in Sudan we do not *have* latrines. Here in Sudan, we just relieve ourselves as we are, for we are a free people."

With that, he grabs me by the wrist and marches me onto the main street of the hamlet, leading the way with his flashlight through the dark. He stops, points emphatically with his flashlight at a spot in the middle of the street.

"This is your place! Here in Sudan we do not have latrines, so you just be free right there!"

What the hell. I drop my pants, squat down, hope desperately I still have some toilet paper in my pocket. He has his flashlight trained on me. That's all right, I say, I'm fine now, thanks a lot, no need to wait here, I'll be back in a . . .

"No, I must stay here and see that you are fine! This is Sudan! You just be free!" He is shouting. "You are our guest!"

"Our"? I realize with horror that a crowd has drawn, the entire population of the hamlet. Who among them could resist? I hear a number of snickers and an unmistakable high, feminine giggle. His flashlight beam is held steady, on my ass. I resign myself, rest my chin in my hands, and make my mark on the village amid what sounds almost like murmurs of approval. And throughout, above it all, like a circus barker, "This is Sudan! You are our friend! We are a free nation! You just be free!"

I had come to Sudan to go on a vacation following the overthrow of Saul by the Gang of Six. The largest country in Africa, one of the poorest, howling empty desiccated wasteland of the Sahara, cut through the middle by the Nile. Chaos, famine, a northern Arabic Muslim half and a southern black animist half that have been having a civil war for decades. Searing heat, flash storms that produce rivers in seconds, hundreds of miles between bridges on the Nile, four paved kilometers of road in all the south, roads impassable six months of the year. Mutinies, coups, refugees from every neighboring country, locust swarms, tribal insurrections. It was in Sudan that I made the worst literary mistake of my life.

I was accustomed to making food mistakes on trips like this. My first backpacking trip ever was a disaster because of a food mistake. In high school in urban Brooklyn, we decided it was time to become outdoor hippies and made plans for an Easter vacation hike on the Appalachian Trail on a stretch a mere forty miles from Manhattan. We had no idea what we were doing. Word spread, and soon twenty-four were in on planning the trip. It turned out that it was going to take place on Passover. We divided into food groups. Those who were Jewish and keeping Passover diets who were also vegetarian. Non-vegetarian non-Passover keepers. Vegetarian non-Passover. And so on. We planned shifts of who would stay awake during which night hours to guard against mountain lions and poisonous snakes. We argued over placement of sleeping bags, determining who got to sleep near whom, rife with titillation over the various pointless crushes that various people had on others. We spent weeks meeting after school daily, planning the one-night trip. As our final stupidity, we wanted some sort of communal gesture to tie us all together into a utopian backpacking collective. We would carry supplies for each other—four or five people would carry everyone's water. Someone else would carry everyone's crackers. Someone else the cheese. We would be strong and united and interdependent. We would strike socialist-realist work poses around the campfire while others sang folk songs.

By the first half mile of the hike, eight people had quit in exhaustion. Within a mile, in some manner that defies spatial logic, the remainder were already scattered miles apart. I wound up with a friend named Kenny Friedman, having no idea where anyone else was. We never saw another soul. Unfortunately, all we carried by way of food was the chocolate and celery, nothing else, including water. We survived our gorging on chocolate but stayed up half the night, torturing each other with descriptions of things to drink and lamenting Alana Goldfarb, the flautist we had unsuccessfully tried to convince to go on the trip with us.

My food luck was even worse on desert trips. My first visit to the desert in Kenya had been by accident. I had hitched out to Mt. Elgon, straddling the Ugandan border, a snowy, 15,000-foot honker with elephants living in its caves. Went with my thermals and woolens, good mountain food as well—oranges and cheese and chocolate. It turned out that Idi Amin's soldiers had been kidnapping foreign climbers, and the place was closed to whiteys. Disappointed, hitched back to the nearest town and spotted a lorry heading north to the desert. Jumped on, spent the next week wandering half sunstroked in the desert on the Ethiopian border with my wool socks and down mittens and liquefied cheese. Oranges, when sufficiently hot, actually shrivel to the point of contracting inward, tearing free of the peel. You open it up, and out pops a marvelous inedible petrified orange.

The next desert trip I planned better, which is to say, I planned for a desert trip. I went to one of the spanking new supermarkets in Nairobi, got my salt tablets and crackers and fluids. I wanted dried fruit; dried fruit is perfect for the desert, I'd decided; I'd always thought of myself as wandering through the desert eating dried biblical fruit. It was damn expensive. The dried pineapples or dried coconut or dried bananas were going to bankrupt me. Clearly not basic subsistence foods around here. Suddenly, I spotted a block of dried *tamarind.* Had no idea what tamarind was, but it was phenomenally cheap. Bought two bricks—two kilos of the stuff.

First evening, hiked off from the only town in the western part of the Turkana desert, made it up to the top of a desolate cinder cone by dusk. Set up my tent, dizzying floating view of the entire empty scorched planet below. Settled down to eat, unwrapped my block of tamarind, and bit off a hunk. A stupefying gustatory sensation screamed through my head at that instant. Imagine opening up an entire salt shaker into your mouth. Quick, before swallowing, pour a bottle of mustard in. Then, just a second, toss in a hunk of Marmite, some fetid French cheese, and an old fish. Multiply by a hundred thousand. That begins to approximate how strong the taste was. "Taste" almost stopped making sense as a term. It transcended taste. It was as if every neuron in my brain had been recruited into gustation, as if each cell were being rubbed with sandpaper made of tamarind. It turned out I had brought enough dried tamarind along to give gustatory hallucinations to every man, woman, and child south of Cairo. Wizened tough leathery murderous desert chieftains would pinch off a tiny smidgen of this sort of dried tamarind and still get queasy and weak in the knees. I lay up all night, trying to spit the taste out. Another ruined trip.

But this time in Sudan, it was a literary disaster that I precipitated. The morning after my night at the policeman's, I caught a quick lucky ride, got to the Nile, and soon was on a barge heading south. I would spend the next ten days traveling upriver, heading to Juba, the capital of southern Sudan, some 800 miles away. This was the only route connecting the two halves of the country much of the year.

We loaded. My barge, along with a few others, was attached to a sort of tugboat. The barge had a center wall, with an awning above it. The passengers sat on the floor, against the wall. I settled in on my pack, next to two large Arab men in robes who smiled and then ignored me. Goats, chickens, sacks of charcoal and food, barrels, crates, were jammed on by sweating black workers who were yelled at by the Arabic foreman. We sagged to about an inch above the water, and still more cartons and drums were piled on. The sun was astonishing, even through the awning. In an inexplicable way, it was exciting to feel awful and dizzy and sick while just sitting still. Yeah, this was the desert, all right.

We finally got under way. I eagerly scanned everything. I planned to watch the passengers and see the transition from the northern Arabic merchants to the southern black agriculturists. I would get someone to teach me Arabic, write down tribal songs on my music paper, learn them on the recorder. I would watch the fishermen and the hippos and the crocs and the nomads with their camels drinking at the river. I would think that this has been unchanged for millennia, the British, the Egyptians, the Turks, the Ethiopians, all the way back to the Romans, all have come here to dominate and have gone, and this has continued, this river has given birth to the world. We would wander through the gigantic maze of the Sud reed swamp, we would travel through the lands of the nomadic Dinka tribe, we would cut across the centuries until there was time no more, until there was only heat and light and the movement of water. After a couple of hours of this sort of nonsense, I was already climbing the walls with boredom.

I got out the book I had brought along. Each trip, I bring one big book. Since this was going to be a very big trip, I had gotten a very big book. In Nairobi, I had shopped for books by the pound and bought the thickest book I could get for my money. It was Thomas Mann's *Joseph and His Brothers,* an umpteen-thousand-page retelling of the Bible story. Within a short while I realized my tragic error. I had come to spend a month in the Sudan and had brought along reading material such that whenever I had had enough of my desert surroundings, all I had to read was Thomas Mann's endless prolix descriptions of the desert, at an impossible pace of one five-page scene alternating with hundreds of pages of description of fig trees and types of camel caravans and, if my memory doesn't fail me, chapters and chapters about drying of tamarind. This was the worst literary mistake I'd ever heard of, except for the earnest German student who was overlanding through Africa and wanted to improve his tenuous English during the trip. So he had brought along William Burrough's *Naked Lunch* as his only book, a book that, I might add for the unfamiliar, is the classic Beat '50s account of out-of-control drug use, with maybe 20 percent of its words being English that has never been used before or since and ditto for about 5 percent of the syntax. He nearly paid me to take the book off his hands. I desperately wished I had bought the *Joseph and His Brothers* in the original German, which I don't know, so at least I could have continued reading it without understanding it. Instead, I settled down in the heat for the next ten days, alternating between staring at the desert in semicomatose desiccation and then rousing myself to read about it in Mann's stiff Germanic convolutions. I would have died for some British comedy of manners to read, or some high-tech spy thriller set inside the Strategic Air Command. Or a phone book. Anything.

The days wore by. We slept on the deck, ate on the deck, sat on the deck, crapped on the deck. At first, I tried shitting off the side of the barge, but the heat and dehydration would leave me so dizzy when I would stand up afterward that I was certain I was about to pitch backward into the Nile and its crocodiles. So I took to doing like the Romans and shitting on the barge like everyone else. Soon, however, that problem was mostly solved, as I was so dehydrated that nothing much more was forthcoming than painful stool rocks every few days. Everyone else shat enthusiastically, and each morning, the deckhands would pour barrels of Nile water down the deck, ostensibly to wash things over the side but usually only accomplishing a thorough mixing of the human and goat shit that would slosh back onto our bare feet and quickly dry in the sun.

The Arab merchants sitting nearby grew fond of me and would guffaw and pat me on the back and spit near my feet and tell me to be careful of the southern black Sudanese. Later in the trip, the southern blacks would tell me the same about the Arabs. One merchant, Mahmoud, took a particular shine to me and told me the story of his one visit to England years before. He told it well, and I welcomed its endless repetition, given the circumstances. He seemed to have a poorly disguised crush on either the queen or the queen mother, hard to tell.

Slowly, my brain adapted to the searing heat and repetition, which is to say that it became stupid to fill the space. By the fourth or fifth day, my major daily task had become to remember the names of all of my elementary-school teachers. I would wake and think, Today I shall remember the names of my elementary-school teachers. This would be followed by a walk around the deck, maybe a painful crap if I was unlucky, a delightful story from Mahmoud about his visit to England, some food, a quick nap from the heat. Then I would be ready. Soon, I would remember the names of kindergarten and first grade. I would fall asleep, nap for a while. Awake, sharp as a knife, kindergarten name at hand, sort of lose track of time after that. By late morning, I would be up to fourth grade, but then the heat would really set in, and I would have enough trouble remembering what phylum I belonged to, let alone teachers' names. More napping. Afternoon, cooling a bit, ready for a big push, up to fourth grade, able to repeat the sequence over and over with confidence, ready for the final assault on the summit, when suddenly two Arabs would start fighting nearby, or a goat would have a convulsion, or some such other distraction that would be the exciting high point of the day. All thoughts would flee except for openmouthed goiterous gaping. Soon time for bed; project to be completed tomorrow.

Somewhere in the middle of it we passed through the Sud, the endless reed swamp that turns the Nile into a labyrinth. I remember little of it except the heat and mosquitoes and a sickening sense of paranoia about getting lost that kept me anxious and clutching my knees the whole time. Improbably enough, you become convinced you can recognize individual patches of reeds and are certain that you've seen *that* one before. That's it, you conclude, we're going in aimless circles. You spend hours wanting to murder the pilot for getting you lost and not being man enough to admit it, and then you quake with terror that he *will* admit it and confirm all your worst fears, and then Mahmoud and the boys in a rage will pull out their scimitars and behead the poor bastard in a ritualistic manner, take over the boat, fall into confused and factional arguments over direction, and all will be anarchy and violence and starvation and chaos as we die horribly, horribly, lost in the swamp.

Naturally, we cleared the Sud uneventfully.

Now it was only a final short stretch until Juba, our destination. Juba figures heavily in the collective emotions of the southern black Sudanese. By all logic, sprawling impossible dichotomized Sudan should have been two countries: the northern Arabic half and the southern black. Instead, it is one unworkable country dominated by the Arabs. If the place were ever to become two countries, Juba would be the capital of southern Sudan. The civil war that had been smoldering for decades was over just that proposition. Juba, fair graceful capital of Nubia, or whatever the future country was to be called, was a boiling, dust-spired collection of huts and refugee tents, with a four-kilometer circuit of paved road, the only tarmac for 600 miles. It was in Juba that I had a major anxiety attack for reasons that could probably not be understood by anyone for 6,000 miles. It was also in Juba that I felt the most alien in all my time in Africa. My first night, I got taken home by American Southern Baptist missionaries.

They were at the dock, waiting for barrels of something or other, and they spotted me immediately, invited me to stay at their center. Now, don't get me wrong—the day I spent there involved not the slightest bit of proselytizing. It's just that they seemed far more alien to me than any of the half-naked tribesmen I'd been hanging out with for the last weeks. They were all older Southern couples who'd spent years farming or dishing soup at the school cafeteria or working in the Chevy plant before suddenly getting the word from god one day that they should go to Juba and eat canned cheese food inside their compound. I couldn't quite figure out what they did with their time, but it sure wasn't pressing the flesh with heathens, at least not Sudanese heathens. No one, including Bud and Charlene, the seeming leaders, who had been in Juba for four years, was able to tell me where the town market was. They didn't know where the road to the Zaire border was, if there were any commercial buses that went from Juba to anywhere, if the Jubanese had three arms each or were photosynthetic.

They didn't know anything about the place. I don't think they ever went out of the compound, except to go to the dock to pick up barrels of supplies from the boat, or to the airport, to get weekly shipments of canned food from their organization's Nairobi-based airplane. My lord, the food! Even I, raised in a world of Jiffy Pop popcorn and Coco-Marsh, was moved. Cans of Velveeta cheese food. Cans of Spam. Cans of chocolate syrup. Cans of imported dates, for god's sake, sitting there amid oceans of dates, southern Sudan's only agricultural product. I lounged around, showered, read old *Life* magazines, hid in my room. In the evening, another novel experience: my first video movie. We sat in their mosquito-netted gazebo, turned on the extra generator, and watched some Clint Eastwood thing, an almost incoherent movie, which, unfortunately, was not quite incoherent enough to persuade you to stop trying to follow the story line. We all got lost frequently, had to stop the film to argue about whether that fella with the glasses was really working for the Russkies or was he just pretending.

Dawn, and Edna emerges with a whopping great boom box, turned up *high*. Male chorus, accompanied by banjo, belting out "Oh, Susannah," "You're an Old Smoothie," "Pack Up Your Troubles in an Old Kit Bag." We all rise and shine, set the table for canned powdered egg breakfast while we sing "Swanee" in lusty voices, and I scram shortly thereafter.

Wandering through Juba, I encountered the incongruous University of Juba, where I had my anxiety attack. It had been built by the northern Arabic government as a sop to the pathetic, systematically underdeveloped state of the black south and then filled almost exclusively with northern Arabic students. There had been some obscure sort of rioting recently, so the place was mostly empty, the students having had their heads bashed in appropriately by someone in a uniform and sent back home to cool their heels in their malarial backwaters. The place had a few students milling about, presumably the counterrevolutionaries who had saved the day. I went into the library, where the librarian slept on the desktop. Looked around. Green peeling paint on the walls, cracked masonry. Looked like an aged Atlantic City bathhouse, complete with an inch of sand that had come in for lack of glass or screens on the windows. Books here and there, mostly English. Some technical books, some out-of-date journals—an Indian botany journal, the *Italian Archives of Experimental Biology*, a few others. I suddenly spotted issues of *Nature*, the British journal that is probably the premiere science journal on earth. And only three weeks out of date. Incredible. On the cover was stamped "Gift of the British Embassy and Sudan Airways." Ah-ha, paid for by the former, delivered by latter. Thus, its relative currency.

I leafed through, excited at this contact with the outside world. And there, standing in my desert robes, with the sands lapping at my feet, I discovered that a group in New Haven had just published the experiment I was going to do when I returned to the States, having to do with a newly characterized stress hormone secreted by the brain. Scooped! Scooped. The very word ran through my head. I've been scooped in Sudan. I started hyperventilating. What was I doing here? Somewhere, somewhere far from here, science was swirling around, people in lab coats were toasting each other, breaking open bottles of celebratory champagne amid witticisms and anecdotes about Bertrand Russell and Madame Curie, all this was happening at just this instant, august old microbiologists were sitting down to pen their obligatory book of essays on ethics and biology, newly tenured associate professors were embezzling their grants, and where was I, stuck in southern Sudan, with unsettling fungi developing on my feet. I had to do something immediately!

I rushed out to look for a pay phone, the nearest one of which had to have been many hundreds of miles away. I didn't know who I was going to call, should there magically be one there, but I had an overpowering need to make a phone call. I walked around, agitated, planning to catch desert rats and breed them for laboratory experiments, use my Swiss army knife to carve test tubes out of wood. At the edge of the campus, I encountered some young school kids who bowed solemnly to me, said, "Hello, visitor," and handed me a flower. Then, they ran away giggling and waving. It broke my mood, and my archcompetitors in New Haven were forgotten for the remainder of Sudan.

I hung out in Juba a few days, getting information on the southern end of the country—what there was to see; what roads actually existed; of those, which were safe from rebels and/or government soldiers; of those, which were ever traveled by lorries. A foreign development worker filled me in on the latest news of the civil war. A Sudanese air force jet with engine problems had touched down in the desert, just happening to land near a rebel base. Hot damn, thought the rebels, let's grab it, but the plane had taken off first. Irritated, with pent-up rebel energy, they grabbed a dozen French aid workers instead. They demanded 30,000 British pounds, sneakers, trousers, and radio time from the government. A heroic Canadian pilot flew in and out as a messenger and voluntary hostage. He brought in secret news to the prisoners as to the night the army was going to attack. They prepared, slipped sleeping pills into the rebels' water that night. Naturally, the army came two days late. When they did, the rebels ran off into the bush, but not before releasing the hostages, telling them, "Get out, run, it's not safe here." So much for the war.

As for Juba itself, it was ramshackle and overrun with refugees from everywhere—Amin's Uganda, the Chadian war, Mengistu's Ethiopia, Bokassa's cannibalism in Central African Republic. Swarms of gentle friendly beaten people. Occasional overlanding Brits with dangerous flinty looks and bits of gangrene about them, always resulting from some machete accident in Zaire, just before they got out ahead of the soldiers. Always swaggering bravado in near incoherent Cockney accents. A big market in the center of town ringed by mosques, women of the agricultural tribes sitting on the ground selling tomatoes, dates, onions, flatbread, warm milk, and sugar—goods spread in front of them on their shawls, piled in geometric shapes. Occasional Dinka tribesmen, the Masai-like cattle people, wander through—tall, thin, cloaked, detached, spacey, aloof. Outlanders, but dangerous ones, clutching their spears.

The big news was at the prison. Sharia, Islamic law, had recently been imposed by the northern government, a big reason for the smoldering civil war having burst into flames again. That afternoon, there would be a first public severing of a thief's hand. A crowd of black southerners, furious at the imposition of Sharia on their animist and Christian lives, was already gathered, a riot predicted. I decided to pass up the show.

The flashiest thing in Juba, however, was the four kilometers of tarmac. It was driven endlessly, pointlessly, and exclusively by the large, air-conditioned vehicles of the various foreign agencies that supplied three quarters of Juba's excuse for existing, as well as most of its discarded cans of Spam. U.S. aid people, British relief groups, UN High Commission on Refugees, missionaries, Norwegian aid people, Bible translators, all driving the four kilometers endlessly to visit each other and have drinks and eat canned cheese food and get on each other's nerves. I don't think I ever saw a vehicle in the main part of Juba that was Sudanese.

Unfortunately, there were probably no vehicles driven by anyone going in the direction I wanted to go, which was to some forests on the Zaire border that contained chimpanzees. Everyone knew about the forest and the chimps, but no one had ever heard of anyone going there. I settled for my second choice—a range of mountains called the Imatongs, along the Ugandan border. This had the highest peak in Sudan and, apparently, a fifty- by sixty-mile-long plateau of rain forest, floating above the desert. At the very edge of the forest was a logging town, a small encampment that constituted probably the most (only) successful enterprise in southern Sudan. There was a road to it, and a lorry leaving Juba to bring supplies.

I got a space on the truck, settled in happily. We filled up, but I had a decent seat on a sack of maize meal. I contentedly returned to Thomas Mann's many-paged description of how Joseph and his brothers would lash sacks of dried tamarind onto their donkeys for long journeys, of the intricate knot work on the saddles of the camels, so on. Inexplicably engrossed, I finally noticed that the lorry was now jam-packed and was still sitting in the yard, at dusk. No petrol. It turned out that we were on line at the sole petrol station in Juba (not counting the private stores flown in for the aid organizations, of course). We were something like seventh on line, and an old pickup truck with a single barrel of petrol had arrived that day, servicing three of the trucks. We all got off for the evening, slept in the sand around the truck, and at dawn, were back at our stations, ready for our streaking journey to the Imatongs. Another day passed, and we were number two in line, and finally the next day, we were gassed up and started off. By then, the crowd on the lorry had swollen, and we were all standing on one leg, barely holding on to a metal bar with our fingertips, being elbowed in the ribs repeatedly by lurching old men, etc., all squeezed in among mounds and mounds of supplies for the lumber station. We were stopped within 100 yards, as we came to the bridge on the Nile. All people and sacks were off-loaded for a military inspection. Bags were poked with spears to determine if people were being smuggled inside, the Arabic soldiers inexplicably slapped around one protesting mama, I was asked in deadly seriousness what the name of the town was that I was leaving. I passed the test and the Arabs were soon interrogating the guy next to me.

Finally, we departed, all of us magically repositioned exactly as we were before the checkpoint. We lurched through 110-degree dust for the next twelve hours, covering 130 miles. Searing heat, rocking violent jolts from the uneven pseudo-road. People barely holding on, no awning, kids vomiting everywhere. The metal bars became too hot to touch for more than a second, yet you grabbed on for dear life with each lurch. I had a desert shawl over my head and carefully-watched bottles of water, which I went through far faster than anticipated. My head began to hurt, to throb rhythmically. I was breathing fast, I noticed. At one stop, at a borehole, I ignored one of the basic rules of desert water, which is never to drink enough of it not to be thirsty anymore, as you will probably become sick from the bad water. I gulped the stuff down and was weaving green and nauseous within fifteen minutes. My eyes began to hurt, my groin started throbbing painfully. The next six hours were spent trying to control the nausea and make the time go by and not scream. Thomas Mann was out of the question; I was pinioned so tightly in the crowd as to be unable to lift my arms. Once again, the sacred list of the names of my elementary-school teachers was conjured up. I spent hours repeatedly reciting in my mind the first two paragraphs of my thesis talk, planned for the coming year. I tried to outline a lecture on baboon social organization, just for the hell of it, but couldn't concentrate. I tried to fantasize about the summer student working in my adviser's lab whom I had had a crush on, but couldn't concentrate on that either—too exhausting and, under the circumstances, so pointless as not even to provide the frustrating distraction I was hoping for.

I wound up staring at the cheek of the tribesman sitting nearest me. As we had gotten further from Juba, we had picked up more people, Kakwa tribesmen, and they had become bushier and bushier, wild naked isolated men with ochered heads and lip plugs and scarification patterns the likes of which I'd never seen on anyone in Kenya. Many lacked nose bridges, which I thought was a particularly rough rite of passage mutilation, but turned out to be leprosy. Some had ears that were serrated. Others had goiter. Most had these ornate complex cheek scars in the shape of seven-limbed starfish—cuts had been made in the skin and sand pushed into the spaces, to form the cameo scar. I stared and stared at this one man's scar, counting the limbs repeatedly. Nah, couldn't be seven, must be six, I'd think, to lure myself into yet another counting to pass the time. The scar pattern seemed to be animate, undulating, probably due to my being dizzy—all this aided my inability to count correctly and motivated yet more time-passing counting. Mostly, as the hours lurched by and I swayed in more and more of a comatose fog of nausea and thirst and stomach cramps, I just wanted to kill the driver, for every bump, for every pause.

I had noticed, amid my heaves, that there was now a massive wall of mountains to our south. The Imatongs. Excitement amid the misery. Around 5:00, we got to the town of Torit, a fairly large one on the main road. Most of the hoi polloi departed, including my scar man and the young tough who had been standing on my foot for most of the afternoon. This left maybe a dozen of us, confused by all the space. Tentatively, we separated ourselves, lay down on burlap bags, and stretched. And something magical happened. The lorry came out of Torit and headed straight south into the mountains. We began to climb, and it got cooler. Some grass and bushes appeared. Some trees. The sun was getting low. Incomprehensibly, from out of nowhere, there was a breeze. A breeze! Everyone looked at each other and started laughing. Spontaneously, people started shaking my hand, people who had been standing next to each other since dawn suddenly recognized each other. At sunset, halfway up the mountain, some of the mamas on the sacks of onions began to sing. I lay on my back, looked at the stars and the trees. It was magic. The sweat on everyone, the tree branches we now had to duck, the smell of the shit of the goats jammed in with us—suddenly, all of it combined, it was summer camp again, I was with all my friends from the Jewish Community House day camp on an overnight trip to a dude ranch in the Catskills, I was on my first hay ride. We swayed and dozed and sang and shook hands and discovered water in forgotten places and I was in love with all the women. We glided into the logging town of Katire, into its dark forest, nestled amid the mountains, and I was delirious with dehydration and pleasure.

I staggered out waving good-bye to all my friends. I smiled at the trees. I marched into the village and encountered my first Katirean, an old man with a hunting spear and a fantastically wry face. Around his neck was a rope, tied to which was a flute made out of a reed buck's horn. He came up to me, fairly prancing. We shook hands; he oohed, aahed, bowed, wiggled, and was overcome with delight when I pointed to the flute, giving him a chance to play. He screwed up his face and blew across the opening of the horn, like a soda bottle, fingering the four notes. He played a simple tune and then sang it, complete with the dum de dums:

> Dum de dum . . . Torit!
> Dum de dum . . . Juba!
> Dum de dum . . . Khartoum!
> Dum de dum . . . *Sudan!!*

Tremendously animated, couldn't keep still while singing. The second time, I sang along, both of us crooning together as if this were a song from our youth together. We bowed again, and he pranced away.

Certainly a good way to start off. I headed over to the police post to report in. The cop was a grizzled old man in a striking green-and-black striped outfit that could have been pajamas, or a leisure suit, or stolen from a prisoner. No one else was there except for an ageless crone sitting outside. I entered, presented the man with my passport and travel permit obtained in Juba. He grunted, squinted at the passport, held it sideways and upside-down, seemed not to know what to do with it. Finally, he spoke.

"Do you have your passport with you?"

It was a delicious African moment that I could not pass up.

"No, I do not have my passport," I answered with deathly seriousness.

"That is very bad, very bad. Where is your passport?" Oh, perfect. I looked him in the eyes.

"You are holding my passport." The ball's in your court, copper. Could he save face? He turned out to be a polished professional—he glanced at the passport now seriously, actually flipped open the pages, looked at my picture, compared it with my face. Finally, he had his comeback line.

"You are right. This one is your passport. Now you can stay."

We relaxed, his job over. Suddenly, he lunged at me, said, "We must go now." Wha, wha, what did I do? It was time for dinner. The old woman outside, his wife, fed us beans and cabbage, and there was all the water one could dream of. I thanked him, and he said, "You are our guest. You do not say thank you. Would you thank your mother?"

The cop's son, Joseph, about twenty years old, appeared. He was a schoolteacher here, just out of high school in Juba, and thus quite qualified. He was wearing a fine white shirt. I had been noticing other young guys in white shirts passing on the road by the light of our fire, women in white blouses. "You are lucky," he says. "Tonight is a dance." What's the occasion? "No occasion, we dance every night, so you are always lucky when you come here." Suddenly, I realize that I had heard music, drums, when I first walked through the village.

After eating, more water, Joseph and I departed for the dance. We walked through a stretch of forest, meeting more and more white-shirted people. The music got louder until we came to a large clearing, teeming with hundreds of dancers in white. Instantly I understood it—it was desert altitude euphoria. Scattered throughout the northern Kenyan desert, insane stinking hot shimmering desert, are occasional mountains, plateaus. On top, higher, cooler, there might be bush. On the larger ones, there are hints of forest. And always, somehow, there is water—a borehole, a spring. Invariably, the people there staggered up at some unknown point in the past out of desperation—to escape a battle, a famine, a plague. God knows what's up on top of the unlivable mountain, but there's nowhere else to go. They make their way up there and discover it's heaven. Cool, shaded. Water! All the people I've ever met living on the desert plateaus are euphoric, slap-happy, dazed with their fortune. On one plateau I went to near the Ethiopian border, where a cold spring poured water coursing through the plateau and down into Lake Turkana, the entire population seemed to live in the water. You'd walk along the river; every forty yards there'd be another group swimming. Join us, they'd shout; do you want some water? Heaven. And here, up in Katire with the cool and the shade and the water, on top of it all, there were some of the only steady cash jobs anywhere in southern Sudan. And every night, everyone danced their heads off.

There were drummers and one barrel-chested man blowing into a hollowed log that emitted a vast single bass note. The dance itself was some sort of female-run mating ritual. The young men were in an inner circle, dancing in place. The young women rotated in a dancing circle around them. At some unpredictable point, the old men on the side would shout, "O-re-o! O-re-o!" and quickly, the women would grab partners. Surprisingly chaste, Sunday-schoolish dancing would ensue, the man and woman circling, the woman establishing a dance step, the man trying to match it, the difficulty escalating slightly. After a while, people (usually the men not chosen) would impatiently start shouting, "O-re-o!" until the old men would join in the shouts, and the circling and scouting would begin again.

Joseph was beside himself with excitement. He had borrowed my flashlight as a prop, stood in the stationary circle next to me, wiggling and shimmying, trying to attract the women's attention, flashing the light on his arms, chest, crotch. "Yeah, yeah, o-re-o, let's go, o-re-o," he would shout, ignored until the old men gave the signal. Irrationally, I found myself feeling nervous that I wouldn't be picked. Once we started, I was picked by the giggly girls frequently and then felt nervous and irritated because I was obviously being picked just because I was a novel, amusing Martian. "Tonight you will sleep with someone, you will find a wife," shouted Joseph in my ear. Why not, anything is possible, euphoria, as long as there is water and shade. O-re-o, o-re-o, dancing for hours, Joseph slapping me on the back, people shouting hellos and shaking my hand, tureens of water being passed around during the dancing, the one rhythmic bass note over and over and over and over amid the drums, everyone in their clean white dress clothes celebrating the end of another day not spent in the desert below.

Silence, dawn. Mist-filled forest everywhere. Hints of antelopes, birds. People emerging from their huts. Spires of mountain everywhere. Caught a ride on the logging truck going from Katire, clinging to the edge of the recently hacked-out dirt road, ascending to the upper edge of the forest that was being logged. Men working entirely with hand tools, cutting down trees here and there. An edge of clearing and the end of the dirt road. Beyond that, forest for fifty miles in every direction. A continuous plateau, thick, mist-filled rain forest forever, 10,000-foot granite peaks soaring out of the jungle, monkeys and hooting birds and bush buck and forest hunters, and every now and then, a break in the mountains, a pass, and a view of the pounding desert, 7,000 feet below. Like being on a huge, lush verdant ship, floating above the ocean of hell desert.

I put up a tent at the edge of the clearing, at the beginning of the forest. I would start exploring. My main goal was the peak of the highest mountain, some fifteen crow's miles away, through the forest. Already visible, floating above, pure straight soaring rock and menace.

I had no maps. There were no maps. There were no directions, no one had gone in there. There were just little forest trails, here and there, made by the forest hunters. They came out occasionally to trade with the loggers, small silent men in loincloths who would then scamper back into the forest.

I developed this pattern of hiking that decreased my anxiety about getting lost and disappearing in the forest. The first day, I followed the first path for about an hour until it came to a major split. I stayed there awhile and went up and down the split until I felt I knew the trees at the junction perfectly, could recognize the path I had chosen (seemingly the one toward the peak) from both directions. I sat there, drew a map of the path past the junction, drew pictures of the trees at the junction. Played my recorder for a while and called it a day, went back.

The next day I breezed past that junction and went two more until I felt too anxious and went back and rehearsed those. It felt calming to know that I was relatively familiar with all but the most distal of the day's choices of paths. A rhythm of anticipation developed; each day, closer and closer to the mountain, knowing the forest better.

It was thick, giddy with overgrowth; you want to scream at its complexity. Dark, moist, sheltering. Twenty-foot-high ferns, archetypal vines to swing from, sections of the narrow paths where you walked on roots and huge rotting leaves instead of ground. Every afternoon, the cooling rains came, light, invigorating, as you stood there with your head back. The smell and crush of decay underfoot. Along the paths, frequently a deep ravine, descending into a stream you could only hear, lost amid the giant ferns.

On about the fifth day, perhaps seven or eight miles into the path, I came onto the first village. It was a small clearing. Maybe an acre of maize hugging the side of the slope, in the edge where the forest had cleared but a granite wall had not yet started. Four extremely simple huts. Perhaps a dozen people— slight, muscular, taut, silent, in animal skins. A few lip plugs. The women smoked long pipes. They bent in greeting, but said nothing. I sat for a while, feeling uncomfortable, and finally pantomimed that I was going to the big mountain, looming ever larger, and they pointed me to the proper trail. And then, as I was about to leave, they brought out a boy, about ten. He had conjunctivitis. They motioned to his eye, pointed to me. Could I do anything about it? Why in god's name did they assume that, just because I was white or an outsider or wore clothes, I would know what to do? I kind of knew what to do. I had antibiotic ointment and tetracycline with me, started him on both. I had them bring water from the river, had the kid wash his hands, had the father wash his own hands before touching the kid. We put on ointment. I pantomimed that I would return the next day with more.

So I obtained my village. I would now pass each day while getting closer to the mountain. I put more ointment on the kid each day, gave him antibiotics. They brought me a man with a badly lacerated thigh, which I treated. They brought me a woman with a horrible tubercular cough, which I implied I could do nothing about; they seemed resigned. They became more talkative, brought me maize. Someone pulled out a plinker—a musical instrument—a small box of wood with half a dozen metal tines of different length. When each one was plucked, a metallic note emerged. They played dizzyingly, with one hand, with a pulsating shifting rhythm and a harmony that I could not begin to penetrate. I played my recorder back. One day, I detoured and went on a monkey hunt with them. We crept through the forest. I felt like a clumsy oaf and giant, all five feet six inches of me, as they slipped through the bush. There were colobus monkeys in the trees above. Naturally, I felt a surge of rooting for the monkeys, only to have it replaced now and then by the anticipation of their actually getting one. One of the men slipped in an arrow and brought down a monkey, with a sickening crash through the trees and screams of others as they brachiated away. We carried it back. It was skinned and cooked in a pot, a subadult male, its hand sticking out. It was then that I noticed the monkey-skin rug, the monkey-skin clothing. I declined the meat but stayed on while they ate, feeling queasy and excited.

More days, pushing closer, the kid's eye looking better. I felt like the father to all of them, like I was the god of antibiotics. About ten days into it, I reached the next village at the very base of the mountain. It had become one of the most ominous mountains I'd ever seen. Vast, looming, silent, craggy, dark magnificently complicated rock formations, rising up straight out of the jungle like some sort of citadel of the ruined jungle empire of Zinj. And at the end of the final valley of jungle, another tiny village, clinging to the base of the mountain as if the people, continuing the traditional task of their ancestors who served the last rulers of Zinj a millennium before, still guarded the path to the mountain.

When I finally reached the village, the people were familiar. My Schweitzer village was indigenous mountain hunters who had been up there forever and were ethnically completely novel to me. But this next village turned out to be made of refugees—desert people who had fled up there a dozen years before during the last bad festering of the civil war. They were Tuka tribe, very close to the Turkana, the Kenyan desert people just across the border. What a homey familiar touch—I'd know those lip plugs and neck rings anywhere. Also the potbellies on the kids, the coughs, the suppurating lesions. I knew about half a dozen words of their language, and we got on swell from the start. A homecoming. Quickly, I arranged to return in two days; a man there named Cassiano would take me up the mountain, this impossible rock now tearing straight up out of the trees behind their huts.

I returned late afternoon two days later. Cassiano insisted I sleep in his hut, instead of my tent. He slept at his brother's, next door.

I had been noting that these people in the second village, desert folk for centuries until a decade ago, had still not adapted to their new settings. They made a fire inside their house, which was certainly necessary with the mountain cold, but they had not modified the architecture from the way it was back down in the desert—still completely shut. Thus, the smoke accumulated to a horrendous extent. The village was filled with red eyes and tubercular coughs from the smoke. As soon as Cassiano had left for the night, I blew out the all-night fire he had left—my sleeping bag was warm enough, and the smoke was sickening. I went to sleep.

Around midnight, I discovered the other reasons why they kept fires going all night. I awoke to a sound that will give me the chills for the rest of my life. I woke up thinking, Oh, it's raining. Then I thought, Oh, it's raining on me— I can feel the drops hitting my sleeping bag, my face. Then I remembered I was sleeping *inside* a hut. Suddenly, I was monstrously awake. Things were moving all over me. My hair was moving. I shined my flashlight around. The smoke was also meant to percolate through the grass thatched roof. This would drive away the giant cockroaches. In the absence of smoke, the cockroaches had poured in, all over the bags of maize meal. But this was not the real problem. Because following the cockroaches were the army ants.

I would contend that army ants are the single most disgusting disquieting panic-provoking creatures in all of Africa. Their mere proximity leads me to twitch and moan and shudder and leap about with a Saint Vitus's dance of agitation. They come in swarms that cover square acres. They are huge with pincers that take pieces of meat out of you. They crawl all over you silently, before a single one bites, and then through some pheromonal alarm signal, they all attack at once. They eat your eyelids and nostrils and soft parts. They attack anything, kill invalids who cannot run away from bush hospitals. Once they dig in your skin with their pincers, they hold on so tightly that when you pull at them to get them off, the head detaches from the body, leaving the pincers still in you. The Masai use them to suture people—bad cut, and someone grabs an army ant, holds the two sides of the cut together, lets the pissed-off ant sink its pincers in, and, quickly, twists off the body, leaving rows of ant head sutures in place.

But the worst thing about them is that when they attack, they hiss. A nightmare sound, the hiss of army ants, in the dark, sweeping over the field around you.

The place was swarming with them, the raindrops falling down on me from the thatching. They weren't bothering with me. Yet. They were dismembering the zillions of cockroaches. There were roaches all over the maize sacks, and, horrifyingly, a three-dimensional bridge of ants, holding on to each other, had formed from the floor to the sacks, pulling off the cockroaches, ten times their size. I was covered, I was just furniture for the moment.

I had to get out. A movement, a stepping on ants on the floor, would trigger all those on me to attack, but there was no other choice. The only question was whether the ant column encompassed the front of the hut. If so, I would just have to run off into the jungle night until I cleared them.

I counted, procrastinated, made my move. By the second step, your body suddenly catches on fire. Flames, little flames, everywhere. You slap, scream, pull at them, keep moving. One on my eyelid, lips, many on my *crotch*, goddamn it. I burst outside, yelling, ripping my clothes off, rolling on the ground. Thank god the swarm was coming from the opposite end. I flailed, yelped, pulled ants off, spastically leapt about hammering a body part against the ground in an attempt to squash the ants. Cassiano and the rest of the village emerged and, predictably, found my plight hilarious. Once I had gotten the last of the ants off, gotten my clothes back on, I sheepishly explained what I had done. Disdainful of the ants, Cassiano leapt into his house, got a fire going, and soon the ants and remnants of the cockroach ocean were swept back into the forest.

At dawn, we left for the mountain. Cassiano, barefoot, led the way, macheteing a path through the forest, for lack of a preexisting one, until we reached the actual rock wall. From there, we began to climb, somewhat straight up. Precarious footings, scrambles across seams in the boulders where a shower of rock fragments would come off. It felt kind of unlikely, but he seemed to know what he was doing. An hour, two hours, exhausting, sweaty, fun, and we cleared the top. The highest point in Sudan. A cascade of dizzying sights below—other granite peaks with birds looping around them. Forest below with the steam lifting off of it. And in the distance, the desert.

On top of the mountain, at the highest point, was a rock cairn. It was pyramidal, with a central core. With rapid motions, almost curtly, Cassiano motioned me away from it. Quietly, reverently, he knelt down. From behind his ear, hidden in his hair, he pulled out a small bird feather, which he placed in the heart of the cairn. At that moment, I deeply envied every animist his religion.

It was time to go. Or rather, it was time to start trying to go. Transportation was so precarious that you had to start weeks in advance. I would go back to the main road, try to catch a ride on some lorry either going straight back to Kenya, or via Uganda.

I left heaven, rode on the loggers' lorry from the mountains down to Torit. I wound up sitting in the truck yard of the Wimpy Company, about the only thing that worked in Torit. Wimpy was a British road construction company, contracted through the British government to build a new Juba-Kenya road as a gift to Sudan. They had already been there for years, fighting to get a road through the desert and the tribal raids and the rainy seasons. The Wimpy truck yard was where things were at.

There was an unlikely turmoil of activity—British managers yelling at Arab foremen yelling at black workers, forklifts and jackhammers and road graders careening about. I spotted my targets from across the yard—six Somalis, sitting in a circle, drinking coffee made in an old oil can, in between two petrol tankers with Kenyan plates. In East and Central Africa, all the real long-distance drivers, the hard-ass crazies who would get in a petrol tanker by the dock in Mombassa, on the Indian Ocean in Kenya, and drive for three straight months through wars and revolutions to drop things off in the Congo and then turn back, all of these madmen, are Somalis. It's some sort of logical adaptation of traditional desert nomadicism to a modern occupation. They are simply tough enough and resilient enough and don't mind a six-month delivery trip across the continent. The crew is two or three guys, a driver and some gofers, austere tapered silent Somalis with a cab jammed with camel's milk and boxes of spaghetti (a taste acquired from the colonial days of Italian Somaliland) and heaps of psychoactive plants to chew. Some prayer mats, some guns, no doubt something or other being smuggled. The Somali truckers.

I approached this group, went up to the senior guy, middle-aged with a goatee and an un-Somali potbelly. In Swahili, I said, I'm looking for a ride, are you guys going to Kenya? He didn't even look up from his coffee. Get lost, he told me. I retreated to the other end of the yard, sat in the sand, read about the embroidery pattern on Joseph's wondrous coat for about thirty-five pages.

Four or five hours later. They're still sitting, drinking coffee, ignoring the other trucks sweeping around them. Now playing cards. I went up again. Do you at least know anyone else who is going to Kenya? Get lost, I told you, he told me again. I retreated back to my book. About two hours later, the senior guy shambled over to me and, in a voice as if he were giving me my last warning, said, Okay, we'll take you to Kenya, but it's going to cost you, believe me. We bargained a bit, agreed on a perfectly reasonable price. When do we leave? Tonight. He shambled back, I returned to my reading. A few minutes later, the junior-most of the gofers approached, silently handed me coffee and a bowl of spaghetti. "The sun is not so fierce there," he said, motioning toward the group.

So I joined the Somalis. There were six of them—Abdul, Abdul, Abdulla, Achmet, Ehmet, and Ali. Abdul and Ehmet were the drivers of the two tankers. Achmet and Ali were the seconds, Abdul the Younger and Abdulla the two kid gofers. They were an inseparable crew and were about to start back from the three-month drive they had taken from Mombassa to deliver the petrol to Juba. It turned out, they were all from the same village in Somalia, possibly the only survivors; the village had been wiped out in one of the obscure wars that had been raging in the Horn of Africa forever, and they, all six of them, walked to Mombassa in Kenya. Despite the possible logic of their feeling grateful to Kenya for taking them in, they commandeered my map and marked the whole northeast corner of Kenya as belonging to greater Somalia. The Somali government's tendency to make the same claim has brought the two countries to the brink of war more than once.

The six of them were mean, quiet bastards. Well, except for the two younguns, the gofers. Abdul the Younger was, uncharacteristically, a mean, garrulous bastard—loud, talkative, bragging bully. He had the air about him of a petty, scheming con man always taken in by better con men. And Abdulla the Kid, the youngest of them all, maybe sixteen, was even more uncharacteristic—he was quiet and meek and had this curious, frightened, overwhelmed air to him, thick sleepy eyes and a seeming desire to be liked. He sat next to me and smiled hopefully, as if I were going to save him from his kinsmen.

Late afternoon came, and the card game continued. We had more coffee. I normally don't drink coffee, and this stuff was sickeningly powerful, but I thought they would beat me if I didn't drink it. Evening, more cards, more coffee, more spaghetti. At dusk, with the tumult of trucks no different from at noon, everyone prepared to sleep. I thought we were leaving today? I asked. Ehmet leaned over menacingly. Are you in some kind of rush? he said. No, no. Okay, tomorrow Kenya, tomorrow Nairobi, he said—an inconceivable goal. He wished me good night, smiling beatifically. Abdul and Ehmet, the seniors, slept in the beds in the cabs. Achmet and Ali got to sleep underneath the tankers; Abdul the Younger, Abdulla the Kid, and I on mats in the sand of the truck yard.

The next day we were up early, and the Somalis quickly formed their circle and started playing cards and drinking coffee. In boredom and irritation, I retreated back to the adventures of Joseph and his brothers, the brothers reminding me more and more of the Somalis. Midafternoon, Abdulla the Kid wandered over, conceivably sick of the coffee and cards himself, and sat next to me. Soon, I was playing recorder, Abdulla trying to teach me impossible Somali songs: modal, short, noodly chanted bursts of near-melody, little rhythmic fragments, quiet whispered parts. In revenge, I tried to teach him "Mares Eat Oats and Does Eat Oats," real fast. He was impressed. Abdul the

Younger sat down, ostensibly to taunt Abdulla for this wimp music stuff, but he was soon singing Somali songs and his favorite melodies from *Saturday Night Fever*.

More coffee, more spaghetti, another day gone by. We slept on the mats again. All night, as with the night before, trucks lurched just past our heads, yellow phosphorus klieg lights burned, pickup trucks screeched past us, spraying us with water from the only muddy potholes for a hundred miles. Dawn, the crew assembled for more cards. It was apparent to me that they had little desire to start the awful three-month journey back and would happily stay there forever. But today, fortunately, one of the British managers bellowed at them, "I want you bloody Somalis to get your asses out of here this hour or else there will be hell to pay." Murderous grumbling among themselves, and we were off.

Adventure, barreling through the desert back to Kenya! I sat on the engine casing, jauntily chuckling good-naturedly at everything. Yeah, moving. We got to the eastern edge of Torit, to the last store in the town. Everyone piles in, buys new sandals, combs. Abdul the Senior Driver, in a seeming ritual, buys an absurd outlandish bottle of perfume and slaps its entire repulsive contents on everyone, including me. Anointed. Yeah, celebration for the long trip we're beginning. Then everyone settles down under the tree next to the store, resumes playing cards. I despair. Twenty minutes later, the Brit shows up again, boots everyone into the trucks, and off we go. It's apparent from the view that that was the last grove of trees for a long long time, so we might as well drive.

Lurching, churneling through the desert sand, each cab pulling an empty double tanker. Desolate howling desert; sometimes the road would be anyone's guess. Midafternoon, when the heat was intolerable, we napped underneath the vehicles. Late afternoon, we stopped for coffee and spaghetti. I was beginning to feel coated with caffeine and starch, queasy at the diet, but no one else seemed to mind. Tonight, however, to celebrate our departure, we had a special meal. This time, Abdul the Senior had the honors of mixing a ton of sugar and some pretty rank camel's milk in with the spaghetti. With the heating over the paraffin stove, it formed a milk-sugar coating over each strand that made each bite that much more sickening. We sat in a circle, Somali style, knees resting on each other's thighs, and everyone ate with their right hand out of the central pot. Then off to bed.

It seemed like we had been sleeping for only a few hours. In fact, we had been sleeping for only a few hours—it was ten in the evening, Achmet was shaking me awake. Hurry, we're leaving. The trucks were already revving up.

I bundled up my sleeping bag, grabbed my stuff, leapt on. Why the rush? Good time to drive, answered Abdul. It became apparent over the days that something dreadful had happened to these guys' circadian clocks. There was no day/night pattern at all. We drove till midnight, went back to sleep. We started an hour before dawn, stopped twice during the day for naps, drove halfway through the night before stopping for a two-hour snooze. The only schedule was the five stops a day, where everyone would pile out, put out their mats, and pray to Mecca. The crazy schedule made no sense, but my head was soon reeling, especially since each day's drive would begin with Abdul confiding in me, "Kenya, today," and each day we would be, perhaps, another ten kilometers closer, lurching and spraying and heaving through the sand.

It also became apparent that these were savagely aggressive men, with the exception of Abdulla the Kid. We would come to some hamlet, and, essentially, the men would go into some house and shake down the desperately poor occupants. The five of them (Abdulla hanging back with me, looking more frightened than usual) would tromp into the decayed hut, find the frightened, half-decayed occupant, and take three onions. Or some cabbage or oranges. Or, our third day, a goat—the angry, frightened man in a tattered pair of shorts and nothing else tried to hold on to his only goat, and Ali and Achmet beat him. These were pathetically poor people, and the crew was just driving through, pillaging and threatening and taking what they wanted. I felt sick, didn't want to eat any of the food, but was afraid to insult them. Abdulla seemed as uncomfortable as I. While Ali and Achmet were beating the goatman, Abdulla looked away and sort of whispered, Well, they don't give us much food to take when we leave Mombassa, as if searching for an explanation.

A lot of the violence seemed to reflect the endless hostility between the Arabs and the Africans. Forever, the Somalis' ancestors had probably been part of the raiders that rounded up the ancestors of these Sudanese as slaves. The slave market in Arabic Zanzibar had continued to operate well into this century. The Somalis had a seething contempt for inland blacks that seemed to be at their very core. "These Sudanese are like animals," Ehmet chuckled to me, after one of their plundering raids of two cabbages from a hut where there was nothing else.

And the Somalis were almost as violent with each other. While they were quite affectionate in a way I've become familiar with from Arabs—holding your hand for emphasis as you spoke to him, sitting next to him with knee on thigh—they were also intensely aggressive. Each day, each meal stop, inevitably, there would be a fight. Achmet, under the truck, trying to get the paraffin stove going, would be criticized by someone for how he was doing it, and he would come up fighting. Ehmet would get us stuck in the sand, necessitating our unhooking the cab from the tankers; Abdul would criticize his choice of path, there'd be a fight. I came to recognize the ritual pattern. The two trucks would be parked parallel, with everyone gathering in between for food/coffee/cards. A tense moment would arise, and two would fight. Savage rapid fighting, grappling, kicking. The loser would invariably make a last attempt at saving face—the intensely calculating, pointy, taut Achmet would take on Abdul the Younger, quickly pummel him into the ground, walk away in triumph, and Abdul would leap up, his boot knife pulled out. And the ritual would continue. Everyone would lumber up at that point, wrestle Abdul down, take the knife away—Abdul *would* have taken Achmet, but he was unfairly outnumbered, face thus saved. Abdul would sulk by himself under a tree at a distance. A meal would silently be prepared. People would begin eating, Abdul still sulking. One of the seniors, Abdul or Ehmet, would yell something joking or conciliatory, and Abdul the Younger would return to the circle.

This happened nearly every meal, every stop, the ritual of fighting—but no conventional ritual—there would be blood half the time. Only Abdulla the Kid was excepted. And me. It occurred to me that I was being treated so courteously, so gently, that I was in deep deep trouble. One day, as we stopped driving, and everyone was happy and uncharacteristically frisky, Ehmet bear-hugged me from behind, wrestled me down laughing. I laughed also, struggled to no avail, and was more than a little frightened. But other than that, I was treated with immaculate detachment. I attempted to pay for things on the few occasions where they bought instead of stole, and they huffily made me put my money away. Every meal, they insisted I eat first. It was all so considerate and ostentatious that I was absolutely certain that this was part of some long-standing Somali custom, feeding me and fattening me on sugared spaghetti until the preordained full moon when they would slit my throat from ear to ear. This fear was more than a little bit serious. I just couldn't read them, and I felt more uncomfortable and frightened each day, as we disappeared into the no-man's-land of desert between the two countries, they pillaging and beating and terrorizing the Sudanese, pulling knives on each other in moments of hideous anger, and placing the spaghetti pot graciously in front of me.

A few days out, somewhere just west of the barely defined border, Abdul rolled the truck. It was a bridge, maybe twenty feet long, spanning what was a deep river for perhaps two days a year during the rains and was now just a deep ravine. The road just beyond the concrete was washed out on the left, and Abdul came into it too close to the washout. Agonizingly slowly, we slid toward the left—"Whoah!" we all hollered—Abdul tried to turn the wheel to the right as we kept moving laterally, but it was useless. We slid further left, and then slowly, we begin to tip. There was even time for all of us to brace, to think, Leap out the window, no, don't leap out the window, your head will get sheared off. Almost imperceptibly, we rolled down and onto our side and completely over.

We squeezed out to inspect our state. The cab was upside-down, the first tanker on its side, the second upright back on the bridge. What a stunningly sickening feeling, to see the undercarriage of your vehicle exposed to the desert sun. We detached the two tankers from Ehmet's cab, which had already passed the bridge, a job that took all seven of us. Ehmet tried to pull out Abdul's cab but instead slid and rolled as well. We were well and truly fucked.

The Somalis did the logical thing. Ehmet criticized Abdul's driving, and they began to fight. Ali, Achmet, and Abdul the Younger began to fight. Abdulla the Kid and I cowered. Things quieted. We sat, felt dizzy in the heat. There wasn't much shade to sit under, the tanker was too precarious. Everyone was tense as hell. Occasionally, we would do ineffectual things like dig at the tire with our hand shovels. By some unspoken decision of group distress, we ate nothing. Everyone was getting angrier. We were thirsty, and there seemed to be little water. Ali discovered poisonous ants nearby that made your foot go numb for five minutes and then throb for an hour. Scorpions turned up. Late afternoon, Abdul and Ehmet had another fight. Everyone seemed frightened in an undefined way.

By the next morning, still sitting there, Abdulla the Kid had defined that fright for me. The Toposa. These were wild-ass tribesmen who lived along the border, making a living, if one could believe it, raiding the Somali truckers. The army had almost gotten them under control until the civil war farther north necessitated the army's withdrawal, and the Toposa had been running amok since then. They had guns (obtained from raids on army units), came in large numbers, took everything, shot the truckers, burned the petrol tankers. Weirdly, despite their growing familiarity with twentieth-century firearms, a moving vehicle was still apparently intimidating to the Toposa. They only hit stalled vehicles or ones stopped for the night—thus explaining the frenetic, noncircadian pattern of driving. Whether it had been an unspoken sense of Toposa around that had been sending the Somalis scrambling from sleeping to driving in minutes, or a spoken sense among themselves along with a gracious sparing me the news, or just general heebie-jeebies each time wasn't clear. It made me faint to consider there was someone out there who could take on the Somalis. It seemed implausible, cowboys and Indians, but if these guys were scared shitless of the Toposa, I was perfectly willing to be as well.

Everyone was tense as hell. Everyone was yelling at everyone, until they were exhausted at that, sat, moping, shifting to avoid the poison ants. Achmet got out the guns, which seemed futile. Abdulla looked as sick as I felt.

Early afternoon, Ali, who had been perching silently on top of Ehmet's tanker, our highest vantage point, scanning the desert, reported that someone had spotted us and had moved off quickly toward the hills in the distance. Toposa, going to a village to report that we were stranded.

We were near panic. Ali and Achmet took positions with the guns. Ehmet tried again, as if with extra desire now, to get his cab out of the ravine. Abdulla the Kid huddled underneath the back tanker. We all breathed fast, felt like we had to do something to prepare ourselves, knowing there was nothing to do. All I could think about was the last passage of Thomas Mann I had been reading—Joseph's brothers had attacked him, sold him into slavery, and had just brought his bloodied coat to their father (one could surmise that Joseph had been done in by lions, but you could never know), and Jacob, old Jacob, was haunted by never being certain what happened to his son. I suddenly decided I really wasn't in a panic about dying, I was upset that I would never be found, my parents would never know what happened to me—I would just disappear, without a trace.

I sat there, clutching my knees, near tears, thinking about my old father. Abdulla the Kid was hiding under the bridge. The others were fighting. Achmet was pummeling Abdul the Younger; Ehmet and Ali were on Abdul the Senior, Ali bludgeoning him with the stock of the gun. It was chaos, sheer terrifying chaos, and the Toposa would be here any moment. It was then that we heard Baker's engine.

From in the distance, we spotted it. It was approaching us from the Kenyan direction, puttering at an imperturbable crawl. It was a huge tractor. "It's Baker," shouted Ehmet, his hands still around Abdul's neck. "It's Baker," all the Somalis shouted, leaping up. "It's Baker," I shouted, Abdulla the Kid and I hugging each other.

Baker, I was soon able to find out amid the huzzahing, operated the biggest tractor for the Wimpy Company, and his job was to trundle up and down the nascent quasi-road, pulling the company vehicles out of their frequent messes. It was a massive vehicle, outfitted with bulletproof glass. A Ugandan refugee rode shotgun, and they did a circuit up and down the stretch from the border to Torit, pulling out stalled and overturned company vehicles.

Baker puttered up, inspected our state, said, "Should be no problem." He was a stocky, tall, intensely black Sudanese with a heavy beard. I fell in love with him instantly. He hooked some chains onto Ehmet's cab, pulled it onto the road with barely a shrug. Fifteen more minutes of unhooking and hooking chains and Abdul's cab and tanker were righted and on the road.

As the Ugandan coiled the chains, I realized that I had just made a decision, without even thinking about it, without even realizing that there was something to be decided. I sidled up to Baker. Could I ride back with him to Torit? I was tired of being frightened, and I had just imprinted on Baker, had decided that he was the safest, most protective human on earth. I wondered if I seemed bizarre, the intensity with which I was asking him to save me. This was a normal workday for him. You bet, he said, in oddly colloquial English. I got my stuff, felt fearful to tell the Somalis, wondered if Baker would protect me if they attacked me for ingratitude or something. Instead, they seemed disappointed, waved away the money I offered to meet Abdul's original price. I swelled with warmth for them when I realized they were not going to beat me.

We departed, heading west again, the Somalis disappearing. We moved at a steady speed. I asked Baker about our progress, our likely destination tonight, and he said, "I don't know. We do about 15 kilometers an hour, but it will depend on how the river crossing is up ahead, and if anyone else is stuck." It was so refreshing—he didn't categorically say, "Torit, tonight," when there was no way to make it, didn't lie, didn't say anything confusing. He had said, "I don't know," and then outlined the contingencies in a way that was completely clear. I fell more in love with him.

A few miles ahead, as I began to calm down, a chain came loose on the back. It was a minor problem, would take Baker and the Ugandan a few minutes to fix. As he got out of the cab, Baker reached underneath his seat, said, Look, a surprise, and tossed me a mango, one for the Ugandan, one for himself. They went to the back to coil in the chain, and I leaned against the cab of the tractor, in the shade.

I may live to be a very old man someday, a lifetime filled with thoughts and emotions and sensations. But no matter how many of those experiences pile up, I will always look back with incredible pleasure and gratitude for the next instant. I bit into the mango, tasted the juice, and my eyes filled with tears, as I felt safe for the first time in many days.

Postscript: Within a few years, the brush fire of fighting between the north and the south had turned into a savage, full-blown war in the south that has produced two million civilian deaths, mostly from starvation, millions more refugees, armies of orphans—and has been largely ignored by the West. The Wimpy Company's partially completed road was destroyed, they and virtually all other Western presences driven out of southern Sudan. Juba and Torit have been alternatively occupied by government or rebel forces and thus subject to a withering blockade and starvation by the other side. The Toposa have become a major raiding force on the Sudanese/Kenyan border, specializing in hitting refugee camps. And as has been well documented by various relief organizations, the enslavement and selling of southern blacks by northern Arabs has, once again, become widespread.

As I read the occasional report about the ongoing war, I always search for a mention of, or for any bad news about, Katire, the tiny logging village on the edge of the Imatong plateau. The absence of such news leads me to conclude that people there still dance in their white shirts and blouses each evening, and that thousands of feet above them in the shrouded forest, my villages are still safe, their residents hunting monkeys and raising maize, free of the scorched planet below them. I am comforted by this unlikely possibility.

Part 3

Tenuous Adulthood

15

The Baboons:
The Unstable Years

Male baboons are not renowned for their self-discipline. Or their capacity for gratification postponement, or their communal spirit. Or their trustworthiness, for that matter. The wonderfully cooperative junta that had overthrown Saul lasted all of a morning before it disintegrated into factionalism and both metaphorical and literal backbiting.

All hell broke loose for months afterward. Joshua, Menasseh, Levi, Nebuchanezzar, Daniel, and Benjamin were clearly the upper-ranking cohort now. For example, in a social interaction, any one of them dominated a subadult like David, Daniel's old buddy. But they didn't have a clue where they stood with respect to each other. Ranks flip-flopped daily. Levi would beat Daniel in a fight and supplant him a dozen emphatic times that subsequent afternoon, but by the next day, the direction of dominance would be reversed. Over the course of months, Menasseh might turn out to be dominant to Nebuchanezzar, but he'd be winning only 51 percent of the interactions, instead of the 95 percent you'd see in more stable times. Chaos reigned. Everyone was scheming, spending hours forming coalitional partnerships that would collapse within minutes of their first test. Nearly 40 percent of the time, when it did collapse, the erstwhile partner would wind up on the other side. The number of fights went through the roof, as did the rate of injuries. Nobody ate much, nobody was grooming, sex was forgotten. Public works projects were halted and mail service became unreliable.

By later that year, things had sort of straightened out, and the dominance hierarchy stabilized, but the next three years saw a series of weak alpha males who held on in their position for only a short time. You want to know how bad things were then? Benjamin actually wound up on top of the hierarchy at one point. It was some sort of fluke, and for a short period, he held sway, had one consortship with Devorah when she was at the peak of her swelling, won one fight with Menasseh that seemed to have been an accident. Not surprisingly, being in the thick of the competitive world turned out not to be his forte. He was a wreck, constantly in a hysterical state. He would threaten someone and then run away. He hid behind Devorah in a moment of crisis. Once, he showed how poorly versed he was in evolutionary theory by trying to kidnap the Valkyrian Devorah when threatened by Menasseh. Devorah responded by slapping him. Benjamin chased zebra petulantly, and after one particularly tense interaction, he spent an afternoon up in a tree, bouncing up and down on branches until they'd snap. One day, he marched up to Menasseh, who was facing the other direction, napping, and Benjamin threat-yawned at him real close from behind his back. And then ran away in panic when Menasseh shifted and looked as if he would catch him at it.

Benjamin hardly inspired much confidence. One afternoon, the troop was on the move, coming through a narrow opening between two thickets. Benjamin was in the lead. Now, male baboons, of any rank, rarely lead troop progressions or, to state things more accurately, are rarely followed. They don't know what they're doing, they've only been in the troop a short time. It's the old females who are followed. So Benjamin comes marching down the opening between the thickets, never glancing back. Meanwhile, the two old matriarchs, Leah and Naomi, decide to veer into the thickets, and everyone else follows. Benjamin marches past the Jeep, proud as can be, finally looks back. Freakout, where did everyone go!? He runs around a bit, hyperventilating, and then in a moment of inspired cognitive addledness, Benjamin walks over and looks for sixty-some baboons underneath my vehicle.

To bolster his rank, Benjamin formed a coalition with Joshua, who supported him in the alpha position. Benjamin's lack of élan proved to be infectious, and soon both of them were weaving around the neighborhood in a hysterical, disheveled state. Menasseh was the main challenger breathing down their necks, and unfortunately for him, it's extremely difficult for a single baboon to take on a stable coalition, even this discombobulated a one. In some classic confrontations, Benjamin would be in a consortship with a female, and all the while, the silent, calculating Menasseh would circle the pair, in ever tighter circles. And one step tighter in the circle throughout would be the stumbling, hyperactive Joshua, somehow pulling off his role of getting in Menasseh's way. Eventually, Menasseh's pressure would become too much, and Benjamin and Joshua would flee the scene, barely holding on to their proverbial straw hats and cardboard suitcases, herding along the unimpressed female, to try to resume someplace else in the forest. And a few days later, Joshua would be in a consortship, with Benjamin giving the less than stellar tactical support.

Charming though they may have been, this arrangement couldn't go on for long. Within about three weeks, Benjamin and his coalition with Joshua went down in neurotic flames, more from exhausted abdication than from an overt overthrow. Menasseh emerged as the alpha male, followed shortly thereafter by the thoroughly premature Daniel. Things flip-flopped even more indecisively after that, opening the way for Nathanial's brief ascendancy after he joined the troop. Nathanial was this huge monster of a baboon, the biggest, heaviest animal I would ever dart—without a glimmer of aggressiveness or ambition in his soul. Everyone was terrified of him simply because of his size and essentially handed him the alpha position. In actuality, he was a big woolly bear who seemed best designed for doing things like enveloping sleeping infants in his huge arms or carrying baskets of gumdrops for all the children who'd been good. In many ways, he was the soul mate of Isaac, Rachel's friend who habitually walked away from any unpleasant social encounter. He had a quick series of successful consortships with females, gave up on this male-male competitive nonsense immediately after. He voluntarily walked away from being alpha male, retiring to spend his time playing with his kids. While I never subsequently spotted him giving out gumdrops, he became very adept at tossing babies in the air and catching them, and was often in danger of having his massive self pinned to the ground under the weight of the kids climbing on him.

So went the succession during the unstable years. It was a wonderful period to take advantage of, if you were a savvy female. An obvious question in watching all this baboon mating is whether the female has any choice as to whom she winds up with. Early in the primatology business, the guess was no. In the strictly linear models of the '60s, if there was one estrus female in the troop, the alpha male would mate with her. If there were two females on a certain day, the alpha and number 2 would; if three females . . . and so on. This would not necessarily be great amounts of fun for the female. Who would you want to spend your time with—the (by now, moderately high-ranking) jerk Nebuchanezzar or the low-ranking Isaac? No question. Female baboons turn out to have perfectly rational preferences for males, like not enjoying hanging out with ones who beat on them, for example. But there are limits to what you can do when males are twice your size. If the alpha male is a strongly dominant, entrenched individual and is interested in the female, she'll probably wind up with him, like it or not. But if there are any weaknesses to exploit, a clever female will spot a way. For example, you refuse to stand still when the male tries to mount you. Or you begin walking away whenever the male, famished and exhausted from maintaining a vigilant consortship with you, tries to rest or eat. Or the most obvious war of attrition: one day, Rachel had a peak swelling and was in consortship with Joshua, while Menasseh harassed and Benjamin weaved in between. Clearly, she was not interested in any of these guys. So for hours, she methodically marched over to Menasseh, forcing Joshua to scamper in between her and Menasseh, Benjamin in between Menasseh and Joshua, until Joshua would move her away or Menasseh would back off to decrease the tension. And then she'd march over to Menasseh again. Inevitably, the trio would eventually get haired out enough by all of this that they'd wind up off in the field fighting. And Rachel would wind up happily with Isaac.

It was also a wonderful period to take advantage of if you were the neighboring troop. Half the males in my troop were injured, moping, off strategizing, or too cheesed off about the morning's fight to possibly cooperate with anyone. The neighboring troop moved in now and then to shove them out of the forest, for no obvious reason other than spite. It would be an amazing sight, if a dispiriting one if you were partial to my team—150 baboons tearing through the forest, screaming, barking, chasing, feinting, fencing. The troop did not do very well for itself in the face-offs. Nebuchanezzar and Menasseh might be making a credible showing of ferociously driving two or three of the invading males out of the forest when they would decide they'd much rather fight with each other. Joshua might abandon his consortship with Devorah briefly to join in the fray, causing Nat to veer off from his chase of a neighboring male to try to herd Devorah over to the quiet end of the forest. There was little evidence of communal spirit, and one morning, the troop was emphatically driven out of the forest by the marauding neighbors by 8:30. They stood around, eventually went and foraged listlessly out in the field all day, and that night, for the first time to my knowledge, they slept elsewhere, perched crankily and precariously in some wispy acacia trees a mile away. A few days later, they were able to regain a foothold in the forest, but for coming seasons, the neighboring troop pushed them around mercilessly.

There were some notable comings and goings during that time. Old Aaron and young Uriah and Levi all disappeared. Levi turned up two years later in a troop thirty miles away, faring quite well; I suspect the other two found new homes also. Weird pathetic Job also disappeared, and my guess for him was eaten by hyenas. Menasseh vacillated between this troop and the neighboring one, never quite distinguishing himself in either. In their place came a number of new faces. Reuben joined, a big strapping male who was destined to go nowhere in the hierarchy. For years to come, he'd maneuver into precisely the confrontation he'd need strategically and, at the critical moment, would flee in panic, tail in the air. Once, when some hyenas were passing near the troop, to no one else's consternation, he crouched down in the grass, to avoid their notice, except for his rear end and tail sticking up conspicuously. One was forced to admit the fact that he was a coward. An ancient decrepit animal with a mangled back leg whom I named Limp also joined the troop. His life was made miserable by every displacing bastard in the troop who would make him pay for their problems. A short time after that, the troop was joined by Gums, who was, if imaginable, even more ancient and broken down than Limp, and had no teeth to boot, which made his survival near miraculous. Gums wound up being slightly lower ranking than poor beaten Limp, who immediately lost any sympathy he may have engendered previously, by beating up on Gums whenever he had the chance. You'd look at these two ancient animals, still being competitive and cagey and maneuvering, albeit at half speed, and you'd have to wonder, Who were they, what are their stories? What part of the Serengeti did Limp terrorize years ago? Did old drooly feeble Gums ever kill someone in a fight? Did the two of them know each other back when, are Limp and Gums the last survivors of some extraordinary event? Can they even remember it anymore?

This period saw two additional transfers into the troop that were pretty atypical—new females. Normally, females spend their entire lives in the same troop, building up a quarter century's worth of complex relations with friends and kin and enemies. It's a pretty good bet that if a female changes troops, she's had some major troubles. Both of these had the air of political refugees or battered wives. One day, the troop encountered the adjacent troop as both fed along the riverbed. Everyone briefly yelled and barked and threatened and made a fuss about the neighbors, who did the same in return, until feeding was resumed. Out of the corner of my eye, I spotted an adult female from the other troop dash along the riverbed and hide in a bush.

A while passed and she darted to another bush, closer to the troop. Her own troop was beginning to drift off, back up the ridge—it was a period where they were no longer contesting the forest. Another ten minutes, another scoot to a nearer bush, and her troop disappeared over the top of the ridge. And suddenly she sprinted into the middle of the thickest crowd.

She had a peak swelling, was probably ovulating. Significantly, she also had two fresh canine slashes on her—one on her haunch, one on her face. Another female who probably wished she had never heard of estrogen. Whatever she was escaping from in her home troop, I'll bet it had something to do with the size of her estrus swelling, and something to do with male baboons being jerks.

Everyone reacted predictably. The females in the troop harassed her, the males came on to her. Ruth and Devorah chased her around, Boopsie supplanted her every time she tried to feed; Jonathan forgot his crush on Rebecca long enough to make the moves on her and got chased away by Reuben, who was pushed off by Nat. She stuck around for a couple of days of this nonsense, it presumably being vastly preferable to whatever grief she had escaped in her own troop. The third morning, her swelling had gone down, the steroid poisoning had abated, maybe she could return to her home and live in peace for a while. She disappeared whence she came, not heard from since.

The second female to show up was even more untraditional. She stayed. Whatever she was running from, it must have been really bad, if she was giving up whatever rank, family connections, and friends she had elsewhere. She also was at the peak of an estrus swelling, had a shoulder slash. And her tail tip was freshly severed. Maybe that was why she decided she had had enough of her hometown. Short Tail joined the troop and, for lack of family or a known lineage to fit into, was shoehorned into the very bottom of the female hierarchy. Where she spent years, unperturbed by her subordinance. Not surprisingly, given the epic and unorthodox life she was leading, she was pretty tough. She regularly predated rabbits, something one rarely saw females doing, and she fought with males for scraps of meat on larger kills. In general, everyone seemed to think she was a weirdo, except for Adam, a new meek transfer male who showed up around the same time and spent the coming years following Short Tail with an unrewarded devotion.

So went the unstable years, amid coups and countercoups and general chaos. I was constantly reminded of a comment of a baboon-watching colleague, after we had seen a film entitled *Chimpanzee Politics* about the Machiavellian brilliance with which those animals went about making each other miserable. "Chimps are what baboons would love to be like if they had a shred of self-discipline." One image stands out in my mind to typify the period. It was after the marginally successful coalition of Benjamin and Joshua had fallen apart, and they were somewhat at odds with each other, or at least nervous about each other. I came into the forest one day and spotted Benjamin crouched down behind a tree, holding on with both hands. He was intent on something, vigilant, nervous. Every now and then he would carefully, slowly lean over, peek out from behind the tree at something or other across the clearing. And then he would jerk back, safe behind the tree.

What's up? I walked over to the other end and found Joshua, also crouching, hiding behind another fig tree. God knows how they got into this, but they were pinned down, each carefully hiding from the other, peeking out from behind their trees now and then, making sure the other wasn't up to something before hiding again. Each seemed to have trapped the other there, but why and how, who knows. They seemed like two maddened, paranoid forest gnomes. They sat like that for half an hour, until Joshua fell asleep against the tree and the relieved Benjamin was able to tiptoe away.

16

Ol' Curly Toes and the King
of Nubian-Judea

$\mathcal{B}$y the end of the years of instability in the troop's hierarchy, I had been making pretty good progress with my scientific research. It was now clear to me that if you had a choice in the matter, you didn't want to be a low-ranking male. They had elevated levels of a key stress hormone all the time, indicating that everyday life was miserable enough to activate a stress response. Their immune systems didn't seem to function as well as did those of dominant animals. They had less of the good version of cholesterol in their bloodstreams, and I had indirect evidence that they had elevated blood pressure. I had some idea about why these rank-related differences occurred. For example, if subordinate animals had less of the good cholesterol in their bloodstreams, was this because they secreted less of the stuff into the circulation or because they secreted the normal amounts but cleared it faster from the circulation than did dominant animals? It looked like it was the former. Or as with another example, people with major depression often have elevated basal levels of that same stress hormone that was elevated in the low-ranking males. I was finding that the hypersecretion in those baboons was due to the same constellation of changes in the brain and pituitary and adrenal glands that gave rise to the hypersecretion in depressed humans. I also observed that in a stable hierarchy, the dominant males weren't the ones with the highest testosterone levels. Instead, it was the jerky subadult males starting fights who had the highest levels. I was pretty pleased with this discovery, as it ran counter to what was prevailing dogma in some corners of my field, namely that testosterone plus aggression equals social dominance.

Amid this scientific progress, I was forced to admit that I was no longer a kid out there. I was nearing the age when Jerry Rubin was no longer supposed to trust you. I now officially had a bad back, which made every hefting of a comatose baboon more than a little hairy, my stamina in the midday heat was definitely not what it used to be, and I had even had a serious, attentive conversation with a knowledgeable tourist on my most recent plane flight over about the salutary effects of oat bran on cholesterol levels (this was the 1980s, after all). And as a measure of my sagging decline into aging, I was finding with each passing year that I was finally being driven crazier by the rice, beans, and Taiwanese mackerel. Wonderfully, fortuitously, I was now getting funded regularly enough that I could afford to diversify a bit in my food supplies, to have a few more upscale items. However, as a measure that my actual tastes had not improved with time, this mostly took the form of buying numerous cans of sardines plus crates of spaghetti, to alternate with the mackerel, rice, and beans.

As the surest sign that I was growing up a bit, I now had my PhD and had started a couple of years of postdoctoral training. Back in my academic world, this meant that you were truly in limbo. You no longer got student discounts on movies and were having to start paying back student loans. On the other hand, you didn't actually have a real job (a postdoc being this penurious journeyman stage of training that is really meant to delay people a few more years from entering the virtually nonexistent job market).

Naturally, my degree was meaningless to anyone I knew out in the bush. My prior student status had always been vaguely confusing to folks there. On one hand, only old men in Africa are able to grow a beard of any note, and my having a full beard had, I'm sure, always unconsciously biased people to assume that I was quite elderly (i.e., at least in my forties). On the other hand, being a "student" was an attribute only of kids less than ten years of age, before their parents ran out of school fees and the child was forced to resume doing something sensible, like tending the goats. So there was always this discordant feature of my being a late-twenty-something who looked like an old man and had the job description of a kid.

Mostly, various Masai men, like my friend Soirowa, wanted to know when my father back in our village of Brooklyn was finally going to give me my presumed inheritance of cows, now that I was no longer a student. Rhoda and friends, however, had some more pressing nosy questions—when was I finally going to get a wife and some kids? This was being asked with such resoluteness that it seemed likely that my mother had somehow put Rhoda up to it.

Questions like that reflected my growing connectedness with Soirowa and Rhoda's village, which was due in part to the recent relocation of my campsite. In previous years, I had been farther upriver, at a site with a wall of bushes alongside the river, blocking the view of my camp from the Masai comings and goings just outside the park, on the other side of the river. This was fine, but a big drawback was that my campsite was, instead, quite visible from inside the park. There was a tourist boom going on, and minivans of Japanese tourists were incessantly barreling into my camp at the most inopportune times (while I was wrestling a baboon who was getting light from anesthetic, while bathing in the river, crapping in the bushes), cameras blazing, wanting to know where they could find a rhino to photograph.

So I'd moved downriver to a site much closer to the village and with far less privacy on that side. The advantage, though, was a mammoth thick wall of bushes and trees between my little cul-de-sac on the river and the main plains of the park, necessitating a complex, twisting path through the bushes for any vehicle. Satisfied that this was impenetrable to all but old bush hands like myself, I set up camp. Naturally, within a day, the first minivan of Japanese tourists had followed my clearly visible tire tracks into camp, searching for rhino.

So I was still being forced with surprising frequency to pose with my anesthetized baboons for pictures for tourists, while now being just a stone's throw from Rhoda and Soirowa's village. Mamas passed through camp each day on their way to find firewood, would stop to schmooze, even though I only spoke half a dozen words of Maa, and they only half a dozen words of Swahili and less of English. The kids would ignore their flocks of goats to hang out in camp, in the hope of my giving out some balloons or blowing soap bubbles. The old men of the village now included my camp in their daily rounds, in order to inquire upon the health of my distant parents and to request the gift of my watch for the umpteenth unsuccessful time.

Thanks to this proximity, I was beginning to be privy to all sorts of gossip. There was the British tour guide operator at a nearby camp who was carrying on with some tourist woman while his wife was in the UK with a dying parent. This was neither surprising nor interesting—a huge percentage of expatriates connected with the tourist trade in the park seemed to follow the grand old British tradition in Kenya Colony, which was to instantly become alcoholic adulterers and, worse, insufferably boring popinjays. What was interesting was the vague approval of his activities by everyone—it was a good thing to see that even white men go about the time-honored task of shopping around for a second wife.

More interesting was the wildly ambivalent gossiping about the kid from two villages over who had been working as a pot-washer in one of the tourist lodges and had recently been seduced and whisked off to America by a ravenous American tourist woman who was viewed as being mad as a hatter. On the one hand, there was clearly a squeamish revulsion at the mere thought of his having to be intimate with her. Race had nothing to do with it. Instead, it was the fact that skin was reported to fall off her face (i.e., she was sunburned), she was ancient as the hills (i.e., approximately forty), and, by being the sexual initiator, she was viewed as some sort of she-witch hyena who probably still had a clitoris. On the other hand, the kid was presumed to be living high on the hog in America, with limitless quantities of water and milk and cow's blood to drink. (The story reverberated in the Masai villages for years to come and, not surprisingly, among the equally gossipy research community in the park. The woman was enormously wealthy and, in fact, even madder than a hatter. She kept this bush kid for years as her pet on her ranch, giving him flying lessons. Just when it seemed about time for her to tire of him and discard him, he made the typically Masai realpolitik move of discarding her first, taking up with an even wealthier, younger, crazier socialite in Montana. He eventually returned to Masai land, wealthy and corpulent, the subject of vast admiration, a man who had survived terrors that made him a warrior among warriors.)

And then there was gossip having to do with the goings-on in the village next door. Rhoda and a few of the women related the deal recently worked out by two elderly men there. Each was in the market for a new wife, and these old lifelong comrades at arms had come up with the fine scheme of each giving their youngest daughter to the other. Naturally, the daughters were not consulted, nor were their first wives (i.e., the mothers of these kids), but wailings and beatings were reported before everyone compliantly went about marrying. What was interesting here were not the particulars of the arrangement, as this was pretty routine stuff for the Masai. What was fascinating instead was the implied consciousness-raising creeping into these parts, as Rhoda and her cohort discussed this in scabrous, horrified tones. "Disgusting old men," they snorted.

And best of all, I was even getting some dirty laundry about the village itself. It was evening, around the time that the mantle of alpha-maleness was slipping from Joshua to Menasseh. Samwelly, Soirowa, and I were hanging out around the campfire. The latest dry ice shipment had come in large plastic bags; Samwelly had stuffed them with leaves, and now we were lounging about on our pseudo-pillows, eating. It was a rice, beans, and Taiwanese mackerel night, if I recall correctly. We had put on chili sauce.

"Good chili sauce."

"Really good."

"Spicy."

"Really spicy." A hyena whooped in the bushes.

"Hyena."

"Yup. That's a hyena all right."

"Good rice and beans. Spicy." It was one of those evenings.

There was a full moon that I was reveling in so much that Soirowa finally asked me if there was a moon in the United States. Yes, but not as good as this one. As a treat, we munched on some dried fruit; a visitor from the States had recently passed through and left the delicacy with us. Samwelly and Soirowa liked it well enough but didn't quite understand the need to dry fruit when you can just eat it plain easily enough. I explained that the winters in the United States are very cold, snow everywhere, and during the harvest, we must dry our fruit so that we can eat the rest of the year when there are no crops, when we are huddling inside. With my lame Swahili, I somehow left them with the impression that Americans live in caves during the six months of winter each year, subsisting on nothing but sulfurized pineapple spears.

We fall into telling each other stories. I tell about the American man who was born on another planet and is very strong and flies, and who fights for justice and freedom but must hide himself and pretend that he writes for the newspaper, and there is one woman who loves him. Samwelly says he thinks he heard that story from missionaries. Then Samwelly and Soirowa tell a story about the Ndorobo, a tribe of hunter-gatherers around here who are shrouded in myth, serving all the same cultural purposes as do the Gypsies. They are thought to steal Kikuyu and Masai and Kipsigi children and raise them as hunting dogs—not feeding them so that they are small, and sending them off on all fours to hunt for reed buck, and that the chief Ndorobo checks on these kids by turning himself into a colobus monkey and following them in the forest, watching from the treetops. "Does the chief turn back to a person from being a colobus?" I ask. Yes. "Are the stolen kids really hunting dogs or are they just acting like hunting dogs?" They don't know, no one knows, because if you actually see them, they chase and kill you. "So how do you know about this story?" I ask. Because the Ndorobo brag about it when they come out of the forest to the trading posts—you see this reed buck here, it was caught by our band of Kikuyu-children hunting dogs, why don't you buy it from me?

We escalate our scary stories. I tell about Cropsey, the wildman in the Catskills who ax-murders little boys, which is told to every Brooklyn Boy Scout, Cub Scout, summer camper, on his first camping trip. It seems that old Cropsey lived in the woods with his daughter. Boy Scouts were nearby, chopping wood, and because of carelessness, an ax went flying off and killed Cropsey's daughter. And Cropsey went mad and ran off into the forest and he spends forever and ever creeping around waiting for Boy Scouts to murder *with the very same ax* and maybe tonight he is even somewhere around here, getting closer and closer, looking—quick, shine the flashlight in the listener's face—*for you!* Samwelly is impressed, keeps saying, "Looking for you," and shining the flashlight in his face. How old is Cropsey? he asks. One hundred twenty years old and he has iron teeth and glowing eyes. Where are the Catskills, near here? No, upstate New York.

Then Soirowa tells the story of the Masai who becomes unhinged and goes to live with the hyenas, living like one of them. He does not wear clothes and forgets the language of people, runs away from humans, and can be seen at a distance at dawn, eating with the hyenas on a kill.

This time we shudder for real, because this story is true. And then Soirowa reveals a recent piece of news about the man, something I suspect that Masai found profoundly disturbing and shameful, something probably most of them would just as soon not have had being told outside the members of the village—he has recently snuck into the village at night, and the smell of this hyena-man in their midst set the dogs to barking. By the time the men had gotten to him, he had killed a goat with his teeth and was tearing at its underbelly. He was covered with hyena shit from rolling in it, and his toenails had gotten so long that they curled up. Just like Howard Hughes when he became a hermit.

It was around the time that the river was haunted by the man who thought he was a hyena that I heard the story of the man who thought he was the king of Nubian-Judea. It could be directly traced as an unforeseen consequence of the aborted coup attempt of a few years before. It was told to me by a wonderfully animated Scotsman, sitting on the porch of Mrs. R's boardinghouse in Nairobi that I frequented.

It seems that the Scotsman was accompanying a fellow countryman who worked at an aid project up at the edge of the desert. They had to deliver some piece of machinery to a colleague way the hell further north, about forty kilometers past the checkpoint that marks the beginning of the desert.

They're in the middle of nowhere, empty, desolate, stinking hot, nothing but heat-crazed nomads now and then staggering around with their animals. They approach the checkpoint, which is a small hamlet. On their side is the last of the provincial districts that are governmental units. Ahead is the other half of the country, the Northern Frontier District, howling empty boiling desert full of nomads and cutthroat desert bandits who control everything except the occasional government outposts and the convoys that everyone must travel in to be safe. They're hoping to get a pass to travel without waiting for a convoy, given that they just have to scoot the short distance past the border and quickly return.

Checkpoint. Some mud huts, comatose-looking Samburu tribesmen slouching in the scattered shade. Palm trees, sand, gravel, one lighter-painted hut with a tin roof and a flag. The government quarters. Normally, at these outposts in the middle of nowhere, the government man manning it is half-naked, forgotten, starved, wasting away. Many a governmental outposter I've met has nearly fallen upon me with a spray of gibberish, crazed sunstroke look in his eyes, delighted to talk to anyone who's not Samburu, yammering and begging for news of the outside world, seeking to pull himself together in the tatters and rags of his uniform. Instead, the two Scotsmen enter the office and are confronted with a man with gelled, brushed-back 1950s American "Negro" pomaded hair, crisp white shirt, tie, pinstripe three-piece suit, and walking stick. This is the government man. They are led, with great formality and silence, to seats in front of his desk, at which he sits. Above his head is a photograph of the president. It is the obligatory official photograph; the president sits at his desk, pen in hand, glancing up from his busy affairs of state. Our government man assumes the precise same posture with his pen, glances up, and announces in superb English that he is ready to hear the nature of their petitioning.

The Scots explain where they are going and how they'd like a permit to just head on, without having to wait to go in a convoy. The government man asks a few perfunctory questions as to where they started off from today, how long they've been in the country, what do they think of the weather here. They answer, and suddenly, with stern finality, our government man announces to them that they are from the south of Scotland. He is correct. He looks at them keenly and identifies correctly the subregion of Scotland that they come from. You see, he explains, I knew many men from Scotland when I was training with the Royal Air Force. This explains a great deal—as a general rule, one only works for the government and gets assigned to a hellhole like this in the middle of nowhere if you've screwed up badly—the Northern Frontier District is full of border outposts manned by men being punished for getting a little too drunk on the job, or for blowing the whistle on some corruption or some such indiscretion. Following the coup attempt of a few years before, led by the air force, everyone who wasn't hung was exiled out to godawful assignments. Thus, our ex–air force government man.

Without warning, he stands, looks skyward, makes some flourishing gestures with his arms, and shouts something in what turns out to be almost, but not quite, correct Gaelic for an old battle cry. This, it seems, is the announcement of the beginning of his inspection. He aggressively demands that they pull up their hair and expose their foreheads, so that he can take the full measure of them; specifically, he says, so that he can determine whether they have a criminal mentality. They comply, feeling nervous and irrationally criminal, as he ponders their foreheads, making humming noises to himself. They are forced to stand and grasp his wrist with their full strength, as part of some test that he refuses to explain. In the heat and the incongruity, it doesn't seem to occur to them to object to any of this. They simply feel alarmed that they might fail his test.

He settles down for a complete interrogation. He looks at the Scots' passports (which are irrelevant to the issue of his letting them go unescorted) and grows excited at one of them having been to Egypt from Kenya. He incorrectly identifies the flight number of the Egypt Air Nairobi-Cairo flight, apparently missing the number and time by only a digit or two. He then gives a short spirited lecture about the ethnic diversity of Alexandria, the type of fish found there, and, he claims, the abnormally late closing of the skull sutures in the children there, allowing the people sufficiently large brains to have built the pyramids.

He grows even more excited when he discovers that the same Scot had also been to Greece, saying that he will now read the passport stamp in proper Greek, will identify the town from which it was issued, and will then tell them about the people of that village. They await this feat. He correctly reads off the word stamped there, his pronunciation apparently being perfect. He proclaims it to be the name of a small town in the islands; in actuality, it is the Greek word for "entry." He says the town has many ruins, healthy goats but small-skulled people, and says that he knows so much about the Mediterranean because in his former life, he was the governor general of Tiberius.

Ah-ha. At last, he has shown his hand; we've arrived at the core of his looniness. He says that there are two Italian missionaries in town whom he is keeping under house arrest because they say it is not possible that he was the governor general of Tiberius. (Later, after departing, the Scots run into these two Italians, who are on their way north to deliver a carburetor to their archrivals, three bearded Coptic missionary colleagues who every now and then manage to actually convert one of the animist nomads, only for the new acolyte invariably to be killed by outraged tribesmen. Their planned outing to the Coptics belies their being under house arrest. They claim no knowledge about the man's claims regarding Tiberius, but say they have not gotten along with him since they corrected his near-correct proclamation regarding the year of the Vatican's founding.)

Emboldened, perhaps taken to assume that the Scots' silent wonder is supplication and loyalty, our government man suddenly stands majestically behind his desk and announces that he, in fact, is *still* the governor general of Tiberius, that he is raising an army of the faithful here in the desert, that soon they will march upon Nairobi in the south, that the president will flee and "run and eat grass like a zebra in the Serengeti," that Nairobi will be burned and razed so utterly that even the wild animals will not venture there, and that he will then return to his outpost, declare the revival of his empire, and become the king of all Nubian-Judea.

He's going like a banshee by then, breathing heavily and looking off into a far distance. He sits, spent, and extracts a pass from one of the desk drawers, allowing them to travel on alone. He rouses his energies again, with a flourish signs his name in phonetic Greek, stating that his signature is known and feared by bandits throughout the northern desert. The Scots depart, he once more lost in his president's pose, consumed with the affairs of Nubian-Judea. When they return through the checkpoint later that day, he waves them through with a distracted, unrecognizing air.

17

The Penguins of Guyana

$\mathcal{I}$ was in a real crappy mood. It had started off as a fabulous morning with the baboons. Young Daniel, prematurely in the alpha position because of the ongoing instability in the troop's hierarchy, was being pushed around badly by huge Nathanial, and I thought this was the morning that their ranks were going to switch, that Nathanial would finally make his decisive move. This is a big deal to a primatologist, actually seeing the transition from one alpha male to another—witness to history. Daniel had spent the morning ostentatiously repositioning himself each time Nathanial came near, so as not to have to see him, presumably trying to will him out of existence. Nat, meanwhile, was inching in closer and closer, threat-yawning all over the place. Showdown was in the air, and I was avidly waiting to see if Daniel was going to fold and simply give a subordinate gesture, signaling the transition, or if it was going to take a decisive fight in which he'd be trashed.

Right when things were getting pretty exciting I had to leave. It was time to drive to the tourist lodge, to meet the supply lorry from Nairobi, as it was carrying an essential shipment of the dry ice that I needed to keep my blood samples frozen. So I had to miss all the fun.

Arriving at the lodge, I discover that, naturally, the ice has not actually been sent from Nairobi—an hour's work later, I finally get through to the ice guy in Nairobi over radiophone. Sorry, he says, we forgot. Forgot? They've been sending it once a week for months, and somehow it's suddenly forgotten. I'm down to my last day of ice before samples start defrosting, and I depart with the less-than-convincing promise from him that there'll be ice tomorrow.

Driving out of the lodge through thorn bushes, I get my third puncture of the week. This is always a misery. First you go to the guy who repairs punctures. Instead of being on the job at the lodge's gas station, he is back in the staff quarters somewhere, sleeping. Head back there, go through the same interchange with the twenty different people you run into, namely first exchanging news with each about the health of their parents and my then reiterating that, no, actually I can't give you my hiking shoes, as I need them. Tire repair guy is located, and after ninety minutes of easily distracted labor, he has fixed the puncture. He gives me a stub, which I take to the cashier at the other end of the lodge, who fills out a note saying "1 puncture, 40 shillings," which the other man signs, which allows me to pay the cashier—all a procedure to keep the mechanic from repairing things under the table and pocketing the money. The cashier goes on a search for scrap paper to calculate that I get 10 shillings back from my 50 shilling note, and I'm ready for the next step: taking the tire to the other end of camp, to find the man who operates the air hose. He, naturally, is drunk in the bar at 11:00 A.M. and, with some effort, explains that he would be happy to fill the tire, but his brother has the key to the shed in which the hose is kept, and he is on leave this week. Bad luck. I express profound regret at the apparent need for me to now live in the lodge's gas station for the next week, and the man, seeing his cue, says maybe, just maybe, he could find another key, but why don't I sell him my watch at the good American price? We settle for his receiving a button that says "Hollywood Bowl," and, satisfied, he turns his prodigious energies toward filling my tire, completing the task in a mere half hour. The man with the pressure gauge to determine whether the tire is filled properly is found easily, and quickly does the job, making me feel as if there might be some hope. The tire is underfilled, however. Fed up, I decide to go with that, rather than track down Bwana Airhose again, he no doubt back at the bar trying to flog his Hollywood Bowl button for a drink.

Task completed, I encounter the depressed Richard—yesterday, the end of the month, payday, meant that the rangers showed up from the gate to shake down the staff for protection payoffs, swaggering around the staff quarters drunk and armed, and Richard had been taken for more than usual, plus half his ulcer medicine that I had brought from the U.S. and had done cartwheels to get through customs. What the hell does some ranger want with an unknown medicine, other than just to be a prick? Richard announces he is going to sleep.

Grouchy and fed up with the whole mess, I do something egregious. I drive a great distance to another tourist lodge where, blessedly, no one knows me, and I spend an obscene amount of money on their all-you-can-eat lunch. I gorge till I am ill and concentrate on red meat. That's how bad it's become.

I sit there and smile at the tourists, hope to be taken for one, speak only English with the waiters. I look for an American to strike up a conversation with. Maybe to talk about the Yankees, or recent movies, or just how goddamn terrific it would be to have a Big Mac right now (a food item that I have, in fact, never eaten in my life).

That out of my system, I drive back guiltily. Somewhere in transit, I usually begin to wonder what the African guys here do when I and my godforsaken culture begin to drive them mad.

Okay, we're all doing a great job learning about each other and exploring the world and being cultural relativists, but this whole place is pretty alien, and I must be pretty alien to all of them, and the charm must wear off for everyone after a while. It constantly amazes me that there isn't more overt hostility between the different cultures and tribes and races here that rub elbows all the time, elbows already pretty scarred and tender from a lot of pretty nasty history. One arena where the hostility is in full flower has been a number of scams I've noted over the years. They all take advantage of the folks from the other culture and are predicated on a robust hostility toward them. Some prime examples:

One particularly well-honed scam has been worked over and over at the airport by African officials against the hated wealthy Indians. Some Nairobi Indian family is returning from abroad, visiting relatives in London or Toronto. Invariably, they arrive at customs with a mountain of boxes, usually highly desirable electronics items bought overseas at far lower prices than in Kenya. The stern customs inspector queries as to whether, prior to their trip, they filled out some imaginary customs declaration form he concocts out of air. Greatly dismayed to discover that they have not, he makes plans to impound all their possessions until hell freezes over. The family, now equally dismayed, wonders in an exploratory tone whether there isn't something that could be worked out that would solve this unfortunate impasse. An appropriate bribe is subtly paid, and perhaps one small trifle among the electronics gifts is left as a token of gratitude and fondness for the customs inspector. Thus, the family is able to clear customs . . .

. . . only to be nabbed by a policeman as they leave the room. He, it turns out, is on a special detail investigating corruption among customs officials, and has just observed them, shockingly, to have bribed a government official. Fines, jail, floggings are threatened, along with the impounding of all the electronics goods until hell freezes over and people are cross-country skiing in the streets of Nairobi. The family, now more than a little panicked, wonders whether there isn't something that could be worked out to solve this unfortunate misunderstanding. Another bribe is paid, another electronics offering is made as a symbol of the love and mutual respect that has been established. Family clears the waiting room . . .

. . . only to be nabbed by an army official in the lobby who is investigating corruption among police officials. . . .

Naturally, I fell for this one too. One of the security guards at a lodge begged me to bring him an American watch, cash to be paid on delivery. I wasn't enthused, as he wasn't someone I particularly knew or liked the looks of, but I decided to be a nice guy. Watch is brought in undeclared through customs, so as to avoid the manyfold import tax, in order to pass on to him the discount that prompted his begging me in the first place. Watch is received, immediate brotherhood is proclaimed, payment is promised the next day. The next day, instead, brings great dismay—bad luck, he recounts, a park ranger just happened to notice his new watch and demanded to see Form IV-7b, or some such thing, which attests to the watch's legal entry into the nation. In the absence of it, ranger is now threatening jail, beatings, impounding of all the Serengeti's baboons until hell freezes over, if he happens to find out who brought this soiled watch into this park, but, good news, the stalwart security guard has refused to name names and has instead arranged a cash gift for the ranger the next day, do I happen to have some money handy? Idiotically, I pay up, only to be told the next day, with even more dismay, bad luck, he and the ranger were caught mid-act in the process of bribing by a cop who, should he find out who started this all by bringing this tainted watch into his land, will . . . It was around this point that I finally told the guy to screw off.

Another time-honored scam was the one I had fallen for on my first day in Nairobi, many years before. That was, of course, the earnest Ugandan student, a refugee from Idi Amin, intent on helping drive him from power in order to establish whatever sort of governmental system was most likely to appeal to the tourist he was attempting to rip off. Thus, when addressing an American: "So you see, I must go back to Uganda and fight for freedom, like your people from the British, so that we can establish a two-party state and two legislative houses, so that my people can be free and have electoral primaries years before the actual election and have conventions where cheerleaders in short skirts and rich old men in straw hats sing songs about the winner. We will be free, and then we will make a new national anthem, 'Uganda the Beautiful.' Oh beautiful, for spacious skies," etc.

This scam persisted for years after Amin's overthrow, reflecting the fact that he was one of the few African leaders whose existence, let alone depredations, ever made it into the consciousness of your average tourist.

Then there was the "Mrs. Mortlake" ruse, which required an astonishing knowledge of the Brits to pull off with verisimilitude. Suppose you are some expatriate, parking your vehicle in the lot of the market in the British colonial suburb. Coming out, you find a Kenyan standing there with a moronic and obsequious grin, the likes of which haven't been seen since the Brit colonials strutted about in jodhpurs here. Bowing and scraping, he hands you the following note on pink stationery with purple ink:

> *Dear Mr. Cheever,*
>
> *I spotted your car in the parking lot and some boy seemed to be trying to break in, so I've left my houseboy, Francis, to watch the car. These boys here are really becoming impossible. Could you be a dear—I'm a bit short on cash—and give Francis the money for the bus back to Karen* [the white bedroom suburb, named for Karen Blixen, author of *Out of Africa*, whose old house there is now a museum]. *Thanks ever so much, and see you at the races Sunday.*
>
> Mrs. Mortlake (Theodora)

Oh hell, you think, I'm not Mr. Cheever (who you imagine as some age-spotted old colonial fart with knee socks, cigarette holder, and alarmingly red complexion) and ol' Francis, who's been watch-dogging your car, is stuck here thanks to the cheap Mrs. Mortlake (Theodora), and you suppose the least you can do is give the bugger the money to get back to the house, where he presumably spends his time serving tea and biscuits. Francis, money in hand, departs, still bowing and scraping, waiting for the next victim.

This, obviously, is not a trivial one to try. It requires the pink paper, purple ink, and the capacity to write like a British matron with flowery loopy handwriting. Also, it obviously takes a lot of eating of shit to pretend to be houseboy Francis. Not for beginners.

This one was going around for a while and appears to have been finally squelched when someone wised up and, rather than give "Francis" the money for the bus, instead forced him into their car and drove him the considerable distance to Karen, leaving him there. Perhaps, to establish his own verisimilitude in return, the driver made a point of confessing his respect, maybe even lust, for Mrs. Mortlake (Theodora).

It was around this time that Laurence of the Hyenas and I were discussing a possible solution to a problem he was having at his campsite, a few miles upriver from mine. The nearby Masai, with whom Laurence was not getting on particularly well, were bringing their zillions of cows to cross the river right next to his camp, of all the endless possible places to cross. Cows would crap up the river water, make a mess of the yard, generally get in the way. No amount of yelling at the kids with the cows was working to get them to move the damn animals away.

The obvious solution would be as follows: Disappear into your tent and, after a dramatic pause, reappear wearing sunglasses and a towel wrapped around your head like Hedda Hopper. Have in your possession one hyena skull, filled with baby powder, plus one marker pen. March up to the biggest cow in the herd, grab it by the horns. With ceremonial menace, begin to sprinkle baby powder out of the foramen magnum and eye sockets of the hyena skull. Sprinkle directly on cow's head. At the same time, loudly sing the chorus from "Oobla-di, Oobla-da." That phase of the cow-cursing ceremony completed, write on the cow's side with the marker pen. I'd personally vote for drawing a heart with an arrow through it and inside, "Vinnie luvs Angela." At this point, the Masai cowherd boys, off in the bushes, would be shitting bricks—they've pushed you too far and you've laid some heavy white magic on their cows. We concluded that cows would be removed from the camp within seconds after end of ceremony.

This was never actually done, for the obvious reason that were it to be, you would be visited that evening by a delegation of elders from the village, informing you that your ass is grass if *any* cow gets sick now for the next month, since you put a hex on them.

Then there was the one that Richard had thought up to get the Masai to leave him alone altogether. While Richard got on great with Soirowa and other individual Masai, there was still a perpetual tension in his living and working along the river. The Masai would never get around the fact that he and Hudson were members of agricultural tribes that were their traditional enemies.

Now, the Masai have established their intimidating reputation by being tall and imposing, and by being known for their fondness for gathering in large terrifying numbers, and for their prowess with spears. But I'm convinced that much of the visceral heebie-jeebies that they give all the agriculturists is from their drinking cow's blood.

In that regard, it is the typical banquet food of most nomadic pastoralists in Africa. Wander everywhere with your cows and goats, live off their milk and blood. Simple, fun. Grab one cow from your herd each day and, while it bellows like mad, cut its jugular and collect a calabash of warm blood. Press a mud compact on afterward and the cow is little more than anemic for the next week. Drink blood fresh, let it coagulate, or mix it with milk, pour it on your breakfast cereal. It allows you to avoid unpleasantries like having to hunt or grow things, apparently provides a reasonably balanced diet, is probably ecologically sound. However, it makes the agricultural Kenyans sick to their stomachs.

Oh, now and then, the braver ones decide there must be something to that Masai blood stuff. Hudson's father, for example, once came home after, no doubt, musing all day in the field, and announced that the family was going to try some cow's blood, those Masai have been beating the pants off us for years, there must be something to their disgusting habit. Everyone is dismayed—comical background music is heard and the whole thing takes on the pretense of a TV situation comedy—Oh No! Dad's Turned Masai and It's Cow Blood for Everyone! 8:00 P.M. tonight on *My Father the Bantu*. The predictable happens. Amid derision and wonder, Hudson's dad hauls over the family's sole (and terrified) moo-cow, comes close to killing her (since he doesn't quite know how to stop the bleeding), makes a mess of everything. No one else will drink the horrid stuff. Gingerly, he takes a few sips, pronounces it wonderful, and never brings up the subject again, as whimsical theme song for TV show comes up at the end.

Other than these occasional odd forays, pretty much everyone in this part of the country leaves the blood drinking to the Masai, and the latter no doubt take a certain satisfaction at how they disturb everyone else in the process. The secret to this scam of Richard's was to beat the Masai at their own game, and make them even more disgusted with his own food habits.

This started off inadvertently. I'd darted Nathanial. Later in the day, I gave a Masai woman a lift home from the clinic at the tourist lodge and stopped along the way to release the baboon. I suppose when you do enough of this sort of thing, you forget that everyone else isn't accustomed to your driving up to a cage hidden in a grove of trees that contains some wild baboon, jumping up on top of it with much hooting and yelling, and letting the guy out. The Masai woman was wild-eyed. To add to it, Nat came out a bit woozy, and was still staggering around a bit, in a placid bovine fashion. In a moment of inspiration, I grabbed a stick from the car and walked along beside the still-disoriented Nat, tapping him lightly on the rump, much as the Masai do when herding their cows. I started whistling like the Masai do when they are herding and led him past the car and the increasingly alarmed mama. After guiding him toward the rest of his pals, I returned to the car and dropped the woman off without any explanation.

Sure enough, by the next day, word was up and down the villages along the river that Richard and I herded baboons like cows and, no doubt, subsisted off them. Richard was soon asked about this by terrified Masai kids. Do you take milk from the baboons and drink it? You bet. Is that all? asked the kids, not willing even to verbalize their worst fears. There's even more, Richard hinted malevolently, beginning to hatch his plan.

We plotted carefully and picked the right day. We were lounging around camp, having darted the new transfer male, Reuben. Masai kids were lounging with us, especially the girls, who seemed to have a teasing crush on Richard in the way the ten-year-old girls usually torture the lifeguard at summer camp. They watched us take blood from the baboons with the interest that they always had—since Masai have to hit veins and control their bleeding for their daily bread, they know more about bleeding than most phlebotomists. They clustered around, advised which vein to poke, marveled at the butterfly catheters and anticoagulants. They were accustomed to us spinning the blood in the godawful hand-operated centrifuge, pulling off the serum, and freezing it away in the dry ice. But this time, we had a different plan.

Richard and I ostentatiously took the remaining red cells, full rich baboon blood, and poured it into the drinking cup we had decided to sacrifice for the ruse. We walked back to the tent, with the Masai kids watching, transfixed and horrified. Along the way, with backs turned, I switched cups. Bowing to each other with the decorum appropriate to the start of a Japanese tea ceremony, we then took turns drinking from the cup, exclaiming at the superb taste, wiping our mouths, rubbing our bellies contentedly in a hammy fashion.

That was it. Forever after, the Masai believed that we drank baboon blood, and I think that played a major role in Richard's not getting hassled by the Masai too often. The kids themselves clustered around Richard asking questions. How does it taste? Good, like human blood. They recoiled, spitting and gasping. Does he pay you to do this? they asked, referring to me. No, he is my friend, I ask him if I can drink blood from his baboons. Don't you have any cows at home? No, my father has no cows, that is why we started drinking baboon blood.

The more charitable of the girls came up to Richard and, in an un-Masai gesture, touched his arm. You must be the poorest man in the world, no cows, she said gently. Her friend had little time for sympathy or understanding. Cannibals! she said huffily, as they departed.

But of course, just when I had decided that all anyone did in Kenya was try to pull something off on someone else, I returned home from a field season and promptly fell victim to the most ornate scam I've ever experienced. The whole thing cost me a chunk of my paycheck and, before it was over, I wound up sitting in the backseat of a two-door car in a truly bad neighborhood very late at night. The front seat was occupied by one of the scammers, supposedly a garrulous New York City transit worker who'd seen it all, the backseat next to me by the other scammer, supposedly a sweet, unworldly woman from Guyana, sent here from the plantations to visit her grievously injured brother in the hospital. I never had a clue what was up and made small talk with the fake Guyanese woman, enthusiastically trying to discuss the flora and fauna of her beautiful homeland. As it turned out, she knew nothing about the subject, but, fortunately for her, I turned out to know even less.

When I reported it to the police, I discovered that this was such a time-honored rip-off that they had an entire notebook of grainy mug shots labeled "Guyanese girl/Transit worker," right next to other books with labels like, "Blind nun with sick Seeing Eye dog," "Siamese twins who have just won the lottery," and "Visiting caliph and entourage seeking good Middle Eastern restaurant at any price." The cops, while filling out the forms, found excuses to ask me repeatedly where I was from—"Now where'd you say your home-town was again, Cornfed, Iowa? Backabeyond, Kansas?" forcing me to fess up, over and over, that I was actually a native New Yorker. They chortled derisively and had a great time.

But that's another story.

18

When Baboons Were Falling Out
of the Trees

Naturally, just when I thought I'd gotten a pretty complete education in the various scams going around, even the ones in New York, I fell for another one. And this one was actually of some consequence, instead of a mere failing to see through some guy who was trying to hustle a watch off of me. It involved a situation where I had two seconds to make a life-and-death decision, and thanks to not having a clue about the nonsense going on around me, I made the wrong one.

It was later in that season of Nathanial's ascendancy—he had indeed decisively grabbed the alpha position from Daniel the morning that I farted away with my flat tire. Richard and I had been making good progress with darting the baboons, and data were rolling in. A research vet from Nairobi, Muchemi, had come out to hang out in camp for a few weeks in order to get some samples. A euphemism: Muchemi was interested in schistosomiasis in primates and wanted fecal samples from the baboons. We were happy to oblige, even acceded to his request for samples of our own. One excellent day, we darted four animals in a morning, a record, and rode into camp yipping like cowboys. A productive pattern emerged—we darted baboons each morning, ran the experiments smoothly, threw a Frisbee around between blood samples, helped Muchemi stuff turds into his little plastic bags. It was turning into a great season.

Then one day, the warden came to camp. One was always a little bit skittish about such things—wardens visiting usually meant your permits had been revoked, or some favor was requested, or some vacationing Saudi princes were coming soon to shoot animals nearby and nosy researchers were notified to get lost for the duration. This time it was a request. It was actually the assistant warden, as the senior warden had been on leave for a while. No doubt trying to show he was a gung-ho, take-charge kind of guy, he had followed up on news of a problem and was volunteering me to solve it. He had gotten some radio calls from the manager of a tourist camp at the far corner of the other end of the reserve. The man had reported that there was some sort of disease outbreak among the baboons living near his camp. They were dying in droves, "falling out of the trees." The manager had requested permission to shoot the dying ones.

The warden had said yes, and now wanted me to figure out what the problem was with the baboons, if it was curable, if it was a danger to the tourists. All very commendable, but I had mixed feelings about it. There were lots of reasons to do it. The whole thing had an air of juvenile excitement: a man in a uniform had come and given me a mission. It sounded interesting and challenging. The timing was opportune, with Muchemi and his veterinary skills on hand. Yet I was sulky about it—Muchemi's time was limited, as was mine.

But of course we would go; the warden was requesting it, and he could shut me down anytime he felt cranky, and it was essential to get some brownie points. And we might do some good. By morning, we had pulled together our supplies, ransacking the storage tent: a cage, blowgun, darts, anesthetics. Vacutainers, needles, syringes. A centrifuge and a backup hand-operated one. A hematology microscope, slides, stains. A powerverter and extra car battery to run the equipment. Tents, sleeping bags. Loads of different kinds of antibiotics, antiseptics, painkillers. Cotton swabs, bacterial culturing kits, gloves, masks, surgical scrub suits, saws for cutting through bone, instruments for doing necropsies, vats of formaldehyde.

We drove off early. Muchemi had done research in this corner of the reserve years before, collecting carnivore shit, and waxed nostalgic for his youth. We all sang. It was a gorgeous day. We were excited, buzzed, anticipatory about tackling this problem, pleased and impressed with ourselves and our preparations. I hoped the powers that be would also be impressed, maybe decide I was useful to have around, stop hassling me about permits. We felt like some sort of veterinary SWAT team, planned strategy, vowed that if things got complicated enough, we would mobilize the whole primate center in Nairobi, have teams of veterinary pathologists parachuting out of the sky dressed in dashing orange jumpsuits. We got giddy until we decided the logical place to start was to have the manager shoot one of the dying ones so that we could carry out a careful necropsy. Jesus, we were off to go kill baboons. The anxiety that had kept me awake half of the night before returned—what would we find, how many would we have to kill before we could figure out something, what if I made a mess of it, what if it was indeed a plague? I wondered if, when it was all over, I would think back on this morning, remembering, It had been a beautiful day, we sang, Muchemi told us about lion turds. . . .

The manager came out to meet us in the parking lot. He was an "old white hunter," actually a young version of the genre. Now, before I go on, I should put my cards on the table about how I feel about those folks. It's certainly one of the epic images to emerge from the colonial experience in Africa—Hemingway's man, the grizzled hunter, tough but fair to the natives, intuitive about the workings of an animal's mind, capable of drinking himself to near coma till dawn in a Nairobi watering hole and then getting up glinty-eyed and sober to begin the safari. Point man for saving the cowardly client at a critical moment in the hunt, seducer of the client's wife, blah blah, that whole scene. I'm sure most of them weren't like that, but that's the persona they try to pass off, so I'm willing to hold it against them. As hunting wound down and was eventually banned in Kenya, a new piece of their mythology came to force. Old hunters don't fade away: the profound respect for their worthy animal adversaries, accrued over the endless hunt, finally leads to a tiring of the killing, a desire to preserve. Turning their vast knowledge of animals to conservation, they become wardens in their later years. Certainly, some of the great epic wardens around East Africa's independence were ex-hunters, now mostly Africanized into retirement or running of tourist camps and safari companies. I don't know. I definitely don't have any careful statistics on the subject—how many became conservationists, how many simply liked blowing away animals, what percentage really did manage to look taciturn and handsome at dawn on the savanna. I'm just clearly not crazy about the whole scene.

The old hunters cum wardens cum camp managers, in turn, seem to loathe the zoologists, as a general rule. I suspect we represent a final affront, the domestication of their Africa. They are old tough Brits who were there at the beginning, didn't have much schooling, and learned about the bush from the bush, understanding the big picture. We, in turn, are generally young Americans, already a strike against us, from impossible places like Ann Arbor or Queens. We come out there and try to turn their bush into equations about vegetation, or talk about ecosystems and niches, for god's sake. We spend only short periods there (i.e., less than the hunter's lifetime) and study tiny slivers—how one species of plant pollinates, how some disease moves through ungulates, how many acres of land is needed for a whatever to survive. We're a bunch of candy-ass PhDs who know more and more about less and less and barely know how to wipe our noses when it comes to the bush. All probably true.

Thus, my biases. On closer inspection, the manager seemed slightly less legitimate as one's old white hunter. It wasn't his being young. An old white hunter is more a state of mind than a chronological fact; there are plenty enough young ones, their incipient careers crushed by the hunting ban. He was simply too pudgy, no doubt about it—stocky, with face and neck and torso going to fat. Too smooth, unwrinkled. Didn't have the dusty leather face that the hunters always manage to make appear most severe when talking about how the whole show in the Serengeti has gone to hell ever since old Jock Murray got pushed out as warden by the Africans. He had a dangerous, aggressive small mustache, and hair that looked so utterly like a bad toupee from twenty years ago that it had to be his own. He had the obligatory khaki shorts and vest, kneesocks and omnipresent cigarettes, puffed-up British accent. I've sincerely forgotten his name, which is a shame, as it would have been one of the few here that I wouldn't have changed to protect his privacy.

The warden had promised to radio-call about our arrival and hadn't. I explained ourselves, made introductions, tried to seem official and in control, as if to spread the word that they could all finally sleep easy tonight, we had come to save their baboons. He said he was delighted we were there, and didn't look delighted at all. He was clearly uncomfortable, but hard to know why. So many possible reasons. Maybe the fact that the colonial days were so far gone that he was now confronted with a black "Doctor" Muchemi, whom he ignored throughout the day. Maybe he was irritated at our descending upon him unannounced; maybe it was the general displeasure that folks who look like me always engender in the old settlers—more barbarians in their Kenya.

We chatted awhile about the volume of tourist business, the recent rains. I asked him about the status of the baboons. Unexpectedly, I found that we were beginning to parry. He said there had been some sick ones, but he didn't know if we would find any now.

I expressed surprise—"I thought they were falling out of the trees?"

"No, no, definitely not, there's just some sick ones."

"Oh, I'm sorry, I guess the warden somehow gave me the wrong impression. Maybe we could go try to find the baboons now, have a look at them?"

"I would expect you'd have some difficulty, they're frequently hard to find, sometimes go days without seeing them."

"But the warden said they were the troop that lived in the camp's garbage dump."

"Well, yes, that's true. I suppose we could look there."

I decided I had probably offended him somehow. Maybe he was irritated at us carpetbaggers turning up when he had the show under control, or he thought I seemed too young and long-haired and unpresentable to possibly be competent. Idiotically, I decided that I would have to mollify him somehow, win his respect.

I explained our plan. We would find the baboons, have a good look at them, try to get a sense of the numbers, age, and sex distribution of the sick ones. Then, if there were any in bad shape, he should shoot some, and we would begin necropsying them, try to figure out what was happening.

He called for his gun bearer and gun, and explained to me his rationale for using that particular rifle. I didn't understand anything he said about the gun, and didn't listen to the reasons why that was the ideal one for shooting a baboon. Not surprisingly, I'm not big on guns. Once, years before, Laurence of the Hyenas and I had convinced ourselves we needed a double-barreled shotgun if we were going to walk safely through the bush. He got one, and one day, the two of us Jewish bearded hippies from Berkeley and Brooklyn went out for target practice. We drove way out to nowhere, put chewing gum in our ears to block the noise, set up buffalo skulls and tin cans as targets. Laurence at least knew how to load it, deal with a safety, that sort of thing, showed me how, yelled when I let the gun point at my foot. The whole thing, even just touching the gun, felt sullying, forbidden and furtive and unkosher. We shot for a while. Somehow, I hit the tin can when Laurence tossed it in the air. I affected a manly indifference to his praise for having done so but gave myself away by jabbering about it too much on the way home. Having gotten that out of our systems, we put the gun away forever and just made sure we were careful when we were walking in the bush. So now I nodded in a firm knowing way, not listening as the manager explained his choice.

We walked through the back end of camp, he and the gun bearer, we with some of our supplies. Past the kitchen, storage huts, staff quarters, through a foot trail in the high grass toward a thick grove of trees. Naturally, hidden in there away from the tourists would be the garbage dump. Every lodge and camp in the reserve had one—even though there was certainly not the consciousness among any of the outfits to try to get rid of the garbage properly. Safari companies that would set up temporary camps would just dump the garbage in the river. The permanent lodges dug big open pits to dump their crap, leaving it for the baboons and hyenas and vultures to fight over. Every lodge and tourist camp thus had a resident troop of baboons living on the garbage. The animals would no longer go out to forage, but would sleep in the trees above the dump, snoozing late and waiting for the daily garbage drop. I had even studied the metabolic changes that the baboons living at another lodge had gone through as they became garbage eaters, feasting on leftover drumsticks, slabs of beef, rotting dollops of last night's custard pudding. Not surprisingly, cholesterol, insulin, and triglyceride levels rose, other aspects of metabolism went to hell in the same way that ours does when we eat the stuff. The other problem with garbage dumps is that baboons are not smart enough to know that custard pudding and drumsticks are okay to eat when they're thrown in a dump, but not okay on the outdoor buffet table at lunchtime—the baboons quickly become dangerous scavengers around the lodges themselves. And when you have concentrations of human garbage, you're just asking for concentrations of human diseases, just the sort of thing that wild primates have no immunity against. I had seen that before, and it seemed a logical reason for this disease outbreak in a garbage dump troop. None of this is any news to people familiar with the problems of bears and raccoons around garbage in the U.S. park system, but it certainly didn't seem to be much concern to any of the lodges in the reserve. But I will tirade about this some other time.

It was your typical lodge dump. So smelly, you felt a bit dizzy, acrid waves of stink heat coming off the garbage, roasting and moldering in the sun. Stale leftover smoky smell from intermittent burnings, soot and ash blown about with every breeze. Vultures and marabou storks picking and sorting, occasional metallic plinkings and clickings as rodents ran about the piles of tin cans. And at the far corner, sitting on the rim of the dump, grooming in the bushes, low in the trees, were the baboons.

Whenever I see a new baboon troop, visit some other researchers and see their animals, I feel something almost like irritation—I don't *know* them, I have no idea who they are. How can I appreciate them without yet knowing who is who, what great fights and grudges are going on, who are the epic personalities? It's like being a few pages into some massive novel and feeling impatient because you're not yet engrossed in it. You look at them and reflexively try to begin recognizing individuals: Okay, there's the one with the really sharp features and the torn ear; then there's that one with the limp; then there's the one who kind of looks like a young Saul, but his fur is lighter. You wonder, Is one of you about to have a life history that would change all my ideas about baboons? Who of you are relatives? What kind of dominance hierarchy do you have here? How long would it take for me to feel as much for you as for my baboons? Could I love one of you like Benjamin?

But that's not what we were here for. The baboons were pretty habituated, from all the humans around the camp. They seemed to be slowly filtering from out of the forest behind the dump, coming into the clearing surrounding it, looking about to see if there was any new garbage. They filed by pretty close, gave us a good view. Occasionally, the manager would point out one of them, suggest a problem.

"That one, over there. He seems to be missing a lot of hair."

"Which one? *That* one? Nah, it's just the wind blowing it at a funny angle."

"What about that one, who's limping. She can barely walk."

"Looks like a broken leg. Probably from a fall."

He repeated again that the sick ones were probably all dead by now, that most of the troop hardly came around anymore, I would never see them.

More filtered through. A female followed by a big kid that she clearly didn't want to carry and who just as clearly wanted to be carried; the kid whined incessantly until the mother finally hauled off and slapped it in the face. Two subadult males who briefly tussled and mock-lunged at each other before they decided to find someone smaller and both chased a screaming juvenile into the bushes. A female in heat followed by a skittish nervous male whom she basically ignored. As each animal emerged from the bushes, all of us would swivel, stare with an intense focus, look like hyenas searching for someone with a flaw, the weak one. It was hot from the dump burning, it felt hot from the smell. After a while, you realized how tiring it can be just to look at something, to really *look*.

What must have been most of the troop had already come out. There was nothing wrong, so far as I could tell.

"Well, so far, they seem okay to me. Can you tell me again exactly how the sick ones looked?"

Unexpectedly, he blew up.

"I can't bloody well tell exactly how the sick ones looked. I'm no doctor. I don't know any of these fancy technical terms. I'm trying to run a camp here and I'm very busy. I thought I could just help you and the warden out. Look, a sick animal looks sick. But I'm no specialist with them."

I felt sorry. I understood, I *had* offended him, us descending on him, my trying to impress him, letting him know he could trust our competence with his animals, giving him the "This is Dr. M. and I'm Dr. S.," reciting our credentials. I must have sounded condescending, made him feel patronized. He must have felt bad and defensive that he hadn't made careful enough observations of the sick ones before they died. I should have had more tact, I thought. In actuality, I should have stopped and been cynical for just a second. Instead, I made another mistake. I tried to walk him carefully through a description, to help him out.

"Okay, did any of the sick ones look thin, were they losing weight?"

"Definitely, definitely. Some of them were skin and bones."

"Were they losing patches of fur, the rest of it looking ratty?"

"Yes, that's why I pointed out the other one, when his coat looked bad."

"Good. Did the sick ones cough?"

He elaborated. "Not all the time, but when they did, it would be for long periods, these really deep coughs, from the bottom of their lungs. You definitely got the impression something was wrong with their lungs."

Oh, why didn't I use my brains with the slightest edge of suspiciousness? Why didn't I ask, "Now, did any of them get this bright purple mange on their fur only on the left side and get these muscle spasms that would make them look like they were dancing the Charleston?" and then watch him agree? Instead, I kept feeding him symptoms.

I felt frustrated. I had tuberculosis on my mind, but it looked like the whole first wave of sick ones had already died. That seemed surprising, it doesn't usually come in clear waves of illness like that, but who knows. Without an active case to necropsy, it would be hard to confirm my suspicion, to figure out what kind of TB, what the source could be, what the best treatment was. We'd have to wait for the next outbreak, or start methodically darting and testing everyone, which would take weeks of work. If only we'd gotten here in time to get an active case, at least we could have gotten a start on this.

It was Richard who spotted him first. Another group of baboons was emerging, probably the last part of the troop. Richard gave a low sibilant sound to get our attention, then pointed silently to one hidden in the rear. Richard bent forward and arched his back, in imitation of the baboon. It was a male, a young adult. He was thin, thin coat of fur, but even. He had a high, delicate step, maybe a hint of a head shake as he walked. The main thing was that his back was arched upward. Not a whole lot, just a slight upward arch that looked intentional, that made the male look uncomfortable when he walked. It wasn't much, but it was atypical. It seemed to be an early sign of TB in a quadrapedal primate—as far as I understand it, I think that once the lungs begin to poop out and fail to exchange oxygen, a baboon begins to try to arch its back and expand its chest cavity, to try to get more air in.

He looked basically okay, a little on the skinny side but not abnormally so. But there was definitely the slight back arch.

He came forward and sat near us, shifting around to look at us, at the garbage dump, at the others, giving us a full view of him. We were alert, excited.

"That's what they look like." The manager.

"Is that how it is at the beginning of the illness?"

"Yes." We were whispering, I realized.

I asked Richard what he thought.

"His back is up, definitely."

"But not much, just a little bit."

"He is thin, but not so thin."

We all watched. I wasn't sure. The back *was* arched, and he was thin. But maybe he was just lanky, is that a crime? He didn't look feverish or out of it, but, then, I didn't know him, didn't know how he normally acted.

Suddenly, the manager said, "Well, should we check this one out?"

He had gone into a crouch and had his gun ready.

"Lemme look at him a bit more."

I went on looking, trying to remember exactly what I had learned that a tubercular monkey looks like. I reviewed the symptoms the manager had given me. I looked some more at him and at the others. I looked at the trees and at the storks and brushed away some soot from the dump that had blown on my cheek. I wondered what kind of lunch they served in this lodge. I looked at him again. He was looking at us.

"Should I shoot him?"

If this was the start of tuberculosis, we would have to get some idea of what kind, what we were up against, or else it would kill all the baboons in this part of the reserve in no time. But maybe he's just lanky. It will help to do this, to let the warden know that I actually did something. Maybe we should come back in a week and see if it has progressed at all with this guy. But the manager is going to be impatient, we're taking his time, and I've gotten him irritated enough already; he wants to get his part over with and get back to his camp. But maybe the guy's just lanky and has a funny posture. It's always interesting to do a dissection, anatomy is pretty cool. God, don't let it be a TB plague. But maybe he's just lanky.

I found myself beginning to wonder what name I would give the baboon if he were in my troop.

"I think he's about to move off." The manager, more than a bit of an edge to his voice, no longer a whisper.

The baboon looked the other way. And coughed once.

I said okay, shoot.

The manager crouched even more, took a breath, and fired point-blank at the baboon. It sounded like a little pop, like a toy sound. The baboon was off into the bushes like a shot, silently. All of them took off, some screaming. The manager had missed. He shouted that we should split up, follow, in case he was injured, going down. He and I went one way, Richard and the gun bearer a second, Muchemi a third. But we knew he had missed. We followed some paths in the forest, baboons moving ahead of us. No blood on the trail, no screaming, just alarm calls from the baboons each time we approached them. They were moving off fast, clearly terrified. The manager was running, in an agitated state, starting up one path and changing to another, alternately crouching on the ground, looking for blood, craning his head upward to look at the baboons in the trees. He would gesture for me to stay back at various points, almost angrily, as he would suddenly slow into a cautious hyperalert few steps, looking every which way, even though the baboons were a quarter kilometer ahead of us by now. Then he would be off running again. I realized that my heart was pounding, that I was gasping; I probably hadn't been breathing the whole time I was watching the male.

They were gone, long into the thick part of the forest; no blood on the trail, no one screaming, no one shot. He had missed and finally admitted as much.

"Missed. Not surprising with that sort of wind." He was sweating. Well, so was I.

Eventually we regrouped. Everyone seemed frazzled, more than a little silent. During the walk back to the dump, the manager had turned cranky. He seemed very impatient with us now.

"Well, they're gone, and I don't suspect they'll be back in here for quite some time," his tone somehow implying it was our fault. "You're welcome to stay here and see what you can do, but I don't expect you'll be seeing any baboons here soon. Now, if you don't mind, I need to go look after my camp."

I said we would track a bit more in the forest, see if we could get closer to them again, see if there were any more we missed. He gave a suit-yourself shrug and left with the gun bearer.

Richard, Muchemi, and I went into the forest. We had all stopped breathing hard, it was quiet again, we were beginning to think. We were beginning to finally figure out what was going on. Richard had wanted to talk to me as soon as we had all reassembled. Once we got in the forest he told me that while he and the gun bearer were looking along their track, they had talked, and the gun bearer said that he had never seen any sick baboons. Richard tried a couple of different facial expressions, as if trying to prepare for whichever one I would have—an instant of looking sincerely confused, perplexed at our conflicting data, then a look of wry understanding at what was going on. We settled on the latter, as it was clear what was up.

•   •   •

We slowly came out of the forest, carried our things back to the Jeep. The manager reappeared as we were getting in. I said that he was right, there probably wasn't much more we could get done today, we had other things to do, would love to stay and sort out the problem, but we probably had to be going. He agreed, thanked us for coming, invited us for lunch once we had the engine on and seemed certain of leaving. We declined, thanked him for everything, shook hands all around, left.

We were silent until we had cleared the bush and forest country around the camp and gotten back into the open savanna. As if we were unwilling to talk that close to his place.

Someone had to finally start talking, to say what we were all thinking. It was Richard.

"I think it was just a story he was saying about the baboons being sick. I think that man just likes to shoot baboons and wanted the warden to let him."

I agreed, and was about to pronounce the manager scum, but hesitated. At least one of those times when he shot at baboons, I was the one who told him to do it.

19

The Old White Man

Hanging out at the tourist camp, watching a group of Americans check in. Amid their questions and calling to each other and "Jambo's" to the staff, I noted an oddly metallic voice. I eventually spotted a tall, gangly older man, with a magnificent long backwoodsy beard, holding some sort of shaver-sized device in his hand. Each time he spoke, he held the device to what I spotted to be a hole in his throat. His lips moved, but a monotonic, metallic voice came out of the object. I assumed he'd had his trachea or larynx removed for some medical reason, and this was a voice amplifier. The thing seemed like a rather helpful, pleasing invention, and I was intrigued to note that, despite the mechanical flat quality of the sound produced, it was still possible to tell that the man had a rich, twangy Southern accent.

By early afternoon, I had discovered that the man was the center of feverish discussion among the staff at the camp. The consensus was that the man's entire throat was actually a machine. Maloi, who had once worked at a hotel in Nairobi and was considered worldly, led the discussion.

"That old white man has no throat, so now it is just a machine. I think he must have been in a car accident, or someone chopped at his neck with a machete, and he had no throat left, so the white doctors put a machine there.

"When he needs to speak, he takes the other machine, in his hand, and he puts it into his throat, so that the throat machine will work.

"That is why he has that beard, to hide the machines there, so that his wife will not be upset to look at him."

John, the bartender and purveyor of drinks during lunch, had important corroborating evidence.

"During lunch, he would not drink anything. I tried to sell him a drink, even a soda, and he would not drink. Not even water. You cannot get the machine wet, like a radio. It will make sparks and rust."

Everyone agreed and sympathized.

"So that old white man cannot even drink water. I wonder what he does when he becomes thirsty."

"There must be another hole, down below, where he can pour in water. That is why his beard is so long. He must do it in his room, when no one else is there." Everyone looked expectantly at Simon, the room steward; it would be his job to track down that piece of evidence.

"But he ate a lot of food, that old white man."

"It is to power the machine."

"With food?"

"Yes, food gives you energy," said Kasura, who had had a lot of schooling. "So the batteries will last longer."

Kamau, who was somewhat of a jokester and usually not listened to, suddenly made a logical extension to the discussion.

"You know, I do not think that old white man is a man at all. I think all of him is a machine."

"We are talking serious here, bwana, we are not kids to be kidded."

"No, I am serious. I think all of him was killed in an accident, and the white doctors have made him completely into a machine."

People snarfled and dismissed this absurd idea, and Kamau was about to defend it energetically, when one of the security guards ran in excitedly to say that the old white man was going up to the gas station, was walking there.

Everyone crowded out to watch from a distance. The man had a loping slow walk punctuated by a limp.

"Look at that, his legs are machines, look at the way he is walking." This was Kamau, whose theory was still being ignored.

"Why is he walking to the gas station?"

"He needs gas."

"Be serious, bwana."

"Look, he is going to the gas station store."

Simon had the answer.

"He is going to get motor oil. He has to pour it down his throat, so that the machine works properly."

"This is true, you have to oil machines," said Suleman, who was a driver and knew such things.

We watched him go into the store and, after some minutes, reemerge and limp back. When he was out of sight, Odhiambo, from the petrol station store, came running. He was excited.

"He bought motor oil, didn't he? Did you see him drink it?"

"No, no, it wasn't motor oil."

"What did he buy?"

"Well, at first I could not understand what the old white man was saying, with his voice machine, but then I could understand it. He bought two camera batteries."

Two camera batteries?

With shock, everyone turned to Kamau, as his face widened in fear.

"My god Jesus, they are for his eyes!"

"Kamau, Kamau is right, he is a machine."

"Oh my god, that old white man is a machine!"

Suddenly, John remembered a horrifying detail that confirmed the theory. Every African I'd ever seen in the bush is capable of picking up the hottest things imaginable without scorching their fingers—tea glasses, pieces of firewood, cooking pots—from years of handling hot things around the open cooking fires. But no one, no one, can tolerate very cold things—still too novel.

"I was bringing drinks for the other white people at his table, and I was putting ice into their cups, you know the way you must do it, with the ice in a spoon because you cannot hold it, and I dropped a piece on the table. And this old white man, he just picked up the ice in his hand."

"In his hands, his hands are machines."

"He is a machine."

"How did they do it?"

"That old woman with him, her husband must have died, and she must be very rich, and they made a machine to look like her husband. From the pictures."

"That's why the white women are always taking pictures. In case their husband dies. So they can make a machine to look like him. These white people can do that."

"And they put a tape cassette into his throat."

"But you can talk to him. I talked to him. It is not like a cassette, he will answer you," said Odhiambo, the skeptic.

"It is a special cassette. I have read about them. They have them in Nairobi," said Kasura.

"The ones that will add numbers for you."

"So that old white man is really a machine."

People were near to panicking; they were no longer amused. Suleman voiced it.

"You know, this is serious, I am really annoyed. I have to take those people out on a game drive this afternoon, and now they are sending a machine. It could be dangerous. I do not like this, I am really very annoyed. I think I will talk to the manager." And he left for what turned out to be a drink to steel his courage before the game drive.

The panic spread. By late afternoon, everyone knew that the old white man was a machine. Simon reported seeing him carrying a luggage bag from the porch of his cabin over to his wife, and the weight of it was greatly over-estimated—"Look how strong those machine arms are." He came into the bar, asking in his cassette recorder voice for a drink for his wife. John, schemer, dropped some ice intentionally and the old white man, in front of witnesses, picked it up. And, John swore, took pictures with his eyes. Not wishing to slow down the pace of the hysteria, I gave impromptu lectures on prosthetic limbs, glass eyes, fetal neuron transplants, and dentures.

Everyone crowded at a distance to watch Suleman, poor bastard, go off on the death drive with the machine and his wife and the other white tourists. Thereafter, there was a palpable air of tension, waiting for Suleman's return. Would he even return, or would the machine malfunction at some point and grab Suleman's face and shred it? Or would Suleman return as a machine himself? The various theories were expounded, and the staff quarters came closer to mutiny. Serving the guests dinner, it seemed, was fast going to be out of the question.

The vehicle returned. The couples exited, smiling, laughing. *Taking pictures.* Even the old white man was laughing, and the tourists disappeared to their tents. Suleman came out, looking okay. Everyone clustered around: What happened? What happened?

"That old white man."

"Yes, yes, what did he do?"

"That old white man. He gave me a hundred-shilling tip." A whopping good tip.

Everyone digested this and, at once, came to the same calming conclusion.

"Oh, this old white man is a good machine."

The panic subsided, and he was given excellent, if closely watched, service for the remainder of his stay.

20

The Elevator

Then there was the day that I discovered that no one knew about the knee reflex. I was sitting around with Richard at the staff quarters at the tourist lodge. He had made a joke about something, I tapped him on the knee while laughing. His leg flew out from the reflex, and he immediately asked, How did you make my leg do that? I demonstrated, he was mystified, and soon a crowd of neighbors had formed. No one had ever noticed it before. Someone got a bunch of old soda bottles from the staff canteen, and soon everyone was sitting around, slamming below their kneecaps with the bottles. "Look at this, my leg flies, I cannot stop it."

Everyone was happy and sore. I suddenly had this guess about something else that was going to be novel—eye floaters. "Have you ever looked at the sky, and seen something moving inside your eye, a little something that you can see through, just floating down?" A number of the guys gasped—it seems that they had seen floaters in their eyes and had never had the nerve to mention it. Richard grasped my arm. "My god, I have seen it, I thought there was a microscope in my eye." Clearly, he was spending too much time around me. Someone else said he always thought that his floaters meant he was chosen by Jesus for a special task. I returned him to more mundane realism by explaining how floaters are sloughed-off cell crud on the surface of the eye.

More things everyone had noticed but never had the nerve to mention to anyone. Déjà vu. "One time, I was walking by these bushes, and it was the first time, I know it, but somehow, in my head, I had already seen that bush," said one Masai, who was indeed likely to remember every bush he'd ever seen before. I hit them with the one about how when you are almost asleep, you suddenly feel like you are falling ("My god, I thought that meant I was dying," said one guy), and then you wake up before your body does.

We were all having a fabulous time—one of those days where you realize how lucky you are, getting to hang out with people from a completely differ-

214 • Robert M. Sapolsky

ent corner of the planet. But nothing held a candle to the time I thought I was taking Richard on his first elevator ride.

It was during Nat's reign, just before he decided he had better things to do with his life than be an alpha male. We had just finished darting in our park, were on our way to freelance dart in another one, stopped in Nairobi in between for resupplying. Richard's first trip to the big city. What a blast. I dragged him from one end to the other, taught him about traffic lights. I tortured him with lectures about urban sociology, showed him his first supermarket, his first cinema, his first rush hour. He was horrified by the cars—"I think there can be so many cars here because there are no buffalo." This seemed sensible enough. A Kikuyu (the city slicker tribe in Kenya) mistook Richard for a Kikuyu and addressed him in that tribal language, and Richard glowed in his implied cosmopolitan status. Even more pleasing was Richard's first bookstore. He couldn't believe it. For reasons unknown, Richard had festered with a passion for books unmatched by almost any Kenyan I'd met, irrespective of schooling. He'd sit and plow through them with his rough English (merely his fourth language), make some headway, and get great enjoyment, although he did toss up his hands after insisting that I pass on my copy of *The Brothers Karamazov* to him ("So, Richard, how's that book going, what is it about?" "Well, it is very confusing. There are these brothers, and they are always talking, and the old man is not a good one, but then they are always talking even more, except when the women are coming in and crying. I think they are white people, but maybe not from America." After that, he gave up on it). But an entire bookstore, I gave him some money, told him to run amok, get whatever he wanted, and my heart swelled with vicarious joy.

Later, it was his first ice cream. He had spotted them first, the people with the funny pipes that they smoked with their tongues—ice cream cones. He held on to my arm in ecstasy at his first taste. Then, Kenya's first escalator, in a spanking new downtown building. It had become a local attraction, the thing for the young Nairobi swells to do, to hang out and ride the escalator, maybe take your date to it. It came with a large poster board of instructions, caveats, and disclaimers—face forward, one direction only, no goats, not responsible for pregnant women. We waited our turn, leapt on, clutching for dear life, survived.

Late afternoon, the surprise. I had decided to pull out all the stops, finagle the accounting on the grant, and splurge on one of the big downtown hotels. We checked in, got Richard his room. We were on the fifth floor. I prepared Richard for the elevator. I described how his stomach was going to feel. And then, unable to resist, I drew exploding diagrams of the various floors of the building with the elevator shaft going up the middle, showed myself to be the son of an architect that I am.

We were ready, headed up. Richard initially noted the Muzak and the lit numbers, but then the stomach lurch began and the Montovani Orchestra version of "Love to Love You Baby" was forgotten. He clutched at me, looked green, seemed close to barfing. Fifth floor, led him out, hyperventilating. A minute passed, he gleamed at me sideways—"Gooood." Again. We rode up and down repeatedly. He warned me not to discuss the elevator with him if anyone else got on—"They will think I am a Bushman." He discovered that you cannot get to Floor 5 by pressing the buttons 2 and 3. I sent him on his first ride by himself and worried like an anxious parent.

I led him exhausted and happy to his room, prepared his first hot bath for him, and left him rolling happily in the tub, singing in his native Kipsigi.

I checked up on him an hour later. He was staring out the window, watching the traffic, shouting advice and directions to the drivers five stories below—"Watch out! Slower! Mind that lorry!" Like gnu, he said, pointing to the cars. It's because there are no buffalo here in Nairobi, I said. When I first brought him into the room and showed him the view, he swayed in vertiginous horror. Now he was leaning out a bit, although his right arm had a solid grip on the wall.

So, Richard, what has been the most interesting thing today? I asked. Maybe the bookstore, and how they cone that ice cream food. Not the elevator? I was surprised. No, not the elevator. Something was up, Richard looked furtive. Can I tell you a secret? he asked. You bet. He confessed: I have been on an elevator before, but I did not know it.

Earlier in the year, Richard had ventured to Nairobi for what was in fact the first time on a mission worthy of Kafka; he was going to change the name of his child. Richard, being modern, had insisted that his wife, in labor, hobble the miles down from their mountain village to go to the obscure bush hospital in their district, rather than just have the baby at home. By the time Richard had rushed there from the game park, some ninety miles away, the child had been born. All along, he (and perhaps even his wife—this is not clear) had decided on the name Jesse, for J. Jackson. When he arrived at the hospital, Richard discovered that the doctor, too impatient to wait for Richard's arrival to fill out the certificate (and, apparently, uninterested in whether the mother had any opinion about a name for the child), had chosen the name Hillary (although it now occurred to me that perhaps that doctor had consulted Richard's wife and this was actually the name she wanted). The certificate was already filed, the child's name was now Hillary, and the doctor threatened Richard with the police when he was churlish enough to express meek displeasure. So Richard was on the implausible mission of sojourning to the capital and its labyrinth of bureaucracy and incompetence to try to correct the name (unsuccessfully, naturally; Hillary thrives now with that appellation, and it occurs to no one, it seems, to simply defy the government and call the child Jesse anyway).

The manager of the tourist lodge where Richard lived heard about the planned expedition. He had always been fond of Richard and could afford a kind, generous gesture to someone of Richard's status in his camp (as opposed to someone who was an employee and would thus appear to be receiving favored treatment). He arranged for Richard to be able to stay at the hotel in Nairobi that was also owned by the family that owned the tourist camp.

Richard reached Nairobi, followed the manager's directions to the hotel. The man was sensitive and urbane enough to know that Richard would need help there but would be embarrassed by that need. The manager of the Nairobi hotel was awaiting Richard, greeted him, and tactfully explained that the entire room was his to use for the night, including the bathroom, explained the best news, that dinner and breakfast would come free to Richard as part of his staying there.

"Then, he took me into a small room with no windows. At first, I thought this would be the room I would be staying in, but it was something else. The door was closed, and suddenly it was roaring and my stomach was hurting so much I thought I was dying from Nairobi already. But the other man did not notice. Then, the door opened, and everything had changed! completely!—somehow, they had rushed and changed everything, the people and chairs were gone, the desk of the manager was not there anymore, instead there was this long path and these many doors. I did not know what was happening then, but now I know that was one of these elevators."

He was deposited in his room. The curtain was already closed and Richard never considered touching it, so he never had a clue that he was no longer on the ground floor. He washed in the sink (assuming that the bathtub was far too huge to possibly hold water to be wasted on washing a person. A cow dip, perhaps?), luxuriated in the bed, had an excited, panicked start when answering the manager's solicitous phone call (Richard had seen pictures of phones and how they were held).

All was bliss until Richard became hungry. He searched up and down the hallway for the dining room. No luck. He figured that the tiny room he had been taken into when his stomach flew had something to do with their changing the whole floor to the dining room, but he didn't know where the little door was, or how to make it open, or how to have the area outside that door changed into a dining room. He wandered up and down the halls, felt too ashamed to ask anyone a question, and eventually retired to his room, hungry and disappointed. By midnight, there was now the added fear of not being sure how he would get out in the morning, let alone get breakfast.

By dawn, he was up, with a plan. He had his things prepared, lounged in the hall, and spotted the first person leaving their room in a similar packed state. He followed them nonchalantly, soon found himself in the elevator. His stomach lurched, he attempted to keep his discomfort to himself, and soon the floor had been rearranged to the lobby. Relieved and with his hunger of secondary importance to his desire to escape, he bid farewell to the manager and fled.

"Aii, I wish I had known it was one of those elevators. I think that food must have been good, because this was a big fancy hotel. And they said I could eat all I wanted."

Later that evening, we went for more ice cream, in the hopes of healing the memory.

21

The Mound Behind the 7-Eleven

I am fairly hardened when it comes to the suffering of animals. Other more euphemistic terms might be used—I am pragmatic, or unsentimental, or internalizing. But I am hardened, I do not feel as much as I once did. When I was a kid, up through college, all I wanted to do was live alone in the bush with wild animals and study their behavior. Intellectually, nothing was as satisfying, as pure, as the study of their behavior in and of itself, nothing seemed as sacred as to just be with animals for their own sake, and the notion of animals being pained was intolerable. But my interests shifted, behavior for its own sake somehow began to seem insufficient. "Isn't this behavior miraculous?" became "Isn't this miraculous, how does it work?" and I became interested in behavior and the brain, and soon I was interested in the brain itself, and soon how its functioning fails. And by the end of the unstable years in the troop, my laboratory work had shifted exclusively to the study of diseases of the brain. Nine months each year I would spend in my lab, doing my experiments, and the suffering that the animals would endure there was appalling. They'd undergo strokes, or repeated epileptic seizures, or other neurodegenerative disorders. This is all to find out how a brain cell dies, and what can be done to prevent it—all to do something for the couple of million people each year who sustain brain damage from stroke or seizure or Alzheimer's disease. My father was nearly half a century older than I. Once he was an artist, an architect, a dean of a school of architecture, a passionately complex, subtle, difficult man. But he sustained one of those neurodegenerative disorders, and there were times that he could not identify family members, or tell where he was, or experience any of the pleasures of living that require an active, pulsating, inquisitive mind. And when I would sit in the laboratory, there were times where I'd think that there was nothing on earth that I would hesitate to do to learn how a neuron dies and how to bring my father back.

I tried to compensate for my work, but probably not enough. I remained a vegetarian when in America. I would work hard to cut every corner I could in my research, to minimize the numbers of animals, the amount of pain. But there was still dripping, searing amounts of it for them. My first day as a student when I was taught to do brain surgery on a rat, I threw up. Now, I was reaching the stage, as a postdoc, of beginning to train students, sending them off to begin the same process. I'd be horrified when my intuitions about the next step in my research would turn out to be wrong and a hundred animals would have paid for that dead end. I'd have dreams where I was Dr. Mengele—I'd wear a fresh new lab coat, and welcome the animals to their "hotel," the euphemistic nature of the word being discernible by them despite my Germanic accent. But unlike some Nazis, I was not just following orders, I was often giving them and was my own agent; but I was at war with the infarcts and ischemic cell changes and pan necrosis in my father's brain, and there was little I would not do to avenge his melting. And I was feeling less and less for the animals.

Thus, each year, I was having more of a need to return to the baboons. Among the dozens of other reasons to be there, it was good to be in a place where I was not cutting up the animals, where I was not killing them. It was good to be in a place where they didn't live in cages. In a perverse way, it was good to be in a place where they were more likely to kill me than the other way around. As an additional pleasure, I might even indirectly do them some good with my research—find out something about how some sort of environmental stressor disrupts their fertility, makes them more prone to an infectious disease. Small potatoes, but at least some pluses for a change.

One of the baboons died during a darting once. I will not tell who it was or how it happened—that story will wait for the final chapter. He died, and he was one of the ones I really cared about. Should one feel guilty about caring more for some baboons than others? Is one allowed to wish it had been a different animal? He died. Of all things, in my arms, while anesthetized, while in trouble. I tried to revive him. I did CPR, I shoved an endotracheal tube down his throat. I pounded his chest and infused an insane amount of epinephrine into him. And still he wouldn't breathe. He had actually made a death rattle, and each time I flung myself on his chest, he made a bit of a gargly sound again, and each time it triggered hope and shivers. Finally, I had pummeled and pushed and pounded and cursed until I was exhausted. I would have guessed that trying not to lose someone would be emotionally exhausting; I had no idea that it could be such a physical battle.

He was lying on his back when I gave up. I was sweating and hyperventilating, and I lay down on my back, with my head on his stomach, as if I were a child again with my father. I thought that if he had ticks, they would be all over me soon, but I did not move. I thought that I should dissect him, add his skull to my collection, but I did not move. Instead, I held his stiffening hand, and I must have slept a bit. I awoke to find a group of Masai mamas from one of the other villages, on their way to collect firewood, staring in frightened fascination. They pointed at my face and pantomimed tears on my cheeks. In Swahili, I said, "He is dead," and that seemed to do nothing to decrease their wonder or fear. It did not seem to explain anything to them, and they ran off.

In my sleep, I had decided. I carried him to a spot under a favorite tree, and dug a hole for him there. I would not leave him for the hyenas. The Masai do that with their dead. And with their dying. For a while, teaching American school kids that such things happened in certain cultures, and might even make a certain sense, would guarantee that abuse would be heaped upon you by some Southern senator, branding you as a cultural relativist or a secular humanist. It does make sense for some cultures, but it is still sad and creepy. Laurence of the Hyenas discovered a dead Masai child, perhaps two years old, abandoned near the hyenas once. She was wrapped in an old cloak, and her head was resting on a drinking gourd. In case she became thirsty in the afterlife? More likely because it was feared that the gourd had become contaminated with whatever illness she had.

I would not leave him for the hyenas, and dug instead. It was punishing work that left me with great respect for grave diggers and grave robbers. I thought the labor would cleanse me, but it just exhausted me. I would stop and rest on him some more, caress his head. The Masai women returned with their firewood and stood awestruck at the sight of me digging a grave for a baboon. They began to approach closer, but I shouted and gesticulated like some madman, and they fled.

The hole was done. I cradled him and placed him in. I arranged a circle of olives and figs, his main foods, around him, and thought, This is not because I believe in an afterlife, this is to confuse any paleontologists who dig him up. Then I sang Russian folksongs from my youth and Mahler's *Kindertotenlieder,* and covered him with dirt and covered the mound with acacia thorns to deter the hyenas, and I went and slept in my tent until the next day.

So that was how my first baboon died in my hands. In the coming months, because of the problem whose story I am not yet ready to tell, I returned to that tree again and again to bury more. But that was the first time. When the coming disaster swept over me, it reminded me viscerally of what I already knew, why, despite my childhood desire to be a primatologist and live in the field, I had retreated from that and spent only a quarter of my time out there. It was just too hard and too depressing. I had my hands quite full enough already trying not very successfully to keep individual brain cells from dying. It was too much to try just as unsuccessfully to save whole species and ecosystems. Every primatologist I know is losing that battle, whether their animals are being done in by habitat destruction or conflict with farmers or poaching or novel human disease or shit-brained government officials bent on harassment and maliciousness. The full-time primatologists I know always remind me of stories I read of Ishi, the last member of a particular Indian tribe, a person whose mother tongue was a dead language. Or they make me think of someone whose unlikely job would be to collect snowflakes, to rush into a warm room and observe the unique pattern under a microscope before it melts and is never seen again. Always a losing battle, and all very sad, and quite a bit too much for me, thank you.

So it was at the end of the unstable years, just after Nathanial had abdicated his alphaness, that I went to where the snowflakes are the rarest and nearest to melting, that I visited Fossey's gorillas and Fossey's grave.

Oh, what new can I say about Dian Fossey? She's been enshrined in the movies, featured in books; there will no doubt be posthumous Dian Fossey exercise videos. She was clearly the stuff of legend. She was a large, imposing, awkward woman who looked not one bit like Sigourney Weaver. By chance, the mother of a member of my lab went to high school with Fossey. The mother related that she was already difficult, withdrawn, marked. The lab member once brought in the yearbook. At age seventeen, Fossey had the hunted, ostracized, unhappy look of the high school weirdo destined to become either a reclusive field biologist or a serial murderer. At a relatively late age, she fell in love with the idea of Africa and of the mountain gorilla—the largest and last-discovered of any of the apes, studied in the field only once, cloaked in legend and misconception. Without any formal training, she decided to go to Africa and live with them. She encountered Louis Leakey, the famed paleontologist and sponsor of female primatologists, convinced him to send her to the Mountains of the Moon to study gorillas for a short stretch, and stayed on for decades. She immersed herself utterly in the gorillas, broke all the objective rules about not touching them, not interacting with them, and managed to observe astounding things about their behavior. In the process, she became more reclusive, more difficult, drove away possible collaborators and colleagues, isolated herself. She did little science of note beyond observing amazing things by sheer dint of her persistence, was openly contemptuous of most scientists doing fieldwork, and clearly wanted little more than to be a gorilla herself.

I met her once, as an undergrad at Harvard, in the mid-1970s. My scientific interests had not yet shifted from gorillas to baboons, and gorillas still resonated emotionally with me in an extraordinary way; during the intermittent periods of depression that plagued me, I was dreaming more about gorillas than about humans. Thus, it was not surprising that Fossey was one of the humans I most admired. On my wall, I kept a poem that Adrienne Rich had written about her. I thought I would swoon with pleasure at meeting her.

Fossey was at the university against her will. Despite her contempt for science and rejection of how most primatologists went about their work, she still knew more about gorillas than anyone, and other primatologists were interested. Her funding sources basically had to force her to act like a proper citizen of the scientific community—to finally finish her thesis, publish some of her information in scholarly journals, give a lecture or two. She was in Cambridge on one of those forced excursions, resentful and sullen. It was an evening seminar in the living room of the senior primatology professor, and it was jammed. Quickly, one had the sickened, guilty, voyeuristic sense of watching a bear forced to perform in some medieval circus. She sat with her knees drawn up to her chest and then suddenly burst out, pacing back and forth in front of the room, bent so that her hands hung near her knees. She mostly talked to herself, in a monotone, and nearly yelled at people when they asked questions. Once, she did yell. One professor had his young kid sitting on his lap, the kid making occasional four-year-old sounds, and suddenly Fossey stopped, pointed, and said, "Child, shut thy mouth or I will shut it for you." She rambled about her gorillas, showed that she was unaware of and disinterested in most of the questions that dominated the field, and was a bit incoherent.

I was mesmerized and more than a little bit horrified. Afterward, I went up to her and asked the question I had been preparing since I was ten—could I go to Rwanda as her research assistant and devote my life to the gorillas? She scowled at me and said yes, told me to write to her. She was allowed to escape shortly after that, I returned to my dorm in a transcendent euphoria and sent her that letter by midnight. Which she never answered. I later learned that this was her standard way of dealing with the acolytes and petitioners who would engulf her when forced into the public; say yes to anything, tell them to write, never answer.

Thus, my sole meeting with Fossey. Soon after that, her difficulties and difficultness began their attraction that was to finish her. In the rain forests of Rwanda, since time immemorial, were Batwa tribesmen, hunter-gatherers who lived by catching forest bucks with snares. Inevitably, a gorilla would step on a snare now and then and be trapped. Gangrene, death. The best evidence

224 • *Robert M. Sapolsky*

indicates that these first deaths were accidental. Fossey freaked. She began to fight the tribesmen, destroying their snares, their source of food. And they began to fight back. Things escalated, and soon they were killing her gorillas intentionally, dumping their decapitated bodies on the paths to her cabin, high up in the volcanoes, while she, in turn, kidnapped those tribesmen's children.

Ultimately, some of those killers were poachers of the worst sort, killing gorillas to sell as souvenirs, but some were just tribesmen living as they had always done. Some of the gorilla killings were savage and intentional, but some were accidents. Undeniably, a more stable, rational person would have dealt with the situation in a less inflammatory way, but a more stable, rational one would never have been there to witness what was happening.

Fossey, in a turnaround, became extroverted. She ran around the world lecturing about the killings of her animals and demanding help. Her gorillas were about to be finished, the last of them—the mountain gorilla is one of the rarest, most endangered of beasts on earth, and her population of a few hundred was one of the last. She opened the field site to students, collaborators—so long as they would fight the gorilla killers. Before long, there was a split in the conservation community. Some said, Yes, let's pour money in there, but not to her. She is too inflammatory, too provocative, as long as she is there, there will be revenge killings. Get her out of there, and pour money into the dirt-poor Rwandan game park service to get some rangers up there, armed, to make the place a real wildlife preserve. And the other half said, Give her money, give her guns, if there are going to be any gorillas surviving, it will be because of her, who else cares? The former group prevailed. Money poured into the Digit Fund, named for her most beloved animal, whose butchered body was left for her to find. A real, functioning, protective park service was established, enough interest was generated to start gorilla-watching tourism that has continued to fund the park and the local economy. The gorillas started to do better, perhaps increasing in numbers. And Fossey was sent away. Some sort of visiting adjunct professorship was rigged up for her at Cornell, where, by most reports, she sank into depression and alcoholism.

The final chapter was set. Against everyone's pleading, she returned to Rwanda and her gorillas. She fought with the poachers and the tribesmen, fought with the rangers who led the tourists that she loathed, fought with the agricultural tribesmen whose slash-and-burning was decimating the remnants of the rain forest, fought with the government. Her health was destroyed by drinking and chain-smoking and emphysema, trying to live in humid, high-altitude conditions. She could barely walk, had to be carried up to her cabin. Where she was murdered one night. The government lamely and unconvincingly blamed an American grad student and condemned him to death in absentia after making sure he had left the country, and everyone felt sure it was poachers or government rangers. The funeral service was held near her cabin, a week after Christmas, and was conducted by a missionary who said, "Last week the world did honor to a long-ago event that changed its history—the coming of the Lord to earth. We see at our feet here a parable of that magnificent condescension—Dian Fossey, born to a home of comfort and privilege that she left by her own choice to live among a race faced with extinction. . . . And if you think that the distance Christ had to come to take the likeness of Man is not so great as that from man to gorilla, then you don't know men. Or gorillas. Or God." And, as per her wish, she was buried in the graveyard of her slain gorillas, next to Digit.

It was six months after her murder that I visited the gorillas. I had tried to hitchhike to Rwanda years before and got nowhere. Now, I had finally passed that maturational stage when you can no longer afford the time to travel great distances by hitching, but cannot yet afford the money for something faster. I flew with two friends into Kigali, the capital, and we headed out toward the gorillas. There was a different feel from Kenya in many ways. For one thing, everyone was speaking French and was named Jean-Dominique and Boniface, which seemed oddly disconcerting to me. Another difference was the brutally dichotomized tribal tension, in contrast to the chaotic and shifting tribal alliances of Kenya. Here, nearly everyone was either of the Hutu or Tutsi tribe, and I could just smell the animosity, which was destined to explode a few years later into a genocide of the latter tribe by the former on a scale that would take the world's breath away, had anyone cared to notice it. And another key difference was a staggering population density, the highest on earth. Endless hills with endless terraces and endless farms to feed the dirt-poor country, people jammed in, every inch under cultivation, up to the very west, the very last edge of the country. There, forming the border between Zaire to the west and Rwanda and Uganda to the east, are the Ruwenzoris, the famed Mountains of the Moon, which continue here to the south as the Virungas, a ribbon of mammoth volcanoes between Zaire and Rwanda, rising up to more than 15,000 feet, rugged, jutting, one after another after another, snow on top spilling into the Congo, wild rain forest below. And because they are too steep for even the desperate farmers to try to squeeze food out of, on the saddles and slopes survive the last mountain gorillas on earth.

We had the typical hassles with the park officials, who had lost the reservations I had made more than a year before to see the gorillas, but who located them for a price. We splurged and stayed in the only real hotel in Ruhengeri, the town at the entrance to the park. It was a ramshackle old jobbie, dripping with colonial nostalgia. Parquet floors and old prints everywhere of Notre Dame, and a five-course meal with things like asparagus au gratin. We slept fitfully, feeling the volcanoes hovering over us, and were agitatedly ready by dawn.

We hiked up with park rangers, the men who find the gorilla groups each day for the eighteen tourists allowed in to see the three groups on display. The rangers were silent men who moved with smooth, frictionless gestures. Throughout the week I spent there, I noticed this in all the rangers who spent time around the gorillas—the need to glide silently and slowly around them.

We set off through the farm fields, already angled steeply where they weren't terraced, weaving our way through huts and rows of corn and kids fairly oblivious to us. At the end, a wall of bamboo and a slight forest path through it. In, winding higher up, steep unstable slopes. Bamboo everywhere, moss-covered hagenia trees that have always looked silly to me unless they are shrouded in mist. Higher, onto a saddle of one of the volcanoes, a view of forest ahead of us, a small lake, fields of bushes. Onward, the rangers macheteing a way through fields of stinging nettles. Clouds and mist and chills and heat, somehow all simultaneously. Sweating and shivering. Sliding down a deep ravine, clambering the way back up the other side, more nettles, more bamboo. A few hours had passed and yet the rangers continued their silent, coordinated movement. One would examine some broken bamboo shoots, another would sniff the flattened grass around there. Gorillas, but from yesterday, they concluded.

Another hour. Misty rain, but somehow warmer. More nettles. Something resembling a real path and a flattened clump of grass to the left of it. Large, fibrous, shredded turds in the middle, the type you would expect from a pro football player gone vegetarian. The gorillas. Fresh, last night's nest.

Pushing ahead, tired and excited and impatient. Down another ravine, and one of the rangers hears a murmur up the other side. We stop, silent, willing to invent the sound to convince ourselves that they are close, and suddenly, we hear the unmistakable murmur, deep, throaty, slow-motion, paternal. We rush/tiptoe up the other side and, on top of the ridge, I see my first wild mountain gorillas.

It was a group of perhaps a dozen. A prime-aged male—a silverback. Some females with infants, a few lurking younger males, some adolescents. The silverback played with the kids. The mothers fed, lumbering about with the infants carried dorsal. The two young males spent most of an hour wrestling, rolling around with each other, mouthing each other in restrained bites. They'd pant as they rolled and tickled each other, get exhausted from the excitement, and have to retreat to their separate corners to catch their breaths. Refreshed, one would pound its chest and they'd launch themselves at each other again. At one point, both ambled over to sit next to me and stare, one leaning in so close that the rangers forced me to lean back. They had a comforting, musty, damp smell to them, like opening a trunk from the mildewed corners of a cellar that contains forgotten beloved objects.

I had a flood of thoughts and feelings. At the first sight, I thought, Now my eyes will well up with tears, but I was too intent on watching for that to happen. I wondered what my social rank would be if I had wound up a mountain gorilla. I was mesmerized by their eyes; their faces seemed less emotionally expressive than those of chimps or even baboons, but their eyes, you wanted to go swimming in. I tried not to make eye contact, not only because it's bad field technique and discomforts primates, but because the act would make me want to confess to unlikely crimes. I found myself with the barely controllable urge to scream, or to gibber dangerously among them, or to rudely kiss one, so that they would stomp me to death then and there and stop my suspense. I thought, They are far less socially interactive than baboons, they're kind of boring in fact—thank god I didn't come to study them, I'd be a fourteenth-year grad student by now. And at the same time, I thought I never wanted to budge from my spot.

That night, sleeping in my tent on the mountain's slopes, I had a dream that summarized my feelings far better than I could when awake. It was a dream so tender, so ludicrously sentimental, so full of beliefs that I do not have when awake, that I still marvel at it. I dreamt that a certain brand of theology turned out to be true. I dreamt that God and angels and seraphs and devils all existed, in a very literal way, each with potential strengths and frailties much like our own. And I dreamt that the rain forests of the Mountains of the Moon were where god placed the occasional angel born with Down's syndrome.

My friends left the next day. I stayed another week, going back to the gorillas repeatedly. It was heaven, but with each day, I felt more depressed. The gorillas were wondrous, but the weight of what was gone, removed, unmentioned, unanswered, irrevocable, became heavier. I felt it in the park headquarters, where the posters on the park's history made more mention of nineteenth-century Belgian colonials than of Fossey. With the rangers, who would say, Yes, we knew Fossey, and then change the subject. With the gorillas, where you would watch a mother hold her child and nibble at bamboo, and all the while hear the farmers, their chickens, the school kids, 200 yards down the slope, where the slash-and-burning had finally stopped. On the miles and miles of empty rain forest paths aching with no more gorillas. And finally, from atop the nearly 15,000-foot Mt. Karisimbi, the highest point in the range, where I climbed to peer down and discover that the massive, endless, magisterial, mythic Virungas were nearly gone, a tiny narrow ribbon of forest engulfed by the infinity of terraces spreading from Rwanda to Uganda. It almost seemed like a domestic conspiracy on the part of the farms—an endless world packed with farmers trying to eke out a living, a world with no room for rain forests or the moon's mountains, a conspiracy to forget them altogether. It was as if just behind a 7-Eleven store in some innocuous Iowa farm town there was a mist-shrouded 15,000-foot mound on top of which was a book listing the dates of birth and death of every person who will ever live, and no one seemed to notice that the mound was there.

It was on top of that mountain that the week finally got to me and I had a night of African paranoia. You weren't allowed to hike alone in the range. Instead, a ranger had to be hired as a guide. Hauling to the top of the highest volcano around was clearly not their idea of fun, and the most junior of the rangers was given the task. From previous days of hanging around the rangers, I had noticed him and already had a dislike for him; even the other rangers seemed to ostracize him. He was a sullen, sloe-eyed kid, with a face like a mask and a tense air of violence about him. He mostly sat off on the side of the camp and seemed to get into a lot of monosyllabic arguments when he did interact. I wasn't crazy about heading off with him, and from what little I could read of him, the feeling was mutual.

As we started hiking, my dislike for my guide began to build. I could elicit nothing more than grunts out of him, as I tried in French, Swahili, English, my twenty words of Kirwanda. I slipped and fell on a wet rock at one point, and he laughed; it had a sneering, dismissive whine to it. Once, he flung stones at grazing forest bucks, probably both to hurt them and to deprive me of the view.

My dislike simmered, and his of me seemed to be doing the same. Somehow, these mutual feelings evolved, wordlessly, into competition, a childish angry race. We began to hike faster, moving more relentlessly, until we were racing up the mountain, seeing who would first ask to rest. We pushed harder and harder, through the rain forest, montane forest, patchy woodland, open moorland where we sank to our knees in mud, to stark open rock with patches of frost, from 7,000 to 14,000 feet in a few hours. The air got thinner, I felt an edge of altitude sickness, my vision got blurry, my chest throbbed. He climbed these mountains for a living, and I had the heavier pack, but sheer anger let me keep pace with him. *"Fatigué?"* he would ask in French, and I would gasp, *"Non."* Once, he spoke his longest pronouncement: *"Je pense tu es fatigué. Tu es mzee* [Swahili for an old man]. *"* I nearly sprinted after him, hoping to kill him. At one triumphant point, I got ahead for a minute, and was able to whisper the same breathless *"Fatigué?"* to him, while he gasped, *"Non."*

There was not even a hint of the mythic camaraderie that enemies are said to feel for each other in a tough battle. He was a stupid, cruel kid who threw rocks at animals in Rwanda's last rain forest, and I wanted to prove something to him, although I was not sure what.

We reached our goal, a corrugated metal shelter near the rim of the crater, just as an ice storm let loose. We lay in there, gasping, as the storm closed in and pounded on the metal. And there we stayed, from midafternoon until the next morning. We ate a bit, rice and French bread, but everything tends to taste sickening at that altitude. Your eyes throb, your balls throb, your head hurts constantly, your chest aches with each breath, everything is straining. At that altitude, my resting heart rate is usually about 110, which means you wake from presumably relaxing sleep already feeling like you've been climbing stairs.

We lay on the wooden floor, as far away from each other as the small shelter would allow. I tried to play recorder, but didn't have the breath; instead, I mostly thought about gorillas. He muttered to himself and scraped his name, Bonaventre, into the metal with his machete, all the while smoking in our closed hut at 14,000 feet, even after I asked him to stop.

So the hours passed, until sometime around nightfall, as I still lay there with my eyeballs throbbing 110 times a minute, it occurred to me for the first time to become afraid. Not only was Fossey murdered just six months before on this mountain, not only was it probably not the American student who did it, not only was it probably a government person, not only probably a ranger (I had now decided), not only was it probably this kid with the very same machete he was now holding, but tonight was almost certainly my night to get it. This may now sound facetious or exaggerated or farcical or just paranoid, but I was suddenly terribly frightened. I was alone on some volcano in a Central African country where I didn't know a soul, shut in this hut in the middle of an ice storm with a ranger, and I felt sure now the rangers had killed Fossey. As I reviewed the day, the week, my every word and action now seemed to have sealed my doom, to have convinced the watching rangers that I must be killed.

I was genuinely frightened, near to panic. I desperately wanted to escape. I struggled to control my breathing, thought to cry out for help. I lay awake most of the night, with my pocketknife opened at my side, and truly thought I was going to die. The ranger, meanwhile, spent the night talking in his sleep—mutterings, and harsh muffled barks.

At dawn, I felt foolish and angry and relieved, and felt I had been lucky this time. We struggled up the ice-coated rocks and were at the summit by

7:00. He sat, looked impatient, and kicked at rocks. I looked out over Rwanda, Uganda, Zaire, and tried to imagine that it was once all rain forest full with gorillas. He clearly wanted us to head down immediately; I could have stayed there forever. He was saved from that fate, as the clouds rolled in, obscuring all view and forcing us down.

If the goal of yesterday's race was to give the other a heart attack, today's was to get the other to break his leg. We ran down, silently; leaping down rocks, twisting and changing directions on the wet steep path. He presumably was in a rush to finish this job and return to sitting sullenly at the ranger station. I was in a rush to be away from this mountain and my sleepless night there, to be rid of this murderer.

We ran down the ice-covered rocks. We ran through the near frozen mud fields of the moorland down past the groves of trees and the rain forest and past the bamboo. And as we came to the saddle of the mountain, coming down a different path than we had taken up yesterday, the ranger slowed down. He didn't seem tired, and I couldn't imagine he was slowing out of concern for me. He suddenly seemed cautious, even uncomfortable. It was the nearest I could detect to an emotion on his face.

The forest had opened a bit, there were longer views, and a beautiful stream running alongside our path. We were walking slowly now, the ground was level. We crossed the stream on a log. Another minute walking, and the grove of trees near us parted. And then, with no warning, we were standing in front of Fossey's cabin.

It was plain, small, boarded. A Rwandan flag was flying over it. I walked over toward it, and the ranger motioned me away. I walked closer, and this silent kid told me in French, in Swahili, even in broken but understandable English, that it was not allowed. I walked past the cabin, and for the moment before he forced me away, I stood at the graves of Fossey and the other primates.

Fossey, *Fossey,* you cranky difficult strong-arming self-destructive misanthrope, mediocre scientist, deceiver of earnest college students, probable cause of more deaths of the gorillas than if you had never set foot in Rwanda, Fossey, you pain-in-the-ass saint, I do not believe in prayers or souls, but I will pray for your soul, I will remember you for all of my days, in gratitude for that moment by the graves when all I felt was the pure, cleansing sadness of returning home and finding nothing but ghosts.

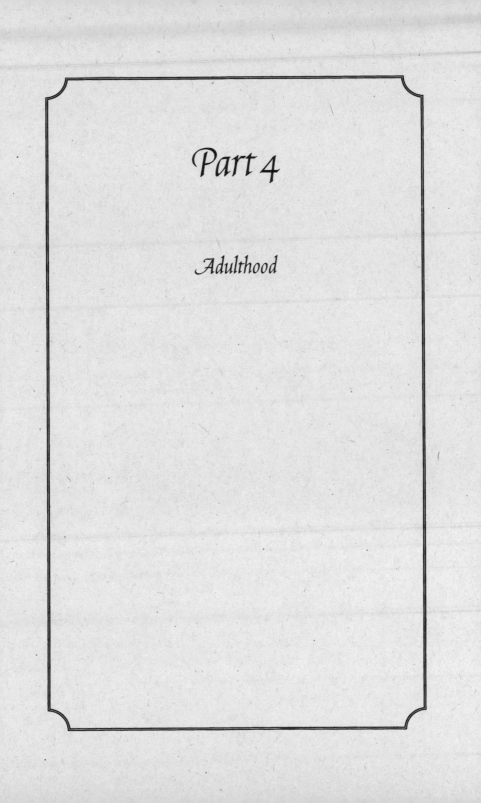

Part 4

Adulthood

22

The Baboons:
Nick

$\mathcal{I}$ didn't much like Nick, and neither did the rest of the troop, in that he had one of the most unappealing personalities I'd encountered in a long time. This was around the time that I was starting to pay attention to personality in a formal, scientific sense. For all those years, I had been focusing on the idea that rank helped determine the health of these animals, that lower-ranking males were more at risk for a variety of stress-related diseases. Rank was destiny, case closed. But my more recent studies suggested that there was more to a baboon's life than his rank. Your physiological profile was indeed influenced by rank, but, it turned out, even more important than that was the sort of society in which the rank occurred—for example, the hormonal profile of a high-ranking male in a stable hierarchy was extremely different during the unstable years. And while rank was important to physiology, an even more significant factor seemed to be whether you had the means to cope when times were tough, whether you were socially affiliated. Thus, independent of rank, males who did the most social grooming and sat in contact with other animals most frequently had the lowest stress hormone levels. This was the realm of an Isaac or a Nat. And, perhaps most importantly, personality was turning out to be crucial. For example, how type A were you?—if your worst rival in the troop showed up and took a nap fifty yards away, would you just keep on doing whatever you had been doing, or would you see it as a crazy-making, in-your-face provocation that would leave you in an agitated state? If you were the kind of baboon for whom a rival napping was a personal affront, you averaged twice the resting stress hormone levels of a male who took it all in stride, after controlling for rank.

So I was thinking a lot about personality, and Nick had a pretty sour one. Basically, he was the meanest baboon to show up since Nebuchanezzar, but, unlike the latter, he was also smart and disciplined and fearless. He was small and slight, which should have made me root for him, but he had a flinty meanness about him that canceled that out. He made you think of taut little guys with tattoos and prominent veins on their arms, the type who in bar fights demolish the big heavy sloppy guys with vulnerable beer guts. He didn't have tattoos, but he had a distinguishing nick on his lopsided face.

Nick joined the troop during the unstable years. He was still an adolescent, and you could almost read the contempt on his face as he watched the foibles of his elders playing Keystone Kops. Just gimme a coupla years, he seemed to be saying. Meanwhile, he dominated his age group. When he began to make his move into the upper echelon, he was confident and unflinching and played dirty. In a fight one day, he trounced the easily intimidated Reuben, who, in a gesture of submission, stuck his ass up in the air. Now, every baboon on earth knows what that means. It means you give up, you're conceding, uncle, *no mas.* And every baboon on earth knows that at that point, the winner is supposed to merely examine your bottom or mount you, or something conventionally demeaning like that, and it's all over with. Those are the rules, posted everywhere, just like three outs to a side. So Reuben sticks his ass up in the air, Nick comes over as if to examine his bottom, everything going fine, and at the last second, Nick leans over and gives him a deep slash in the ass with his canines. Those happy-go-lucky unstable years were over with a vengeance.

The guy simply wasn't nice. None of the females seemed especially crazy about him, particularly when circumstances put them in a consortship with him for a few days. He harassed the females, swatted at kids, bullied ancient Gums and Limp. On one memorable day, he took exception to something that poor nervous Ruth had done and chased her up a tree. Typically, at this point, the female takes advantage of one of those rare instances when it pays to be smaller than the males—she goes to the farthest end of a flimsy branch and hangs on for dear life, depending on the fact that the heavier male can't crawl out to where she is and bite her. And, typically, the male, thwarted, positions himself to at least trap the female, keeping her screaming on the precarious branch until he gets bored. So Ruth gallops up the tree, Nick after her, and Ruth leaps out to a safe edge. Nick promptly climbs onto a stronger, thicker branch directly above her. And then urinates on her head.

To make matters worse, Nebuchanezzar was in his prime now and had not mellowed over the years. He wasn't challenging Nick for the alpha position but was merely up to making lots of other baboons miserable. There were few saviors in sight. Reuben might have been a match for Nick, but he kept chickening out in every critical fight and even slunk past Nebuchanezzar.

Shem, a muscular new transfer kid, was still a few years away from the big time, as were the other new transfers, Jesse and Samuel. Adam was pathetic and hadn't a hope in the dominance game. David, Daniel, and Jonathan could each fight Nebuchanezzar to a draw but didn't have a chance against Nick. Isaac and Nat were disinterested, Benjamin and Joshua were no match, Saul was a crippled spectator from afar.

About the only hope for the troop was Gideon, but it was going to require some pretty clichéd script writing for him to save the day. Gideon was Nat's kid brother and had recently joined the troop. I had spotted him years before in the neighboring troop—a strikingly muscled kid hanging out with his big brother, the then adolescent Nat. Nat had done his migration years before, had had his brief disinterested reign over the troop before retiring to star in *Father Knows Best*. Then, just as Nick and the Reign of Terror was settling in, Gideon transferred. The scenario was set: Gideon, the young Jedi knight; Nat reluctantly comes out of retirement to be Obi-Wan Kenobi; they form a coalition, overthrow Nick, truth and justice triumph, Han Solo and Princess Leia have a consortship as the movie ends.

The only problem was that Nat was having none of that. Gideon had read the script perfectly, would challenge Nick, and, in the heat of the strategic moment, would barrel over to Nat and solicit a coalition. And Nat, distractedly, would groom Gideon, paying no attention to the hubbub and assuming his kid brother was there merely to reminisce about family picnics. Another day, Gideon would be midbattle with Nebuchanezzar, the outcome seesawing, our hero needing only a hand from his elder brother at a critical moment. Gideon would sprint over, try for a coalition, and Nat would earnestly hand him one of the infants clamoring all over him, hoping Gideon would just settle down and discover how much more rewarding fatherhood was than this fighting nonsense. More than anything, Gideon seemed disillusioned. What had happened to his idolized big brother? Nat, who had taught him everything he knew, goes off to a new troop for a few years and now just look at him—not eating red meat, attending antiwar rallies, hanging out with these girls with no bras. His bewilderment was palpable.

So Gideon seemed unlikely to take over the dominance hierarchy just yet, although he still seemed a shoo-in for Rookie of the Year. A far less auspicious debut in the troop was made by Absolom. He was a meek, squirrely kid who seemed way too young to have already made his adolescent transfer. I didn't recognize him from any of the neighboring troops, suggesting that he had wandered in from a long way off and had spent quite a long time by himself before gaining the most peripheral of footholds in this troop. His open, guileless face was marred by a large abscess next to his muzzle, which must have been painful, as he chewed only on the opposite side of his mouth. Absolom was atypically friendly, spending an inordinate amount of time eyebrow-flashing and face-pulling at all and sundry. With the exception of Benjamin and of Rachel's family, his greetings were generally ignored. Once, in a particularly adventurous moment, he face-pulled at me; I returned the gesture, clearly a surprise to him that I was conversant in baboon. He face-pulled again, I reciprocated, and we established an almost daily interspecies ritual.

As of late, Absolom had discovered girl baboons and festered in an adolescent voyeurism. The troop had grown accustomed to a certain degree of this obsessiveness in recent years. Jonathan still had a bad crush on Rebecca (who showed increasing foolishness in disdaining him, as he was growing into an impressive young baboon), Adam was still a follower of Short Tail, such that when either of those females was in consortship with some other male, Jonathan or Adam would shadow them at a discreet, forlorn distance. But Absolom took this to new heights. *Any* consortship in the troop, and he would be lurking around in the bushes nearby, trying to catch sight of the good stuff. Daniel would be in consortship with Miriam, who had never really made any of the males' blood run hot, and Absolom would be ten feet away, craning for a view of the action, holding his tail throughout. And let someone who was really hot stuff in the troop come into estrus—Devorah or Boopsie, for example—and Absolom was beside himself. One afternoon, Nick and Devorah, who was sporting a huge estrus swelling, sat quietly grooming each other. They were peripheral to the rest of the troop, secluded, no doubt building steam for a moment of even greater intimacy, when Absolom, who had silently slithered his way out to a branch of the tree just above them for a *really* good view, collapsed it under his weight and came crashing down on top of them. Naturally, despite his obsession, Absolom had not so much as been groomed by a female since joining the troop, let alone anything more exciting, and when I darted him, he was covered with skin parasites.

While Absolom may have been wishing away a few of his years so that he would be closer to his intimidating prime-aged years, some of the other animals must have been feeling the shadows lengthening. Saul was now an old baboon and had taken to limping the quarter mile over to the tourist lodge to contest the local baboons there for garbage scraps in the cans and lodge dump—an easier diet than foraging for hours a day. Aaron, even older and worse off, had retired to that garbage dump troop entirely. Inconceivably, the salacious and youthful Afghan was beginning to look tattered and worn by life, as were Miriam, who seemed to be aging fast from too many kids simultaneously throwing tantrums, and Ruth, no doubt done in by her constant skittish anxiety, which had only worsened with the years. Old Naomi was older than ever, and even middle-aged Rachel was beginning to look as tattered as her mother, sufficiently so that more than once I made the mistake of referring to her as Naomi in my field notes. And it was the season that I was shocked to discover that Isaac, and even Joshua and Benjamin, were beginning to get old man's veins—their skin was getting loose and brittle, their veins rolly and difficult to hit with a needle when I was taking blood. And they were beginning to get age spots, of all the disturbing things.

Some of the most remarkable behavior of that period was centered around aging as well. One actor was Gums, who, in his few years in the troop, had generated no anecdotes, seemed to have no notable traits beyond his vast decrepitude. The other was ancient Leah, mother of Devorah, number one–ranking female in the troop, no-nonsense, unlovable. Prior to that season, I am fairly sure I had never seen Leah and Gums so much as look at each other once. Nevertheless, I believe those two fell in love, or fell into each other's hairy arms, or at least fell into a set of behaviors unlike anything I have seen before or since. First, they simply disappeared. The troop slept in the forest, a grove of trees covering a few acres, and it was easy enough for me to lose track of a few animals in the underbrush there, or when the troop would be out foraging on the edge of a thicket. But when the troop was marching across an open field, during the dry season when there was nothing growing but stubble, you couldn't miss a soul. And Leah and Gums just up and evaporated one day. For an adolescent or prime-aged male, this would not be surprising—he was transferring, or at least checking out the possibilities of some other troop. Let one elderly animal disappear, and the hyenas or a lion would be the inevitable suspect. But the two oldest animals in the same day?

There was no sign of them in the neighboring troops, nor of them rummaging through the garbage cans of the tourist lodge. Neither was back in the forest, too sick to come out and forage. I checked the hyena dens for bones, dodged buffalo in the streambed of the forest searching for a fresh skull. Nothing. No one seemed to miss Gums (the fate for most males), but Devorah seemed distracted with the absence of her mother. Days went by, then a week, and I had given up on them, assuming that both had been predated on the same day.

Then, a few days later, I left the baboons midday and drove back to camp via a circuitous track through the backcountry behind the thickets that the baboons frequented. And at the far end, in a field the baboons would go to once in five years, I found the two of them. Together, neither foraging nor grooming, but sitting near each other. As I approached them, Leah, an animal habituated to humans observing at close range for nearly two decades, glanced up wild-eyed and stiffly loped off to the nearby thicket, followed by the equally wild-eyed Gums.

The next afternoon, as the troop took a route in the opposite direction, placing them ten miles away, I returned to the same remote corner, tracked them even farther up the back end of the thicket. And I spotted them in silhouette at a distance, sitting exposed on a windswept ridge in an area teeming with wildflowers and lions. I never saw them again.

Another event during that period would have been extraordinary with anyone as the protagonist, but was made even more so since it involved an astonishing display of heroism on the part of the unlikely Benjamin. It was midafternoon and the baboons were lollygagging along. Hot as hell, the time of day when predators were most likely sleeping, and everyone's guard was down. The troop came over the top of a streambed and barreled right into a semi-dozing lion. Chaos, screaming, everyone scattering every which way, as the lion leapt up. The big males, naturally, did their thing, which was to hightail it up the safest trees around. The females, in contrast, sprinted to grab their offspring before heading for the trees. The lion was acting somewhat like a kid in a candy store, starting to sprint after one animal, changing her mind and starting in another direction, overwhelmed by choices. The net result was that she managed to grab no one and stood in the middle of the field, exhaling in exasperation, surrounded by a troop of screaming, treed baboons.

Then all of us—the lion, the baboons, and I—noticed the two kids. They were yearlings, off on the edge, who had climbed up a tiny sapling of a tree, one that bent nearly horizontal within about five feet of the ground, one that would deter a lion for about ten seconds. They were Afghan's and Miriam's, and both moms had been cut off at the opposite end, the lion between them and their kids. General panic and hysteria, as the lion began toward the sapling. Now, the outdated primatology textbooks would go on about how the alpha male would now come to the rescue, as per his job description. And, as I've noted, what actually happens is that a genetic self-interest holds sway—someone will usually do something self-sacrificial only if it involves saving close kin, saving someone who shares lots of genes with them. Tough luck for these two, neither had a really obvious father who had been claiming them—in contrast to the paternalism of, say, Joshua, for Obadiah, Ruth's child from their adolescent dalliance. Most of the big males wa-hooed their heads off at the excitement of having a good view of what was going to happen next, the females were alarm calling, Afghan and Miriam were running up and down the trees frantically, when, from out of nowhere, Benjamin comes tear-assing in. If during his brief reign as the alpha male he had shown how little he understood modern evolutionary thinking by trying to kidnap the adult Devorah against the menacing Menasseh, now he was showing a similar lack of scholarship—there was no way in hell either of these kids was his. But he comes roaring in, yelling, threat-grunting, gets to the base of the sapling before the lion, and plants himself there. The lion approaches, Benjamin begins snarling and lunging, canines bared. I'm horrified, stunned, mesmerized—as is everyone else. The lion approaches, Benjamin begins to back up the tree, and you can basically see him will himself forward again. He could jump down and run to safety in a second, but he lunges forward, snarling like a lunatic. And it's working. The lion has stopped, now about five feet away, flinching each time Benjamin lunges. She tenses for a spring, lifts a paw . . . and paws at the ground a second and then walks off. Screw it with this crazy baboon in my face, and she returns to where she'd been napping. The two kids run down the tree to their moms.

I'm not sure what I was expecting next. That Miriam and Afghan would groom Benjamin for the rest of time, or at least organize a parade for him. That all the guys would slap him on the back. Everyone continues alarm calling at the lion for a while and then abruptly returns to feeding, while Benjamin bounces around up in a tree, breaking branches in some form of agitated displacement. The rest of the day passes without incident.

During the reign of Nick, most of the changes of membership in the troop were among the younger animals. Obadiah came of age and pushed off for parts unknown, never to be heard from again. Scratch, named for the deep gouge on his nose, was an awkward loopy subadult who joined the troop and went nowhere in the hierarchy, was even pushed around by the hapless Adam, and therefore contented himself to lethargically dominating Absolom and Limp. Jesse, another adolescent transfer, introduced a new behavior, giving credence to the notion of "cultural differences" among different populations of the same species of primates. He came from a troop two territories to the south, living along the river that formed the Kenyan-Tanzanian border, and had clearly spent a lot of time navigating streamlets. He introduced the habit of walking upright across water. Whether this was his own invention or a habit of everyone in his old troop, whether it served some obscure adaptive purpose like reducing exposure to water-borne parasites, or merely saved a baboon from the discomfort of getting his hands *and* feet wet, I never knew, but soon all the younger baboons were crossing streams bipedal.

It was the season that Rebecca had her first child (alas, almost certainly not by the heartbroken Jonathan, whom I never saw get close to her throughout that estrus period). Primiparous mothers—those with their first child—are rarely particularly skillful, but Rebecca was plain awful. She forgot the kid when she left a group of other females, slapped him frequently, couldn't seem to learn how to position him to ride on her back, so that he sprawled sideways, clutching the base of her tail. One day, as she leapt from one branch to another in a tree with the kid in that precarious position, he lost his grip and dropped ten feet to the ground. We various primates observing proved our close kinship, proved how we probably utilized the exact same number of synapses in our brains in watching and responding to this event, by doing the exact same thing in unison. Five female baboons in the tree and this one human all gasped as one. And then fell silent, eyes trained on the kid. A moment passed, he righted himself, looked up in the tree at his mother, and then scampered off after some nearby friends. And as a chorus, we all started clucking to each other in relief.

So passed that season, with Rebecca slowly learning how to mother, Absolom lurking in the bushes, Nick harassing everyone. He put me in my place in the dominance hierarchy once, and in a particularly galling fashion. It was early morning in the forest, and I had just pulled off a particularly pleasing darting of Reuben. He had been plodding along in a sleepy, just-woke-up manner, and I timed the darting for the instant when he came through a break in the bushes—the dart caught him squarely in the haunch just as his front half disappeared behind the next bush so that he didn't have a chance of seeing what happened. The plan then was for him to obligingly walk a few feet, sit down comfortably in a secluded spot, and pass out. Instead, Reuben lunged at the nearby Adam, zigzagged across the forest, and crossed the deep stream that cut through it, right past an unsavory-looking buffalo. Pain in the neck. I watched until I was certain he was beginning to go under to the anesthetic and unlikely to wander off further, and then began the five-minute drive around to his side of the stream, since the buffalo kept me from crossing on foot.

As I rounded a bend, with his now-prostrate body in view, I suddenly spotted a large male baboon moving toward him quickly. I tensed; it was Nick. It is essential to keep very close watch on a baboon when he is going down, not only because he is likely to wander off and get lost in the bushes when the anesthetic hits, or because he might hurt himself going under to the anesthesia, but for fear that a rival male might maul him during these vulnerable minutes. And now here was Nick barreling down on the semiconscious Reuben and there was no way for me to get to the latter and protect him in time.

I scrambled to get another dart ready to try to hit Nick, but I was too far away. I thought of leaping out of the car yelling and waving my hands. I hit the horn repeatedly, but Nick still kept coming. Reuben managed to lift his head and focus on Nick, now just a few feet away, and gave a barely conscious fear grimace.

Slowly, forcefully, Nick placed a hand on Reuben's shoulder, the other on his haunch. Then, Nick leaned back and bellowed a wa-hoo call audible throughout the forest, one that would draw the attention of all the baboons still up in the trees. After holding his pose, Nick marched back into the underbrush.

I couldn't believe it. That bastard had just taken credit for my darting.

23

The Raid

$\mathcal{B}$y the criteria of all sorts of different tribes, I was now an adult. In America at large, this could be proven by my finally possessing a credit card. Within my tribe of eggheads, I had actually gotten a real job as a professor. And among the Masai, I returned during the reign of Nick with the most palpable symbol possible—after all those years of responding to any hint of intimacy by fleeing to my tent, I had finally found someone whom I wanted to flee to my tent with.

I had met Lisa toward the end of my postdoc in San Diego, just as I was about to move to Stanford. In my first conversation with her, I was already scheming, trying to convince her to move to the Bay Area—"You, of all people, would appreciate San Francisco," I said, knowing neither her nor the first thing about San Francisco, but deciding that a pronouncement like that might be effective. And, ultimately, it was.

We were a funny combination of partial similarities. We were both lapsed field biologists, with me spending more and more time each year in the lab. Lisa had started off as a marine biologist, winding up doing some deadening research study on hermit crabs or some such thing, enough to convince her that this wasn't her full-time destiny. Since then, she had moved into clinical neuropsychology. We both came from old-left families. For me, back in Brooklyn, this meant growing up with elderly relatives screaming at each other in Yiddish about Stalin's betrayal of Trotsky, whereas for Lisa in Los Angeles, this meant hanging out with the likes of Pete Seeger and Joan Baez. We were both firm atheists. For me, it represented the outcome of much Sturm und Drang and twisting of my innards, while for Lisa, it had the relevance of rejecting the Easter Bunny. And we both came from multicultural communities—but for Lisa, this meant marching in Cinco de Mayo parades, whereas for me, it had meant knowing all the proper ethnic slurs by some precocious age.

She had a wonderfully sardonic sense of humor and sang like a dream. She actually knew about how the real world worked—in contrast to me—but that

244 • Robert M. Sapolsky

hadn't soiled her sentimentality. She worked with her patients with Alzheimer's disease or head injuries with an effectiveness and gentility that moved me to tears. We turned out to have a similar fondness for Old Testament names. And she was beautiful. Soon, we were passing the time on a flight to Kenya, Lisa planning our wedding invitations, me figuring out what I was going to tell Soirowa when he asked how many cows I had paid for Lisa.

It was wonderful, getting to reexperience Africa for the first time, vicariously, through Lisa. It was also impossible to resist playing the old Africa hand, given my weathering years of experience. I tried to give Lisa some sense of what a maneuvering, predatory place Nairobi was and promptly fell for an entirely new scam that she saw through in about five seconds. Once we got to camp, Lisa was extremely nervous about the army ants that she had been warned about, and I laughingly told her that we would go weeks without seeing one. Naturally, our second night in camp signaled the start of a half decade of virtually nightly army ant tidal waves that repeatedly rousted us from our tent. And she was a better darter than I within about two weeks.

Lisa's presence opened up all sorts of new vistas. Camp was suddenly filled with all the kids from the village, hanging out to play, which made me realize that when I was there by myself, I must have seemed like a forbidding weirdo. Rhoda and the women also now made daily appearances to fill Lisa in on gossip that I hadn't had an inkling of—who was sleeping with whom, who wasn't sleeping with whom when you would have guessed them to, which man was spending each night rushing from the hut of one of his wives to that of another and another, convinced he was finally going to catch one of them with another man. . . . What did I know about any of this? Soon, Lisa got her first invitation to a clitorectomy, something I'd never so much as heard a whisper of before. Then there was the day that two prostitutes from the staff quarters at the tourist lodge came to camp, one of them hoping for some sort of medicine for what seemed like a venereal disease. Soon I'm sitting there with my medical books and Swahili dictionary, dead white male, arduously preparing the sentence, "Have you been having any discharge from your vagina as of late?" when Lisa just pantomimes blowing her nose, holding her hand as if it were wet, and then as if that wetness were flowing from between her legs—and got an emphatic "Yes" from the woman.

Having failed dismally to come off as an old Africa hand based on skills, I attempted to pass myself off as one the more traditional way, which was to go on constantly in a tiresome manner about how everything had changed from the good old days—"Why, when I first got here, the nearest whatever was forty miles away, and there was no such thing as a . . . , and you couldn't go twenty feet without being chased by a . . . and now the whole place is just Disneyworld." Lisa didn't pay a whole lot of attention. Which was just as well, since within a few weeks of her arrival, we got a pretty emphatic lesson about how little had actually changed.

It was the year that Samwelly had moved on, having decided that he really needed a job for more than just the three months a year I was around. He took a job at the local tourist camp, sharing a room with Richard in the staff quarters, running security, designing the gardens, reconstructing the cabins, diverting the river when necessary. He would still drop over in camp at every opportunity to help with any architectural problems that might arise.

It became natural for Soirowa to move into camp with us. He brought along a distant relative, a kid named Wilson, who had come from the other end of Masai land for a prolonged stay with Soirowa's family. They were your proverbial city and country cousins. Soirowa is the nearest I've met to the sort of noble, taciturn Masai who hangs out with the likes of Robert Redford in the movies. Wilson, in contrast, bordered on the effete, at least by Masai standards. He came from a different branch of the Masai, from a clan north of the county seat, which had long ago abandoned traditional ways. He spoke a considerable amount of English, dressed in Western clothes, came from a family that prided itself on its ability to farm maize, of all the un-Masai things. We suspected that in the local village, he was regarded as somewhat of a sissy. He was barely out of adolescence, gangly and loopy and uncoordinated, and his emotions spilled out all over the place in the most un-Masai fashion. He became downright doleful when he was unhappy, he giggled nervously when he watched me take testicular biopsies from baboons, he flapped his hands hopelessly and fell all over his feet when Lisa would tease him about something. One evening, Soirowa told us about his coming of age, his killing of a lion as part of his warriorhood. We asked Wilson whether he had done the same. No, I had to go to school, he lamented. We wondered if Wilson had come to stay with distant cousin Soirowa in the hope of some real bush Masai rubbing off on him.

Thus, we passed our days, Soirowa being the one to venture into buffalo-infested thickets for firewood when the rest of us were too chicken, Wilson the one to climb excitedly all over the car engine, checking the spark plugs daily. Then, one morning, the wailing began.

Richard, Lisa, and I were darting in one of our least favorite places, weaving through tourists, tents, vehicles, as the baboons wandered through the camping sites. We were getting ready to dart someone or other when the wailing began on the ridge behind the campsites, up where the villages began. Richard, who knew the Masai pretty well by now, immediately tensed. There is trouble, he said. The wailing continued, built, seemed to float between the two villages, a strangulated rhythmic cry that would only occasionally take on a human quality. We stood transfixed, breathing hard, trying to figure out what was going on; the tourists, taking our cue, were beginning to line up behind us, concerned, vigilant. "Maybe we should go over, see if someone needs some help," Lisa suggested. "Maybe we should get ready to get the hell out of here but fast," I retorted.

Masai women were pouring out of the village, running to the next one, all the while wailing, waving their hands above their heads in a histrionic stagy way that was all the more unnerving, since the Masai are rarely histrionic or stagy. We thought that there might have been a murderously awful fight in the village, the frightened lamenting women pouring out to seek shelter in the next village, until we noted that the women were running back and forth. Soon the wailing was piercing from both villages. To our considerable alarm, we saw that men were now running around like headless chickens as well. More villages joined in the wailing, up and down the river. "They are calling for help," said Richard.

We all stood watching the inexplicable tumult, as if it were a tableau, something colorful and excited and native, captured in this rare *National Geographic* footage. We stood there gawking. The tourists behind us stood there gawking. And something reasonably terrifying happened to the camp guys standing behind them. The camping companies that would bring the tourists to these sites would send out guys from the agricultural tribes, based in Nairobi, as the tour leaders and cooks. But up and down the river, local guys from the Masai villages were hired for the scut work—guarding the camp, peeling potatoes, putting up tents. These were men usually fairly soiled from the detritus of their cross-cultural experiences—dressed in worn hand-me-downs discarded by the tourists, University of Somewhere shorts, El Paso chili bake-off commemorative T-shirts; ex-warriors who habitually took on the subservient, watchful air of people obsessed with handouts from the tourists.

So we and the tourists are standing there, and Joe Blow Masai, whom the tourists were earlier putting through the silliness of learning to do the bunny hop or something, Joe Blow, who is supposed to be peeling potatoes while this wailing is permeating everywhere—something happens to Joe. He runs behind a bush, and suddenly he tears out—his torn Waikiki Open T-shirt is discarded, he's wearing his red cloak, he grabs a spear that has materialized from out of nowhere, and he's gone. Up and down the river, at all the campsites, all the meek potato-peeling Joes run into bushes, emerge as warriors, and, wailing, run off into the *National Geographic* film.

It was a Kuria raid. Once the Kuria were just another tribe that got savaged by the Masai with regularity. But because they live south of the arbitrary line in the Serengeti that separates Kenya from Tanzania, their luck has changed. Tanzania is poorer than Kenya, the army is paid far worse, and some Kuria discovered that army guys could be paid to "lose" their weapons. Frequently, Kuria tribesmen who were army men themselves would lose their guns just before their discharge. And suddenly, the Kuria had automatic weapons to use when paying their respects to the Masai.

This time they had raided during the moonless night. Most of the cows were about twenty miles west, at a temporary corral. The Kuria had hit there, doing some shooting, stealing the cows. A Masai runner with the news had just covered the twenty miles, reached the village as we began our darting, and the wailing began, spreading from village to village.

The Kuria had had a few hours' start, but they were lumbering through the grasslands with hundreds of cows, protecting them from predators, abandoning the slow ones with calves. The Masai warriors were grouping now and were about to do something perfectly traditional, if outlandish: they were going to run the thirty-odd miles after the Kuria and their cows, chase them down to the Tanzanian border, and, with their spears, face off against the guns to get the cows back.

Warriors were running every which way with spears. A first group sprinted past, crossed the river, began their run. Other groups were forming. Richard, Lisa, and I did the logical thing. We drove the car into thick bushes and hid. It seemed perfectly logical that our Masai neighbors would, any moment, confront us excitedly with their spears and volunteer us to drop them off at the battlefront. The last time the Kuria hit, two Masai got killed. The time before that, when the Kenyan rangers (predominately Masai) responded fast enough to get into it, twenty-two Kuria were killed. No, thank you, but I thought they'd be unimpressed if I tried to explain that my insurance policy explicitly forbade driving into battles against men with automatic weapons. So we hid in the bushes.

Eventually, the coast seemed clear and we scooted for camp. Halfway there we ran into Soirowa. His cows were gone too, and he was about to run to Tanzania with his spear. The usually stoic Soirowa was crying with rage, shivering with emotion and anticipation. He was waiting for us, not for a lift (we later realized, a bit shamefacedly but with relief as well, that the Masai would no more think of asking us to drive them into battle than to ask for advice on bleeding cows. This was a purely Masai affair), but to tell us of his departure. "I am going to get my cows in Tanzania," he said, remembering to reassure us that he had collected firewood, before sprinting off to face the men with guns.*

Impressed, shaken, excited, we went to camp, where we found Wilson puttering about, making tea. Hiya, Wilson, so what do you think of all of this? He was not from here, it wasn't his cattle. "Those Kuria, those people are fuck." He was just learning how to curse in English. "They take the cows with guns, and now the Masai have to run to Tanzania. Even Soirowa, all his cows. Maybe he will get killed fighting them." Incongruously, he chuckled a bit, passed us more tea.

Throughout the day, Wilson went about life as usual. Lisa was more than a bit astonished at the whole spectacle. She kept grilling Wilson. Are they really going to run to Tanzania? "Yes, maybe for two days." How can they do that? "They are strong, they are warriors." Just like that, they run to Tanzania and have to fight. Wilson, does this happen in your place also, people come and take your cows and then you have to fight? "Oh no, we are not like these Masai, running around in their cloaks. We raise maize," he said proudly. No cows at all? I thought all Masai have cows, love them. "No, myself, no cows. I do not like cows, not like these dirty Masai, always thinking of their cows."

She probed. So you do not care about these cows and the Kuria, you would not go running to Tanzania now. "Oh no," he said with sudden emphasis. "I would go, myself, I would run to Tanzania right now." But why didn't you go? "Someone has to watch camp," he said in a disappointed, petulant tone, as if he had to stay inside to practice his violin while the other boys got to torture cats. "I would run to Tanzania too, I would fight the Kuria."

Wait, people are going to get killed fighting, why should you go, these are not your cows.

"I would fight them, I am not afraid to die."

But you don't even like cows.

"No, I do not like cows. But I am not afraid to die for the ways of the cow."

And with that, he turned his attention to more pressing interests, reminding Lisa of her promise to teach him how to make the toast of the French.

---

*The Masai rangers and the Masai warriors converged on the Kuria at about the same time and routed them—one injured Masai, two dead Kuria, all but six cows retrieved.

24

Ice

Oh, bliss! Euphoria! Lisa and I climbing up an African mountain to reach a farming village, haul up a guitar and recorder, and then spend an evening by the fire, clustered in close with the entire village, teaching them Paul Robeson songs. Ecstasy! Socialist-summer-camp/Eastern-European-folkdancing/free-the-Rosenbergs/Passover-prayer-for-Palestinian-independence/don't-eat-iceberg-lettuce-don't-shave-your-legs-or-armpits *heaven!!* Sitting, watching the fireglow of excited faces, kids sleeping in their parents' laps, people holding hands, leaning against each other, learning to sing "Go Down Moses," "Blowin' in the Wind." "Got no penny to my name, you hear the whistle blow one hundred miles." Nobody here knows what pennies are, or miles for that matter, but who cares, I can't understand the Kipsigi tribal songs that they are teaching us back, *it doesn't matter,* everyone still sways and claps hands at the "Ain't gonna study war no more" part. Oh, more pleasure than I can stand, dip me into agar right now, freeze this moment for the natural history museum, put me in the display case as the euphoric liberal.

Going for a visit to Richard and Samwelly's home village. Hardly even the term for it. Drive through Masai country, empty flat grassland, and eventually, a hundred kilometers in, the hills start, the farms start, Kipsigi tribal country, until finally, endless rolls of gentle mountains, and every inch being farmed. Hard to tell what constitutes a village. In each valley, a trading post—a spring, a store with sugar, milk, and flour, a school, a dispensary manned once a week. And then, all over the mountain, a mud-thatched hut for every half dozen acres or so of maize. Can't tell if, when they say "my village," they mean each of their houses, the houses of their immediate family, or everyone on that mountain. Everyone related in complex near-incestuous ways, one village idiot per mountain, one wife beater, one young Turk building the first tin-roofed house, one old shaman, everybody else just up to their ears with maize and chickens and nondescript dogs and cows wandering through the hut and donkeys hauling up water and endless kids and big excited hellos. Hours to get to the top of the mountain. Drive in from the last gravel road, five kilometers away, and then just bash through the cow path, people pouring out excited, never been a vehicle this far up before, certainly never a vehicle carrying whites intent on singing rounds and old union songs. Whooping, huzzahing, people running alongside the vehicle, kids in school shorts pouring out to clear the rocks out of the way, to help heave us over the tough spots, fight our way up the mountain over the old cornfields in four-wheel drive. Eventually, we give up, start hiking up with a caravan of people wanting to carry the sleeping bags, the guitar, the box of surprises. Excited marching line snaking up the mountain past the distant relatives hollering from the field to come have tea, Richard and Samwelly proudly leading the procession, prodigal sons returning with their pale friends. People start singing on the slopes, cows come up to nuzzle you. Heaven!

Up top. Maize and trees and views of everywhere and shade underneath Richard's house. Lisa and I try surreptitiously to hug each other—"This is so wonderful it's unbearable"—and the kids catch us, giggle, come and hug us too. People give you flowers, shaking hands with the parents and sisters and brothers' wives and the folks just passing through. Tons and tons of roasted maize brought out to you to be eaten, and you haven't even sat down yet. The sick kids are soon brought in, vitamins and antibiotics and ointments passed out, appropriate cluckings and lectures about cleaning the kid's eyes or making sure he gets milk each day. Balloons passed out. The kids run away in fright, and we have to teach them how to bounce them around and slap them, but not too hard. Universals, as based on observations of Kipsigi, Masai, and Brooklyn kids: all kids, within ten minutes of understanding the principle of blowing up balloons, will blow one up, untied, go over to their friend, and let the air expel by the friend's rear end, making a fart noise. One kid discovers that you can blow up a balloon, let the air expel through my recorder, and make it play—reinventing the bagpipe. We tie a balloon to the roof with dental floss, and everyone plays tether ball with it. One kid, off on the side and moping after being yelled at by his parents. In a salute to his pre-agricultural ancestors, the kid had dug a hole in the path, covering it with fronds and leaves, and trapped the neighbor kid in his pit. No poison spikes, though, just some minor excitement and a good spanking. "You do that to elephants, not to Kimutai next door." He still sniffles but eventually plays.

More things we've introduced to the mountain, in addition to balloons and dental floss: rice, watermelon, eyeglasses, Band-Aids, soap bubbles. The possibilities are endless. By the afternoon, Lisa is helping one of the guys study for his high school exams. Basic geometry, English grammar, how to decide if a field should be planted in straight lines or contours. What do we know about that? I, meanwhile, am inundated by a kid who wants to quiz me on geography. "How many kilometers in your river, The Mississippi? How many cows in your province, The Minnesota? How many metric tons of maize in your district, The New Jersey?" I get irked, as I decide he's just trying to show me how much more he knows about The New England and places like that than I do. As revenge, I have announced that I will teach him the important words in English that he must learn to get ahead, and I am soon drilling him on 1920s gangster slang. Fedora. Rubout. Gun moll. Running board. Bimbo. Speakeasy. B-girl. Richard catches on, lectures him solemnly on the need to learn the terms, teach them to the other kids on the mountain. Later in the day, as we describe how we dart baboons to the interested crowd, the kid says, "Oh, so you rub out on the baboons." Yes, indeed; we congratulate him.

Late afternoon, picture time. Up and down the mountain, families pouring out as we take photos and promise copies next time we're there. Pictures are still novel enough here that Kenyans are subject to the same photography heebie-jeebies that Americans had in 1900—no photo is ever candid, no subject ever smiles, only the finest of clothing is worn. People have been changing clothes all afternoon, everyone in this dirt-poor village washing and sewing and patching. Group portraits, beloved babies held high, favorite cows at the centerpiece. Those who've been to school invariably insist on being photographed holding an open book, arm lifted in the air, orating at the mountain. All these vibrant multicolored crowds exploding with energy, reduced to deathly serious, near-poignant daguerreotypes.

Evening. Mounds of potatoes and cabbage; one child and one donkey have been dispatched down to the store to bring up the main treat, bottles of soda for everyone. A goat has been slaughtered, and various distressing and unidentifiable organs are passed to us first as honored guests; Lisa, who came to Kenya as doctrinaire a vegetarian as I had been years before, who had recognized that the juncture would come of having to choose between the morality of not eating meat and the morality of being a good guest in a place like this, plows into her goat innards with gusto and praise. Pleasure, intimacy, everyone leaning in and happy, eating like hogs. We start to sing, teaching the songs. Julius, cherubic teenager whom Lisa had been quizzing on geometry, leads the countersinging, teaching us Kipsigi tunes, in a delicate near-whispered voice, face contorted with concentration. Three tough-demeanored, near-thuggish men, distant cousins, have sat silently at the back of the room throughout, not really participating. They suddenly fall into serious, whispered, sustained discussion of considerable intensity among themselves before announcing, with Richard as their messenger, that they have a song, a special song, that they would like to sing. This turns out to be "Three Blind Mice," sung with near-religious fervor in astonishing falsettos. More singing; we are taught religious songs about Babylon and Zion and facing the Lord. It occurs to me that if you are the sort of missionary who, instead of trying to cure river blindness or build schools by hand or promulgate liberation theology in the face of right-wing death squads, merely sits around with some happy folks and sings songs, you have a fairly easy, pleasurable life.

Finally, a break in the singing, time for the main event of the evening. I hate magic tricks, always have, have no capacity to figure out what is going on, am irritated by the whole process. But I will admit it, I have a magic trick to do. The old "make a handkerchief disappear into your fist while you've actually stuffed it into a fake thumb that no one noticed." These are people who have never seen a movie, a TV program, or a magazine, never heard a machine-derived sound except for a car and radio and some turbine that grinds maize at the village store. They are simply flabbergasted. In the paraffin lamplight, I stuff the handkerchief into my hand, while mesmerized faces watch closely. Clump my fist up, blow into it three times, and—hand opened—*gone*. Gasps. Over and over, people alarmed each time, backing away from me. Irresistibly, I have to begin hamming things up, pulling off cheap chintzy flourishes and low-rent carnival histrionics. I begin to moan and shake when the handkerchief disappears, make gargly sounds, act as if my hand is not my own, make horrible silly faces. People begin to clutch each other, a first child hides under the table. One time, instead of pulling the handkerchief out of my obviously empty fist, I slowly, laboriously, seem to pull it out of Richard's ear (who knows the trick). He clutches his head, cries, "Empty, empty," causing more panic. Next time, I get the shakes, point all over the room until I settle on the girl who's been sassing us all evening. She trembles, cowers, but it's no use, I come over and, moaning and yelping the whole time, pull the handkerchief out of her ear. She drops to the floor, clutching her head. Anguished requests that I do it again.

Finally, it is time for the ice. We've brought a Styrofoam box filled with dry ice from camp. I feel like a whimsical García Marquez character, or a Theroux obsessive—we have brought ice to the mountain. We hauled up the sealed box, shooed the curious kids away, and now it is time to reveal its contents. I place a piece of ice on the table. "Hot," everyone agrees, looking at the smoke. Everyone reaches their hands close. "Hot . . . cold?" Confusion, edginess. It is passed around, people holding it contentedly for a second before it stings, then tossing it about in alarm. "Don't kill my brother," shouts Samwelly's oldest kid as it is passed to the younger. Perplexity, people craning to see what's next. I fill up a cup with water. I display it to everyone, pour half of it out on the floor. "Water." Obviously. Place it in the dry ice, make everyone count to one hundred, then pull the cup out, turn it over—the water doesn't run. Screams again, kids flee the room. Everyone passes it around. "It's become a rock." "It's a cold rock." "It's ice," pronounces Julius the student. "What is ice?" "I don't know," he admits.

Then the coup de grâce. I have snuck a pocketful of dry ice. Take a cup full of water. Everyone leans in. Once again, I begin to make horrible spastic tremors and babble in tongues. Throw in the handful of dry ice. Bubbling smoke, pouring all over the table, the miracle of dry ice mixing with water that makes the most sophisticated scientists I know stop in their tracks and play happily for minutes (while I hope that I won't get asked the tough question that Julius has just boggled, since I haven't the slightest idea what dry ice actually is, or why it causes the smoke). "It's soup," shouts Samwelly's kid. Others are not so sure and are backing off again. Then I reach up my sleeve— god help me, I've actually done something so hokey as to hide something up my sleeve. It's a plastic snake, about a foot long. I reach into the bubbling cup, tilt my head at an autistic angle, roll my eyes up into my head and drool a bit, and convulsively coax a snake out of the boiling froth. I hold it back as if I'm fighting it for my life, wail, bite into its head, and run from the house with it hanging from my mouth, amid wonderfully satisfying shrieks.

Inconceivable though it may seem, we get even more pleasure out of the dry ice at other times. We make ices. It's my greatest concession in the face of this moronic rice and beans and mackerel asceticism. Early morning, clouds clearing. Lisa, Richard, and I confer. "Looks like it's going to be hot today." "Yeah, hot." "Hot enough for ices." "Could be." We make a quick calculation, see if there's enough dry ice until the next shipment to squander on the ices. Yeah. Dart the baboons, come barreling into camp, before anything else we run like drooly idiots, tongues hanging out—"Ices, ices." Fill up cups with water, mix in the orange powdered drink, ever ever so gently place the cups into little concavities in the dry ice. And wait. Lifting the lid. "Ready?" "Almost." "Soon." "Ices." "Yeah." Finally, by midafternoon, when it's roaring hot and there's never enough shade, the ices are ready. We each get our cup, spoon, and begin to scrape at the solid block of flavored ice. My god my god my god it is so good you want to scream, to never finish. We scrape and nibble for hours, between blood samples and centrifuge spins.

We tried experiments; Richard led the way. "If we can make ices from the orange drink, how about soda?" he wondered. We tried it, fabulous. "If soda, how about cocoa?" We made cocoa, cooled it off, froze it. It was so good, we all hugged each other. "If cocoa, why not tea?" Not bad, thought Richard, although no one else was too enthused. The next day, Richard suggested freezing onion and cabbage and goat stew—he was within a hair's breadth of reinventing the TV dinner. Lisa convinced him we would just be disappointed.

Ices. We dream about them, we finish some and wonder if we can make more, we spend half the evening anticipating the next day's. Not everyone is as enthused. Eh, too cold, says Samwelly, who, visiting in his off-hours from the tourist camp, lets his ices melt back to a lukewarm drink. Are you mad?! we yell, we'll *make* you your own warm drink, don't waste the ices next time, give them to us. Soirowa thinks it's just plain weird, won't have anything to do with it. Or so we think until one day we barrel into camp early. There is Soirowa, just fishing out his cup of ices made out of cow's blood. Big hemolyzed block. Scrumptious, is his description, after translation.

25

Joseph

Lisa was introducing Richard to musical theater. She had a cassette player and a tape of *Les Mis,* and was walking Richard through the plot and lyrics. The bestial ways in which people were often treating each other made perfect sense to him. He leapt up with agitated concern when told that the white man Javert had revealed his identity. He found it hilarious that a policeman—typically a pretty malevolent and corrupt individual in these parts—got to sing also. All in all, he was mesmerized, as Lisa prepared him for each new song. It was easy to imagine him moving next to grand opera, maybe even *Aïda,* complete with the elephants.

It was right around the part that was certainly not going to make much sense to anyone here—the downtrodden rising up against injustice to man the barricades—that word reached camp: Joseph has gone mad! Joseph, a Masai security guard at the tourist camp, thwarting off raiding fellow Masai, protecting somnambulists from elephants, a silent innocuous man who had toiled for years in the vicinity without generating even the flimsiest of anecdotes, Joseph had gone mad.

First was Charles, the tourist camp laundry man, of the same tribe as Richard and Samwelly. Charles came in a rotund excitement reporting the undeniable evidence that Joseph had gone mad. That very day he had quit his job, a clearly lunatic act. Or at least Joseph himself reported such a brash move, as he gathered his few belongings into a bundle, for he had decided to kill himself for unknown reasons. And he was gone.

Soon Soirowa hurried in worried. He was a relative of Joseph's in some way that we could never quite get straight from one explanation to the next. Joseph had indeed gone mad and was roaring up and down the river region, going from village to village, proclaiming that he was about to kill himself. But why? we asked. Because he is mad, explained Soirowa, departing anxiously.

The Masai children appeared soon, frightened. Joseph had indeed been seen, the innocuous silent Joseph lurching about the grassland between villages. "I will see you in heaven!" he shouted to the children, who shuddered at the retelling. We distributed balloons and made powdered fruit juice to comfort them, as we huddled in wonder.

By late afternoon, a murmuring crowd had gathered to gossip and speculate. Would he really kill himself? Of course, because he was crazy. But how did we know he was crazy? Because he had quit his job. But why any of this? People were replete with theories.

"You know, Joseph has an ulcer which is always paining him, so perhaps he is killing himself because it is too much pain." This was Richard, who had an ulcer of his own.

"But he drinks so much, so that he will not feel the pain of his ulcer," retorted Simon, the waiter.

"But drinking makes an ulcer hurt worse," retorted Richard.

"But the drink makes you feel it less," answered Simon.

We teetered on the edge of that unsolvable argument until Charles suggested that maybe Joseph had gone crazy from drinking too much.

Soirowa thought there were larger schemes afoot.

"At the ceremony at the village, the shaman said that Joseph had too much beer in his calabash for one man to drink and that he should give the rest of the beer to the shaman, and Joseph refused. So the shaman put a curse on him."

"For a beer?"

"But that shaman demands beer from everyone and they ignore him."

"But Joseph said he was not frightened of that shaman, so the shaman cannot curse him."

"Of course he can. The shaman can do it. He can change you into a hyena if he wants, he can make your penis fall off," said Charles, the room steward. It was not clear which was a worse fate.

"That shaman is not so strong, he is just an old drunk."

"That's why he would curse Joseph for a beer."

So it went. Everyone was pleased and excited, and we scared ourselves speculating on whether Joseph would come that night, as a hyena, and murder us.

The next day, more rumors. Rhoda rushed in to say that he was still going to kill himself. Soirowa reported that Joseph was trying to borrow money to buy poison from a rare plant. The oddity of asking for money to be returned after you were dead lent peculiar credence to that story. The rangers were seen out patrolling with guns, and it was thought that Joseph had become so mad and dangerous as to require such an armed response, until it became clear that the rangers were merely searching for poachers. The warden was seen driving in the vicinity, and it was thought that he, the final authority, had been called in to track down mad Joseph, until it became clear that the warden was merely going for free lunch at the tourist camp. Joseph was reported seen by all, but never in the same place, speaking many different languages, making mysterious gestures that might have had meaning.

The next day brought reports from all over of the most shocking news: Joseph had become "somehow a white man." The witnesses said he had become "somehow white," his skin had become "somehow rough." We cross-examined aggressively and forced everyone to the rational conclusion that he had been rolling in the whitish sand found on some parts of the banks of the river. Yet he was still proclaimed to have become somehow a white man. The children were kept inside the village that day, as were the cows.

The next day brought a resolution. In front of everyone, Joseph had emerged from the bush, somehow unwhite, had paid for a bus ticket to his hometown, and had bid everyone adieu without mention of seeing them next in heaven. But, Joseph, how are you? everyone had asked. I am all right. So now he is not mad, everyone agreed.

Upon questioning, the manager of the tourist camp said that Joseph had requested his annual leave, and reported that he planned to spend a few days visiting people at the local village before going home for the remainder.

Other than the, perhaps, occasional nocturnal shudder of the children remembering his warnings of the afterlife, the case was promptly forgotten.

That was the season that Lisa, nearing the completion of her PhD in clinical psychology, and I went on her busman's holiday, as we visited every mental hospital in Kenya. And we asked the same sort of question to every staffer that we could find. How do people here decide when someone is mentally ill? You can have a Masai schizophrenic, from a culture where people are very nonverbal, where they spend most of each day alone with the cows, or a schizophrenic from one of the coastal tribes, from a highly sophisticated, verbal, urban setting. What symptom finally pushes the Masai family over the brink to bring their troubled kid to the authorities, what symptom for the coastal people? What are delusions of grandeur like in a desert camel herder? Does he claim to have twice as many camels as he actually has? What voices do people hear? What makes people here paranoid?

And every staffer gave us pretty much the same answer that Rhoda had given me many years before, after the incident with the psychotic woman with the goat in her mouth. They just act crazy, they all said. People just know when someone is acting crazy. Various academicians make their whole careers studying those cultural differences in symptomatology, but we never got a nibble from anyone; no one thought it was an interesting set of questions.

The patients themselves were plenty interesting. No elderly depressives, the types that fill American psychiatric wards—old age is anticipated with eagerness, the height of respect and power. Why get depressed then? Plenty of younger depressives, who seemed to be doing quite well—"Except when the hospital cannot afford antidepressants, then we get many suicides," we were told by the doctor giving us the tour. Poignant. No teenaged viper-eyed killer-of-old-women-with-no-remorse sociopaths. They wind up in jail, in this society in which psychiatrists are not common fixtures in courts of law. Lots of epileptics—an illness classified as a psychiatric disorder in America only during the dark ages. Lots of kids with cerebral malaria. Lots of paranoid schizophrenics.

The most amazing thing was the lack of violence. The staffers thought we were exaggerating when we described how a major problem in American psychiatric hospitals was patients assaulting each other, assaulting staff. No such thing here. No locks on the doors to the hospital. No one trying to escape. It made sense after the first visit—everyone gets their own bed, three meals a day. Unheard-of luxuries for most bush Kenyans. Why run away, why fight? In the yard, patients of both sexes, naked, with shaved heads, lounged around, slept, babbled, gesticulated. Some chased the chickens in the yard, some were chased by the chickens. One, a bent old man with gleaming eyes, hobbled over excitedly to Lisa, like a tortoise with a pleasing secret, and grasped her hand. "Mama has finally come, Mama has finally come," he kept burbling.

26

The Wonders of Machines
in a Land Where They Are Still Novel:
The Blind Leading the Blind

Wandering the city of Mombassa. Wonderful place. Ancient port on the Indian Ocean, black Islamic Swahili people. Minarets, souks, mullahs, donkey carts, dhows made of reeds. Graceful angular men in white gowns selling painfully sour lemonade for relief from the dizzying heat and humidity, the thick soupy ocean air. Narrow twisting labyrinth of alleys, choked in with centuries-old multistory houses, with stucco walls two feet thick and wooden doors carved to an intricacy beyond reason.

One of the great crossroads of the world. Arabs, Indians, Goanese, Portuguese, Swahilis, upcountry Africans; well-fed kids of every shade and hue in this relaxed languid air of intermarriage and procreation.

Best of all, everyone is dignified and happy in a way that people never are in the inland African towns. Inland, the town is some artificial place that started as a colonial railroad depot half a century before. Everyone there has left their farm and is embarrassed by their past; half the people are stuck in the shantytowns on the edge of town without work in the cash economy and are embarrassed by their present. No one knows who they are and everyone is trying to become something new, and you are inundated with the twitches of it— the guys demanding you give them your watch, sell them your blue jeans, the ones who practice their bad American slang and wear the Bruce Lee *Kung Fu* T-shirts and act cool and don't know why. In Mombassa, instead, everyone seems to know who they are and no one is embarrassed or trying to change. It's not an artificial city—it's been there for centuries. There's no disconnected urban alienation; families have lived in their homes for centuries. Plus something else that as a native New Yorker I recognize—it's the almost arrogant indifference, the superiority and self-containment of the port dweller. The Portuguese and their domination came and went. As did the Omani Arabs, the British Empire. As will whoever is hot this week; and afterward, there will be the same dhows and minarets and carved doors. No one is going to overvalue you just because you have a digital watch, and for once, you are left alone.

So it was particularly odd when, one afternoon, the woman began to speak to us in the street. She was from one of the scary, more alien sects, dressed in black robes and veil, one of those who glide through silent and detached from us infidels. And now she was speaking to us, in marginal English. Americans? Yes. So now you will come to my house for tea.

She led us through the alleyways, with a purposefulness that began to make Lisa and me nervous. The house was ancient, dark, leaden, reeked of roasted goat and prayers murmured five times a day for aeons. We were seated in an anteroom filled with children who studied us from a safe distance. She removed her veil, revealing nose rings and henna and a no-nonsense face. She plied us with cups of insanely sugared tea and began questioning us—So, how are your parents now? They are very fine and send salamias. You will be having children soon, yes? If it is to be. You will bring them here to receive my greetings? Of course. She was not interested in our answers or her questions; it was something else, she was working up the nerve. The transparency of this unsettled us. Was she awaiting the signal from the berobed men to pour in with their scimitars and hack us to bits? It seemed perfectly plausible, as some noodly Arabic singing from next door floated over our fourth glass of tea.

She had decided. So now you come to the back, grabbing our wrists. We did not protest; we would face our fate bravely.

The next room, underneath the domed roof, was illuminated by a single bare lightbulb. There was an old, venerated table at which, no doubt, countless family councils had been held concerning wars, uprisings, births, deaths, betrothals, potential heresies, feuds, festivals, infidelities, financial schemes. And on the ancient table sat this object. It was some sort of combination ice cream maker/food processor/rotisserie oven/salad slicer dicer and shooter/sausage maker. Her brother, who was studying in Germany, had sent it a year ago and it had sat on the table, honored and untouched, ever since. No one knew how to use it, what it was even for.

"You are Americans, you must speak German."

There was a profusely detailed brochure with it, filled with umlauts and "achtungs" concerning the many sharp blades, and numerous exploding diagrams showing the electrical innards of the thing. A cabal of neighboring women had magically gathered, to see if anything was going to come of this object.

The refrigerator was unplugged from the sole outlet, the monstrosity was fired up, and for the rest of the afternoon, surrounded by increasingly demonstrative kids and tureens of unavoidable sugar tea, we toiled ineffectually, knowing nothing of German, electricity, or sausage making. It turned out neither did the woman, nor did she particularly care much either about making creamy smooth ice cream, frying chicken all around equally, shooting salad straight into the bowl, or making potato jubilees. We got the knife blades to whir around dangerously at one point to much acclaim, were pressed into tossing in a nondescript chunk of meat, which was minced and flung about the room for lack of our having placed some sort of catchment bowl in position, and the woman's status in the neighborhood was thus assured. All were impressed, the woman grasped our meat-soaked hands in hers in gratitude and dignified pleasure. We returned to the winding alleyways of this ancient city, picking our way in the twilight over debris tossed there half a millennium ago.

27

Who's on First, What's on Second

$\mathcal{I}$t had turned into a tough season for Rachel. First Naomi, her mother, the oldest animal in the troop, had disappeared, no doubt picked off by a predator. Rachel seemed mopey and depressed. Then Isaac, Rachel's friend, goes and starts spending a lot of his time at a neighboring troop, clearly contemplating transferring. This, after I'd been extolling to Lisa his unique male sensitivity. Just when Rachel needs him most, Lisa'd fume, and he's off checking out the junior high school girls in the next troop. . . . Honey, you know, it's appropriate for them to act like baboons, I'd muster weakly in his defense. He ultimately decided not to transfer and settled back in the troop, but the whole episode made him seem like kind of a jerk.

So we were discussing Isaac's disappointing behavior, sitting in camp at dawn, drinking tea before heading out to the baboons. Richard had just wandered in, walking the mile or so from his site to join us. How are you? How was the night? It's not so cold this morning. How did you sleep? We slept fine. Did you hear the elephants? Do you want some tea? All the usual. Just as we're finishing the tea and getting ready to head out, Richard offhandedly says, There is a small problem. Oh, really, what?

Further downriver there was a campsite where tourists could stay in pup tents. Some Masai guarded the site, a couple of cooks rustled up communal meals for everyone. Low-rent safaris and more fun than staying in the fancy lodges. The latest group of tourists had left a few days ago, and the guards and cooks were minding the store until the next group showed up. Richard nonchalantly relates that during the night, a hyena ripped into the tent of the old cook, dragged him out for dinner, and, after a great tussle and much injury, the hyena was driven off.

We leap up, excited, alarmed—Is the old man okay, we have to go get him, let's drive there immediately, get the medical supplies, so on. Richard, the picture of calm, says, No worry, he is on his way over right now.

We run over to the river crossing to find that, indeed, there he is, this little old man, limping toward camp. We rush toward him. He is totally lacerated, ripped apart on his arms, his chest, his forehead. Oh my god, old man, are you okay? I am fine, how was your night? How did you sleep? How are your parents these days? Bizarrely, he forces us to go through the various greeting rituals before settling down to the more pressing fact that he's been shredded by this hyena.

We get him into camp. We are galvanized into action—pulling all the medical supplies out of the tent, ready for anything. We want to drive him to park headquarters immediately to get him air evacuated by the flying doctor's service. Nah, he says, it's not so bad, I'll be fine. Not so bad? You're a mess, you're bleeding everywhere, you'll need hundreds of stitches, we need to get you some morphine. Richard, glancing up from his second cup of tea, suggests some aspirin for him. Sure, an aspirin would be nice, the old man agrees.

Feeling useless and thrown off kilter by all this nonchalance, we meekly give him an aspirin and some tea. After drinking some he adds, Oh, another thing, do you think you can put my finger back on?

He has a ripped piece of cloth wrapped around what we assumed was his injured ring finger. Removing the cloth, we find that said finger is now gone. Uh, just where is your finger, old man?

He fishes around in his pocket ("Okay," Lisa and I say to each other, "let's just brace ourselves now"), and out comes his finger. In a plastic bag. Filled with salt. Good bush camp cook that he is, he knows about preserving meat, and after the hyena was driven off at midnight, he searched around in the grass with his flashlight, found his finger, and then proceeded to salt it.

We break the bad news to him. Sorry, we don't know how to put fingers back on. He takes it bravely—"That is all right, can I have more tea?"—and puts his bag away.

While he luxuriates with his drink and continues to bleed all over everything, we press him to let us take him to headquarters for air evacuation. No need. Before walking the three miles to our camp, he walked over to another tourist campsite and arranged for a driver friend, who is returning to Nairobi today, to give him a lift to the hospital in Nairobi. We offer to drive him to that other campsite, an offer he accepts, but first he has to stop at his own camp—he needs to change into his dress clothes, suitable for a trip into the big city, so that he can spend the next six hours in the vehicle ruining them by bleeding all over them.

Driving over, we get some more details. The hyena ripped into his sleeping tent around midnight, seized him, and dragged him out, intent on dinner.

He had fought the hyena, and the Masai guards came out and speared it. We listen to this with increasing trepidation. The only reason we can sleep peacefully at night is with the thoroughly inculcated belief that when you go inside a tent, you stop existing, as far as the animals are concerned. Over and over, we tell ourselves that the animals can't figure out where you went, they haven't reached the Piagetian cognitive stage yet of understanding "insideness," and we are safe. And now he's regaling us about the hyena tearing into the tent. Anxiety.

We reach his campsite, and while he is changing into his Sunday best, we inspect the tent. Which puzzles us. There's blood here and there, all over camp, in fact, but the tent is perfectly intact. No rip. We begin to question him, he gets sheepish and evasive, and eventually we get the answer. After a mere decade being a camp cook in the bush and learning what you do and don't do, last night for some inexplicable reason he had decided to get his forty winks sleeping in the food tent amid the sausages. A tent that, for some equally inexplicable reason, had no floor on the bottom so that an inquisitive hyena could just slip underneath the walls and raid the refrigerator.

Ah-ha, so now he's sleeping in the food tent, the hyena slips in, starts munching him until the Masai spear him. We are relieved at having our safe-in-a-closed-tent rule reinstated and marvel at his foolishness.

So the old man was in the wrong tent, but that is fine. Soon, however, a complication arises. He returns to his dressing under the watchful eye of the Masai guards, standing there stolid and silent with their spears—the heroes of our story, two guys we don't know, from a few villages over. And off on the side is the other camp cook, a younger guy who, like the old fingerless man, is from a non-Masai agricultural tribe. He is clearly agitated about something. We schmooze with the Masai while Richard talks to him. And the story comes out—the Masai guards didn't save the old man after all. The Masai guards had abandoned their jobs, were off drunk as skunks in the village, carousing. The second cook was the one who had come to the rescue, barreling out into the middle of the wrestling match and bonking the hyena over the head with a rock, driving it off. And now the Masai, fearful that the word of their AWOL status would get around and they would lose their jobs, were threatening the life of the second cook.

Oh, great. All this is being told to us in a way that makes it perfectly clear to the Masai that we know what's up. To cover our asses a bit, we spend some time scraping and bowing before them and their spears, telling them what brave heroes they are, they are real warriors, and so on. It seems to calm things down a bit—we have made it clear that we are not blowing the whistle on them. The old man departs with his ride, the second cook is mollified, the brave warriors return to the village to resume their stuporous drinking, and we pass the morning up and down the river telling all concerned what saints these guys were, spearing and killing the rogue hyena.

So the old man was in the wrong tent and the Masai weren't really there doing their jobs, but everything still seems okay. Then late afternoon, a complication arises. It seems that after the second cook had bonked the hyena over the head with the rock, the hyena took off, ran a mile to the Masai village, killed a goat, and attacked a man. Who did indeed spear it to death. And now, amid great attention and clucking, there is a dead hyena in the middle of the village with only a single spear wound in it. Late afternoon, the drunken heroes return to the campsite to threaten the poor second cook with murder once again until a new version of the events is worked out that is reconcilable with the inconvenient evidence in Exhibit A, the dead hyena. So the story becomes that the brave warriors had leapt into the battle with the hyena the night before without time even to grab their spears. Instead, it is now they who had bonked the hyena over the head with the rock.

Dutifully, we spend the rest of the day passing on that version of the story and expressing our boundless admiration for the stalwart pair. So the old man was in the wrong tent, the Masai weren't really there doing their jobs, and the first version of the cover-up story didn't work, but the second seems to be a big hit and everything is fine.

Two days later, a complication arises. An acquaintance, a bush pilot, has just flown in from Nairobi, and he passes on the latest newspaper to us. And there on page 3 is the old man in the Nairobi hospital, smiling, displaying his mangled hand and his now-famous plastic bag. One of the hospital staff, no doubt spotting a good story and hoping for some money, had called the newspaper, which sent someone to interview the man. "Camp cook single-handedly fights off hyena in game park." In this version, the old man had been in his sleeping tent, the hyena ripped in, the other cook and two guards were nowhere to be seen, and it was now the old man who reached for a boulder and bashed the hyena a good one. Somehow, within an hour, everyone knows about the newspaper article, even the Masai, who've never seen a newspaper in their lives.

So the old man was in the wrong tent, the Masai weren't really there doing their jobs, the first revisionist story hadn't worked, and now the published version contradicts everyone else's. Irritation roils up and down the river that day—everyone had worked out something tolerable in terms of saving face for the guards, and now the dumb-ass old man grabs the limelight and makes everyone look bad. And because it is in the newspaper, the tourist company in Nairobi will be sure to notice and somebody is going to get raked over the coals.

A few days later, the company speaks. Surprisingly, it is via the newspaper, delivered by the bush pilot chancing through the reserve again. In a follow-up story, the newspaper reports that the company categorically denied that the old man was their employee, claimed never to have heard of him. He was obviously just some guy passing through the area who had gotten drunk at the Masai village and, while staggering out afterward, was attacked by a hyena. And now he had claimed to be an employee just to stick the company with the medical bills. Or, the company hinted darkly, maybe he had even chopped off his own finger and then claimed that he was an employee in order to hustle insurance money off the company. But the company stoically refused to be bamboozled by such an obvious scam. And since the old man didn't really work for them, the company was paradoxically free to now fire him for no particular reason. The whole problem was taken care of, things along the river now could settle down—neither the old man nor the hyena had ever existed.

28

The Last Warriors

In my first year in the bush, I had spent that sweltering afternoon inside Rhoda's hut, forced into the ineffectual role as mediator in the battle between Rhoda's cohort of women, arguing for school fees for kids, and the old men, holding out for their right to spend every shilling in the village on booze. And now, nearly fifteen years later, came the day Lisa and I participated in a Masai ceremony that showed that Rhoda's side had won and things really were changing. When I first arrived on the scene, the nearest school was some fifty miles away. Along the river now was a schoolhouse for the kids. This was the last day of school for the year, so, to celebrate the occasion, Simon the schoolteacher took the kids on a class trip. He walked them a mile from the schoolhouse, crossed the river, and brought them to camp to see Nick, the baboon we had darted that day. The kids (all boys, except the daughter of the chief) clustered around, asked questions, giggled uproariously at Nick's penis and when he had a bowel movement. They wore schoolboy shorts and jerseys. I showed them how to take blood, Lisa demonstrated the workings of the centrifuge. They asked many questions: can a baboon mate with a human, do they have a language, do they eat their dead? At the end, Simon gave an unlikely inspirational speech, commending them on having worked hard and finishing a year of school and urging them to continue in their difficult studies so that someday they could study baboons for a living. They were charming, well behaved, appreciative, and thankful when they left; it was a nice way for them to celebrate the end of a school year, and I was glad to have participated. Afterward, I was depressed as hell.

That season when Rhoda decked the drunk Serere and thus began the great education debate, the older brothers of these kids became warriors, and I attended the ceremony that ushered them in. For Masai boys, the first dozen years or so are spent wandering the fields tending the cows and goats, hunting birds, ferreting out beehives for honey. Then, after years of preparation tha don't remotely understand, the boys enter the warrior period, lasting perhaps a decade. It is an intensely militaristic, communal period. The warriors live together in separate quarters, eat every meal together. It is only after they have finished their years of community service as warriors that they become elders— at age twenty-five or so, marry their first wives (perhaps age fourteen), settle down, have kids, and complain about the poor quality of today's warriors.

Thus, at that ceremony, one warrior clan was being mustered out as another was coming in. The village drank and feasted for days. Warriors-to-be, with bird-skin headdresses to symbolize the long warrior hair that they were about to grow, were trance-dancing. Shouting, spear-throwing, deep-throated choruses with falsetto soloists that sounded like '50s crooners, dancing, chanting, a central core of elders in animal skins and ocher. I found myself with an anxiety that I hadn't felt since, at age eight, I went alone for the first time to services at the synagogue for the Jewish New Year and did not know what was happening. The old men then had told me I would be given an honor—to open the curtain for when the Torah was taken out of the ark, and I did not know when I was supposed to do it, or which side had the rope for opening the curtain, or if I was supposed to say something, or why I didn't know anything that was happening, and just as I was about to run away and burst into tears, an old man grabbed my hand and walked me up to the ark, pulled the curtain with me, and told me I had done well, and all the old men shook my hand with solemnity and I felt dizzy with pleasure. And now, I felt myself with the same anxiety at not knowing *what* was going on, or what, if anything, was allowed or expected of me, what I was doing hanging out with these Masai, and just as I was about to find some excuse to drift away, an old man, maybe even the same one as at the synagogue years before, grabbed my wrist and dragged me into a circle, and it became clear that anything I did during the dancing was amusing and ridiculous and welcome and praised, and we danced the rest of the day and I felt like a Masai for weeks afterward and always felt as if that generation of warriors were my boys.

And such a ceremony has not occurred here since. There is a crisis in Masai land. The government has outlawed the warriors.

Now, don't get me wrong. I'm not about to start praising cultural stasis and the need for living museums. If that sort of trend were to catch on, the logical extension would be for me to live in a shtetl in Poland, fixing shoes, in an arranged marriage with a woman who's been picked for her skill at ritualistically slaughtering chickens. No, thank you.

And even more than that, I cannot truly lament the passing of the warriors, cause they were a royal pain. My first years, here, I had lived on that distant mountain, and the Masai were occasional visitors from the plain. Gosh, were they groovy that first year. I wanted nothing more than to be a Masai, to drink blood and milk, to know eleventy different words for "cows" and to care enough about cows to want that many terms, to be proud and unchanged and un-Westernized. Soirowa gave me my first spear and I practiced with it till my hands bled. I would spear an old tire lying near my tent. Then, I would have someone roll it across my field, and I would have to spear it as it sped past. Then, I graduated to having the tire rolled *at* me, then rolled at me with my back turned—sneak attack. I felt certain I was becoming skinnier and taller and blacker and more angular every day.

But since the subsequent years when I had moved down to the plains, in close proximity to the Masai villages beaded along the boundary of the park, my feelings about them had grown more ambivalent. Rhoda and Soirowa had become close friends, and my relations with their village were usually good. But in a more general way, I was discovering what every agricultural African has known for centuries—tall angular folks with the cows are a pain in the keister. Like their relatives the Dinkas, the Nuer, the Watutsi, and the Zulu, the Masai have been successfully ranging up and down Africa with their cattle, at least in part, because of their predatory militarism. Since time immemorial, the lauded warriors have swept down on the agricultural tribes, pillaging, looting, kidnapping. Masai believe that all cows on earth belong to the Masai and have inadvertently wandered off into someone else's hands; the job of the warrior is to rectify that unfortunate situation. Thus, the community service for the warrior consists of raining terror down on everyone else. It can be big time—Richard and Samwelly's grandfather was speared to death in their village a mere decade ago in a Masai raid, and their people still construct their houses with an architecture explicitly meant to be Masai-proof. Or it can be separate of epic, time-honored tribal battles and take the form of plain old hooliganism and banditry—within a month of working for me, Richard was roughed up by warriors, his binoculars smashed just for spite. Warriors coming into camp, laconically examining my possessions and demanding gifts of things, forcing me to say no to men with spears. Petty pilfering, threats, tourist camps brought into compliance with the old protection racket—hire a Masai to serve as a guard at night because if you don't . . . who knows, maybe your camp might just get raided by Masai.

While the rest of the developing world succumbs to emulating the tawdriest lowest common denominators of Western culture, part of the beauty, the majesty, of these people and their related nomadic tribes has been their capacity to pass through other cultures for centuries and to emerge unchanged uncompromised. And what became clear to me was that the prerequisite for such immunity from other cultures is to have utter contempt for anyone who is not Masai.

Thus, the rest of Kenya, the agricultural majority, had been changing at lightning speed—cash, schooling, Western clothes, watches, television repair schools, satellite relay stations, ice cream, posters about the dangers of tooth decay. Imagine the incongruity, the bizarre juxtaposition, of some Nairobi sharpie, cutting-edge businessman, visiting the old family back on the ancestral farm and, for crying out loud, they're recovering from a Masai raid? Get with it, this isn't the nineteenth century, isn't there even a place to get some Tagamet around here?

Thus, one day, not long after the time that Masai warriors up and down our river had grabbed their spears and run off to Tanzania to wrest back their cows, something extraordinary happened in Parliament. The pinstripes there, backed by the police and army and all sorts of unlikely institutions, did something their grandpas never accomplished with their arrows, something the Brits in their worst excesses of cultural imperialism would never have dreamt of doing—they signed a piece of paper, and that was it, no more warriors. Walk around with ochered hair or a spear and it's off to the hoosegow with you, or maybe even a fine from a magistrate with a powdered wig and an agriculturist's Bantu face.

Oh, I'm ambivalent about it all. I'm charmed by the memory of the warriors, now that they are fast becoming a memory instead of an intimidating reality. But I can see how everyone else wants them finished. Maybe they should have kept the warriors and instituted ferociously competitive Masai Olympics to channel that energy, have the games be dangerous enough to make it seem legitimate, get the same number of young men killed as would have been back in the old days when warriors had to prove themselves by killing a lion. I've read about such games having some success with New Guinea headhunters, turning them into nicer neighbors. What has struck me most is how fast everyone has complied. By the time the school kids had tromped into my camp to snicker at Nick's penis, warriors were disappearing. And the school kids snorted derisively when I asked them if they were going to go live in the bush and kill a lion someday.

Of course, not everyone has complied. The crisis in Masai land is what to do about the old men who have taken to the bush to kidnap boys and raise them as warriors in secret. Everyone knows about it, no one is talking, and it's impossible to guess if the men in the bush are an embarrassment or a great source of pride, a last gasp or the start of a revolt.

• • •

About a month later, after the end-of-school visit, Lisa and I sit in camp, working on the anesthetized Joshua, while one of our favorite Masai kids hangs out. A sweet kid, probably around twelve, whom I have watched grow up over the years. He has a shaved head, and the elongated ears of Masai, but keeps them folded up, as if to hide them; underneath his Masai cloak is a pair of school shorts. Lisa runs the centrifuge, he says, "Bird waking up," in Swahili—but that is an idiom for an airplane engine coming to life—to describe the hum of the centrifuge. Why does he know about airplane engines? He blows soap bubbles and plays with a balloon we've given him, and then it is time to head home with the cows. We watch him cross the river and head to the field beyond the camp, and suddenly, from out of nowhere, a band of warriors sweeps out. They have spears, long ochered hair, are a bunch of scary bastards and they know it. The boy begins to run away, but they easily swarm all over him. He struggles. They attempt to hold him, lift him, but he flails and lashes out until they beat him on the head, seemingly knocking him unconscious. And he is taken away by them. We see them on the horizon, the shimmering heat making their stick legs seem even more elongated and alien than usual as they run off to the bush, carrying him to his training. And we never see him again.

29

The Plague

During one season, I took some time off from the baboons to visit the researchers in one of the other national parks in the country. I made the rounds, seeing the baboon people and the ecology people and the elephant people. I've never known much about elephants, but they are inspiring and moving, as is the devotion of elephantologists. Such researchers are renowned for being as obsessed with their animals as are most primatologists, and it is understandable when you consider elephants—large, smart animals who live for three quarters of a century and fill their days with familial complexity and caring. When I visited them, the elephant people were amid a week of distress that all wildlife biologists immediately empathize with. One of their best-studied, most beloved animals was missing; a matriarch, the mother of a dependent seven-month-old. They had been searching for days, becoming frantic for the panicked and weakening child. We all fretted and imagined bad scenarios.

A few days later, we stood over the body of the missing elephant. The search had not been all that difficult. She died about a quarter kilometer outside the garbage dump of the main tourist lodge. She had eaten considerable amounts of the garbage—no doubt fruit and vegetable remains, chunks of various starches being the main attractants—left the dump, collapsed, and died. The vultures had already transformed someone the elephant people had known for years into a gaping carcass—skull sticking out, most of the really yummy organs already eaten. Her stomach and bowels had been ripped open, the contents scattered over ten square feet in front of her torso: mounds of grass and leaves having nearly finished the process of being transformed into elephant dung; the leafy top of a pineapple, courtesy of the garbage dump. And the cause of her death: shards of broken glass, a broken soda bottle, bottle tops, bits of metal, all also courtesy of the garbage dump. The elephant people had been begging the lodge for months to make the dump inaccessible, had helped make a fence for them, which the lodge never bothered to close, had appealed to the

275

warden to do something. At the point when I left the park, the fate of the child was uncertain.

I will not tell the names of the researchers or the park, and it is not clear if mentioning the name of the lodge and its scum owner will make it more or less likely that he will act responsibly in the future. I will leave it to the elephant people to decide what the best strategy is to avoid repeating that particular tragedy. But I have decided that it is time to tell how my baboons ended. I have tried throughout this book to give some attention to the style of writing, to try to shape some of these stories. Here I will not try. Things unfolded in an odd, unshaped way. There were villains, but they were not quite vile enough to satisfy. There was no showdown. These are not a crafted, balanced set of events, and the telling of them will not be particularly crafted either.

It was a season when I was mostly alone—Lisa's professional obligations had caught up that year, and she had stayed back in the States, Richard had an extended family illness at home, Hudson was still working at a baboon project at the other end of the country. Soirowa, Laurence of the Hyenas, Rhoda, and Samwelly were around, but I was alone most days.

Over the previous years, I had come to avoid Olemelepo Lodge. This was not the lodge where Richard lived. His was a small tented camp, secluded in a river's bend, some five kilometers away. Olemelepo was "town," one of the bigger lodges in the park, a big sprawling mess of a place. It held hundreds of tourists, had three times that many workers and related people—staff, spouses, children, teachers of children, nurses, wardens, rangers, prostitutes, endless cousins and nephews looking for work. In my first year, 1978, it had been the place to hang out. My mail was sent there, which made the place the emotional center of my life. You could waste time there with the invariably unsuccessful goal of trying to get some group of tourists to buy you a meal. There was also an odd pleasure in getting to know all the staff there, becoming a regular, feeling comfortable dropping in for tea in the staff quarters. And over the years, most of the charm had worn off, as I had indeed become a regular. Now, whenever I stopped there, I was embroiled in people wanting loans, wanting to know where was the stereo they had demanded last year that I bring from the States, could I drive them immediately sixty kilometers for an important ceremony at their village, could I sell them my watch and jeans right this minute. People wanted driving lessons, jobs for their kid brothers, scholarships to my university. All perfectly understandable, given the general dire economic straits, but still, after a while, the charm had worn off, and I had taken to voiding the place.

Thus, I procrastinated for many days when the pilot of the tourist balloon offhandedly mentioned to me that there was a sick baboon behind his house. I had other things to do, I didn't really want to have to spend time at Olemelepo tracking down a sick baboon; I assumed that it was actually a zebra who had been sneezing there one evening. But when he mentioned it for the third time in a week, flagged me down on the road to tell me, I decided to check it out.

Later that day, the pilot led me to the back of his house. The baboon had been there for days, hiding between the wall and some diesel tanks, coughing constantly. I nosed around each end of the row of tanks, couldn't see anything, could just hear an occasional, dry, weak cough. Finally, I squeezed between two of the tanks and found myself a few feet away from her.

She was from the troop adjacent to mine, the troop whose territory encompassed the lodge. I knew some of the animals in that troop, but I didn't recognize her. I'm not sure if I would have, even if I knew the members of her troop well. She was transformed. Nearly a skeleton, with huge patches of fur missing, large necrotic lesions all over her. And enormous, glowing eyes. We stared at each other from close range, and it occurred to me that she was delirious. Her eyes would rest on me, seemingly unfocused, and now and then, they would shift slightly, as if she were suddenly noting me for the first time. She'd tense a bit, pull her head back in consternation. She seemed not to have the strength to do more than that. Then she'd begin to cough and the eyes would lose focus again.

I decided to dart her—once I could examine her, I'd try to see if I could make any sense of her illness with my profoundly rudimentary knowledge of such things. I'd also take various samples—blood, saliva, mucus—to store for some wildlife vets who might actually know something.

I decided to try to anesthetize her by hand with a syringe, instead of trying with a blowgun in these close quarters, but she was a smidgen too alert and mobile. We spent some time with her laboriously moving away from me as I laboriously tried to squeeze close enough to inject her. Actually, I was probably trying to herd her out from behind the tanks in order to use the blowgun rather than to actually inject her—I was more than a little afraid that she might bite me and that, overnight, I would become necrotic and delirious myself. I noticed that she was coughing up a bloody foam.

She was out in the open now, as I prepared the blowgun. A crowd of gawking staff had developed. This was the last thing on earth I wanted: the crowd seemed on the edge of sufficient gawking enthusiasm as to trample her or me. And whatever she had might be contagious.

I darted her at close range under her dull, glazed stare. She walked away a few steps, and I noted that one hand was necrotic as well. She went down quickly, quietly, as I pulled on a scrub suit, gloves, and mask. Her pulse and breathing were extremely weak, her temperature was 105 degrees, and as I prepared a vacutainer for a blood sample, she died.

I felt it prudent not to advertise this. I covered her "to keep her warm," announced I was taking her to my camp for an examination, and scrammed.

Laurence of the Hyenas was in camp, and he quickly joined in the planned autopsy. I'll admit it—we were pleased and anticipatory. I'm perfectly capable of getting grossed out by dead things, but if you are a certain type of biologist, this is basically your idea of fun. You skin something, dissect it, study how the musculature works; do a good job cleaning a skull for display, articulating a skeleton; you practice a new type of surgery on a carcass until it's a clean set of perfect reflexes. And this time, it was a mystery, even better—you got to combine scientific puzzle-solving with good old mucking around with something dead.

We decided to act like good, careful scientists. We laid out the ground rules for the game. We had some medical reference books with us, which we had made constant use of, trying to figure out the cause of the nonspecific fever or stomach crud of the week. But we decided not to consult the books, to first go through a full dissection, description, and whatever guesses we might have, so that we wouldn't bias our subsequent observation to fit our book-based theory.

We opened up the belly with my Swiss army knife, the best instrument available. The whole abdominal cavity was filled with a yucky fluid. So sue me, I'm not a pathologist; it just looked yucky. We started slicing open organs. Normally, this is one of the more conflicting, assaultive olfactory experiences you can have. The intestines, naturally, smell like feces with an odor so thick and goopy that you are sure that the shit smell is forming a precipitate on your eyelids. But what is always surprising is the stomach, because it invariably smells like a garden salad—a fragrant mulch of leaves and grass and fruits and just enough stomach acids to give the ensemble a hint of vinaigrette.

The stomach always smells kind of good, except this time—there was no Mother Earth salad smell and no stench in the intestines either. She hadn't eaten in days.

There were small, dark nodules all over the place, in her gut, stomach, liver, pancreas. We cut down further into the groin, and they were in the lymph nodes also. They were hard and compact. Following the tendency of pathologists to, perversely, use food descriptions for the rankest of things possible, it struck us that they looked like watermelon pits. Maybe she ate too many watermelon pits, we theorized wryly. We continued in this vein—"Ah, but note that there are pits in the lymph nodes. How did they get there, Herr Professor?" "So she must be suffering from ectopic watermelon pits" ("ectopic" is the term used for things that are in the wrong place. If you grew six fingers coming out of your forehead, the savant who described it first might call it ectopic polydactylism or something). "But, my esteemed colleague," we continued with each other, "where did the watermelon pits come from, since watermelons do not grow here?" "Ah, thus, I diagnose she is suffering from idiopathic ectopic watermelon pits" (meaning watermelon pits in the wrong place for god knows what reasons); case closed. We were having a fine time.

We cut open some of these nodules. The inside was granular, powdery, lighter colored. We took careful notes and couldn't think of anything clever to glean from that. I started drawing the whole thing—the nodules in the gut, stomach, beadlike sequins throughout the veil of connective tissue. We rummaged around with the knife and managed to cut out two vertebrae. Nodules in the spinal cord as well—central nervous system infection. It occurred to us to begin to feel a little bit spooked. We put on another pair of gloves and noticed how damn warm it was under the masks, dissecting out in the sun. She was beginning to stink a smidgen as well, especially the necrotic hand.

We started to open up the chest. We cut through the skin and then sawed through the rib cage with tools from Laurence's auto mechanic's toolbox. And normally, if you slice through the diaphragm, the whole rib cage should just lift off, like magic, displaying a luscious pair of lungs and heart below. We cut along all the dotted lines, but the rib cage wasn't budging. We pulled at all sorts of angles until we could see—the lungs were completely adhered to everything—to the diaphragm, to the rib cage, to the heart. This was drastically wrong. We yanked at the rib cage, cut underneath a bit, yanked some more, and suddenly it pulled loose along with all the adhered lung.

We leapt back. Jesus fucking Christ. Fluid was oozing out every which way. It was thick and milky and smelly and fibrous and splotched, with pieces of things in it. If you were to find yourself in hell and you got thirsty and ordered an ice cream soda with blood and cherries thrown in, this is what you would get. Then we realized—this wasn't some fluid oozing out of the lungs. This was the lungs themselves oozing away. Her lower lobes had just melted.

Our bravado was gone. We procrastinated before getting up the nerve to examine the remnants of the lungs. There were the nodules everywhere, i? the chest wall, the trachea, the tracheobronchial lymph nodes as well. But t? lungs. Nodules. But also splotches, hemorrhages, explosions of blood and here and there, implosions, and more lung melting away all the time. We eventually touched them. The lungs were bony. Maybe not even bony. They had some sort of cartilaginous superstructure, pockets of rock hardness, other parts that were like hard eggshells that then burst, dripping away more of the lung. This was insanely wrong, as wrong as eating yogurt and having to stop to pick the bones out of it. We began to dissect out and cut open and palpate and scrape. There were chunks of cartilage-type stuff connecting nothing to nothing. There were white parts and black parts and hemorrhaged red parts and garish yellow-green parts. There were hard spheres that split open to release thick yellow ooze that left behind little soft kernels of coagulated hemorrhage with gray powdery centers. And then spheres of things in which the layers seemed to be just the opposite. The remaining lung was adhered to everything, there was no definition to the lobes anymore. There were gaping holes in the trachea, a plug of blood and sputum and yuck clogged at the bottom. It was a mess, and we flailed and wrote down and drew and had no idea what we were doing. Eventually, we decided we were finished, buried her at the far end of the field, left our scrub suits hanging in a far tree and the dissection knife sitting in the tree's crook, far from our camp.

It was Laurence who first mumbled "tuberculosis." Once we had washed, we checked our books, and the description of terminal-stage TB matched perfectly. Anyone who works with captive primates gets the willies from TB. You can't even set foot in most primate centers without passing a TB test, people are so scared of outbreaks. The disease will jump from cage to cage, room to room, will wipe out entire colonies. It doesn't work like in humans, where Hans Castorp can malinger for years, jotting down his prolix philosophic thoughts. It just tears through primate labs. I hadn't a clue whether it moved that quickly through wild primate populations. And as the start of an answer, a few days later, a ranger flagged me down to say that there was a sick baboon at Olemelepo Lodge.

The second case was much like the first. This time, it was a prime-aged male, from that same Olemelepo troop. He lived through the darting and, with next to no reflection about it, I overdosed and autopsied him out in the field again. With him, there were even more nodules throughout the digestive system and liver, maybe a bit less disintegration of the lungs.

The third case was a few days later, a crazed, wailing, coughing female behind the water pump house at the lodge. The symptoms were the worst —her back was arched, her hands were so necrotic, so stinking and putrethat she walked on her elbows when she tried to get away from me.

Apparently, the back arches in an attempt to increase lung capacity. The hands decay because, as the lungs rot and oxygen exchange plummets, the amount of oxygen delivered to peripheral tissues declines. She died within a minute of darting, and an hour later, her lungs were melting away in the corner of my field. That night, I had my first nightmare about being unable to breathe.

These were all from the Olemelepo Lodge troop. They had always shared the forest with my troop, and in the mornings, they would go their separate ways, this troop foraging around the lodge. This was the troop that had pushed my guys out of the forest during the unstable years. As Olemelepo grew, the lodge started generating more garbage and got sloppier with their garbage dump, and soon the lodge troop was spending its time eating among the refuse. And soon, they had moved their sleeping site to the trees above the dump, and they passed their days eating garbage. Their behavior was distorted, their foraging nonexistent, and I had washed my hands of them in disgust. As of late, they had been getting into trouble. Some tourist would toss them food from the verandah in order to get a picture, and when a more aggressive animal would then lunge for food that was not necessarily being offered, there'd be nervous shrieks from the tourists. Later that day, a ranger would shoot a couple of baboons. Or some mama in the staff quarters wouldn't feel like walking over to the garbage can to toss out the leftover maize meal and would toss it to a waiting baboon instead, and the next day, the same male would lunge for her maize meal as she prepared it outside, not yet having mastered the subtlety of distinguishing between maize meal before and after humans have decided they're done with it. An uproar would ensue, and the ranger would go and shoot a few baboons. The previous season, one of the prostitutes at the staff canteen had given birth to a deformed child, and the rumor ran around that she had been raped by one of the baboons. I kid you not. And the rangers shot a couple more.

So this was the troop, and now they had something like tuberculosis breaking out everywhere. As I noted, I had no idea how TB moved through wild primate populations, and the sense I was getting from my cursory reading in the prior week was that no one else did either. It appeared as if I were about to find out. Already, I was spending half my nights wondering how long the TB would take to reach my troop.

I radioed the primate research center in Nairobi. They were in the process of turning from a charity plaything for colonial matrons, an animal orphanage for cute abandoned pet monkeys, into a first-rate research institute. Their director was an American vet, Jim Else, a man with miraculous organizational skills. I liked and respected him and hoped it was mutual. I explained the situation to Jim within the maddening format of the radio call, filled with static and fadings in and out and the necessity to push a button and say, "Over," each time you finished a statement. I shouted the symptoms, the autopsies, the emerging pattern, and amid the static and the metallic monotonic voice, I heard Jim being concerned. Yes, he said, it sounded like TB, but it was absolutely imperative that they be able to culture the lungs to confirm that, and to find out what kind. Absolutely imperative. I was enough of a scientist to recognize the scientist's edge to his voice—"This is imperative, because this might be really interesting and informative" (i.e., neato, this is going to be fun). I'm no clinician, so I couldn't tell if I was also hearing his vet's voice saying, "This is imperative because you might have the start of a plague." Regardless, it was clear what he was asking. They had to be able to culture a piece of the lungs. Therefore, I had to get a live, sick baboon to them in Nairobi.

It had to be an animal who was sick, but was early stage, so that it would survive the transporting. I thought I was getting good enough with the symptoms to spot an early case, but the whole thing still seemed difficult. I had no idea that the difficulty was about to be with the humans involved.

Everyone at Olemelepo knew that something was up with the baboons. People began to ask me whether the baboons were dangerous, whether we shouldn't be killing them all. Then, in the time-honored tradition of shooting the messenger, people began to decide that it was somehow my fault that the baboons were sick—after all, they were my animals, they were sure I could do something about it, and thus I must have decided not to do anything and to let everyone be endangered. I started spending a lot of each day explaining that these were not my animals, that not all of them were sick, that it was not clear yet if it was dangerous to people, that I was trying to do something, and so on.

Another case popped up, someone too far gone to survive the drive to my camp, let alone Nairobi. The next morning, while surveying the garbage dump for a candidate animal, I spotted Saul, Shem, and Jonathan feeding there—they would apparently slip away from my troop for a quick run on the garbage, where they were big enough to hold their own for scraps among the bloated garbage dump males. I got the chills—now there was a vector for carrying the TB into my troop. That afternoon, I discovered a group of the staff at Olemelepo flinging stones at the baboons, trying to drive them away from the lodge.

By the next day, the shoot-the-messenger philosophy had been taken one step further. The manager at Olemelepo had let it be known that he didn't want me on the grounds anymore. A security guard acquaintance met me at the entrance and apologetically explained that I wasn't allowed to dart the baboons there.

I switched vehicles, I took to lurking there only at dawn and dusk, just outside the grounds, hoping to spot a possible animal. The third day of this, I found one, an adult female with a definite arch of the back, a cough, and one hair patch, but not much else wrong.

I darted her on the edge of the stream that ran into Olemelepo. She remained stable and seemed likely to survive a trip to Nairobi. And now began the utter misery of getting permission to take her.

The difficulty revolved around one of the basic animosities in national parks the world over, namely between park officials and researchers. The two groups occupy fairly different worlds. The former are government bureaucrats who, when based in the field, wear uniforms or, when based in government offices, suits and ties; the latter, by contrast, tend toward torn jeans. The former think about issues like how to increase the flow of tourism in their park, while the latter would just as well get rid of those irritating tourists entirely, so that they can study their one species of ant in idyllic peace. The former tend to be pragmatic realists who function in a realpolitik world; the latter tend toward hysterics and causes and pride themselves on having no social skills. The former typically have wildlife management degrees, while the latter tend toward more prestigious degrees from fancy-ass universities and then, in a way that the former seem to find to be almost viscerally offensive, choose to live like Luddite pigs in leaky tents. And most of all, the former seem to exist merely to cite restrictive rules, while the latter seem to exist merely to shit on the spirit of every park regulation they can get away with.

Thus, the two groups don't typically have much fondness for each other or go out of their way to cooperate with each other. This knowledge should have prepared me for what happened next.

On two consecutive days, I went to the warden's office to get permission to transport the sick female to Nairobi, and both days, a sullen ranger with a rifle told me that the warden was out patrolling and I should come back the next day. On the third day, the same ranger informed me that the warden was actually home for a week on leave. The female, meanwhile, sitting in a cage in my camp, had developed more lesions, a cough that kept both of us awake at night, and the start of a fever. I had bought a few cabbages and was hand-feeding her through the cage. She was clearly terrified of me, and not all that hungry, but she was gradually beginning to take the food from me.

I could not wait for the warden to return. I tried the head of the antipoaching unit, who assured me that he would give me permission to take her out of the reserve if I brought him a gift the next day. I obliged, at which point he cheerfully informed me that he had just discovered that he really did not have authority to let me remove her. That afternoon, I returned to my camp to find a group of the rangers standing around, laughing, poking at the female with sticks through the cage bars. By that evening, she was looking less panicked by me, whether out of habituation or delirium, and she was readily taking cabbage and allowing me to groom her. Her left hand had become too necrotic to use.

The next day, I tried the warden's again, by chance, and discovered that he had actually returned two days earlier. This was told to me by the same ranger who had been giving me the resentful, incorrect information earlier in the week. This time, I actually knew that the warden was there. He kept me sitting for an hour before sending a message that he was too busy to see me; throughout, I heard him and some other men laughing behind his closed door, the sounds of bottles being opened. By that night, the female was losing the use of her right hand and was coughing up blood.

The next day, grinning and scraping and bowing copiously, I saw the warden and begged him for permission to drive the female to Nairobi. With a straight face he said, Of course not, that would be depleting Kenya's parks of its wildlife. Are you serious, I said, she is going to be dead in a few days. No, he said, if you remove her, you are poaching, and then we will get you. This from a man who had already been arrested twice for poaching in his illustrious career and would be busted a year hence for rhino poaching (and who, because of his superb marital connections with the Masai political leadership in the district, would receive a promotion as a result). That night, she was slumped against the side of the cage, delirious.

Finally, Jim Else came through. I had been radio-calling with each daily setback, and he was working frantically at his end through the labyrinths of power and inertia. I believe he got his boss, Richard Leakey, then the head of the National Museum (of which the primate center was a part), to get the head of the Game Department to grant permission. A critical radio call was made, the warden balked until it was in writing, a document empowering me to transport up to three sick baboons to Nairobi arrived on that afternoon's flight.

The road out of the game park was too dangerous to drive at night. By evening, she was comatose, and I doubted if I would reach Nairobi before she died the next day. I raced out before dawn, and in a final piece of misery, I was stopped by an impossible ranger at the wildlife checkpoint on the border of the district. Why, you have a baboon there, he exclaimed. Yes, yes, she is sick and dying and here is the permit. He examined it and suddenly noted, Why, it says here you are supposed to have three baboons, where are the other two? No, no, it says I can bring *up* to three baboons. No, it says that you are supposed to have three baboons, but two are missing, what have you done with them, bwana, have you sold them, this is serious. Jesus Christ, she was sinking fast, and I was contemplating killing this guy, who was gleaming at me sideways with slack-jawed malevolence. Finally, he makes it clear what he wants. "Bwana, you have the wrong permit. It says three baboons, and it is supposed to say one baboon, so now you must pay me the fine for the wrong permit." Fine, you corrupt shitbag, why didn't you ask for your bribe earlier. I paid, roared off, drove far too fast, got caught in Nairobi rush-hour traffic, all the while hearing her irregular, labored breathing next to me stop now and then. I argued with the security guard at the gates of the lab, who did not want to let me in because I was not on that day's appointment list, and finally reached the pathology building.

For reasons I don't understand, I felt compelled to clean away from her lips the last flecks of cabbage that I had fed her, and I dried her eyes that had become teary from the dust of the trip. I had a brief, anthropomorphic thought: Because she's from the garbage dump troop, instead of from my own, she's never had a name. Then, I carried her in my arms into the building and, a few minutes later, helped to remove her rib cage. And again, the lungs melted away.

Jim had warned me that it would take weeks for the microbiologist to confirm whether it was TB from the lung cultures. But the vets were unanimous about the diagnosis the second her lungs began pouring out, from the examination of the lesions, from the first histology slide that they made. All the microbiologist would let us know was what kind of TB it was and, for the moment, that was irrelevant.

We sat around the next day, Jim, I, and a group of his vets. It was TB, that was certain, and everyone knew it wasn't a general threat to the humans there. Humans are relatively resistant, anyone in good shape around Olemelepo— well fed, well clothed—would be fine. Anyone who wasn't probably had TB already; the disease was endemic in Kenya. Jim would use all his powers to get the word out to everyone in the game park that there was no human threat.

But it was a shitter of a threat to the baboons. It was disastrous for them. We sat debating for hours. If this were going on in a primate lab, the procedure would be obvious. Every monkey in the room in which the TB was found would be killed that day. Every animal in the colony would be tested, and every time someone came up positive, everyone in the room would be killed. Otherwise, it spreads like wildfire. A sickening word popped up over and over. To stop a wildfire, you need a firebreak. Kill every monkey in that room, anyone who is in the slightest bit suspect, who has breathed the same air. Form a gap, a firebreak, keep the disease from reaching the rest.

But this wasn't in a primate lab with animals in close proximity. As I had guessed, no one knew the first thing about the dynamics of tuberculosis in wild primates. Hooray for us, we were about to find out. Maybe it spread more slowly, because animals weren't jammed into a single room with a high population density. Maybe it spread more quickly, because the animals in the wild could actually come in contact with each other. Maybe more slowly, because they weren't immunosuppressed by the stress of captivity. Maybe more quickly, because they weren't as well fed.

We went around in circles and didn't know what to do. We couldn't treat the disease in the sick ones—tuberculosis requires daily medication for eighteen months. The only option was to try to contain it. It would help if we knew where it came from. There had been no obvious baboon die-off in the Mara reserve recently, this wasn't the tip of an iceberg of a plague that I had stumbled on. The most plausible thing was that some male baboon had migrated up from Tanzania and brought the disease with him when he joined the garbage dump troop. They were only one troop away from the border, and things were chaotic enough in Tanzania that no one would have noticed a baboon die-off there in the Tanzanian side of the plains.

If an émigré male had brought it into our park, and I had already observed a vector to carry the disease from the Olemelepo garbage dump troop to my own troop, it could spread throughout the whole reserve. On the other hand, suppose an alternative scenario: maybe the tuberculosis had been sitting around in reservoir in the Mara population for years, coming out now and then, with most baboons having a natural resistance. This wouldn't be some novel disease breaking out, but rather a flare-up of an old, familiar one. On the other hand, in laboratory colonies, TB doesn't sit in reservoir, and there is no such thing as natural resistance. But, on the other hand, this wasn't a laboratory colony.

Circles and circles. We didn't have a clue. The vets, trained in lab animal medicine, with all the appropriate fire alarms going off in them at the mention of tuberculosis, were pushing for an aggressive approach. "Firebreak" was said more and more. Kill all the baboons in the garbage dump troop. Kill all the baboons in the adjacent troops. Form a no-baboon's-land to stop the disease before it runs amok in the whole reserve. But these were my animals they were writing off as a firebreak. And even though I'm not a vet, not a clinician, knew nothing about TB, I was enough of a scientist to know that there wasn't any science here. Biology in the laboratory is not biology in the wild—that was the scientific justification for my studying baboons in the wild in the first place—and no one knew anything about TB in the wild.

I won a temporary victory. We wouldn't do a firebreak. We would make this somewhat of a scientific investigation, in addition to its being a clinical intervention. I would go back, start darting every damn animal everywhere that I could get hold of in the reserve, give them a TB test, hold them an impossible four days in a cage waiting for a result. If the garbage dump troop was running anywhere near 50 percent positive, then they would be on the edge of an explosion of the disease, and a firebreak would make some sense. But there was an alternative bit of information to look for that would allow a much more optimistic interpretation: if I could find a single positive case of TB in any of the remote troops that I had seen around the reserve for years, troops that I knew were not undergoing a catastrophic population decline, then we would have proven that the disease doesn't always take off like wildfire in the wild. It would mean it works more slowly, like in humans, infecting vulnerable individuals, instead of wiping out whole populations. If it was not spreading like wildfire, a firebreak would not be necessary.

The vets were not too happy. Science is fine, they seemed to be saying, but believe us, we know about TB, if it takes off, you're going to lose every baboon in the Mara, you'll be sorry. They and Jim forced a logical promise from me: if any animal came up TB positive, I would kill it, even if it was one of my own.

My research was forgotten, all I was doing was darting. I promised that I would start TB testing in my own troop, but for starters, I was concentrating on the garbage dump troop, to see just how many were infected, and on a troop at the other end of the reserve, in the desperate hope of finding the one positive animal in a troop without an overt plague.

You don't realize how well you know some baboons until you try to dart strangers. You don't know their personalities—you don't know who will jump up, look around, and sit back down again after darting, who is going to climb a tree or sprint a kilometer or try to kill you. You don't know the grudges within the troop, who you have to protect from whom when they pass out. You don't know their body weight or the vagaries of their metabolism when you are guessing how much anesthetic to put in the dart. You don't know the neighborhood, where the buffalo or the snakes hang out. And the baboons don't know you, so you can't get as close.

Nevertheless, I slowly started the dartings. I hauled back a bunch of cages from the primate center and some tuberculin for testing. The latter required refrigeration, which was a problem, since I didn't have any—the dry ice was too cold, the Styrofoam box buried in the ground too warm. Fortunately, thanks to Jim's reassurances about the lack of human health risk, Olemelepo was welcoming me again, and the assistant manager let me put the vial in his refrigerator. So I'd go dart someone, run back, get a smidgen of tuberculin, and inject it in the eyelid. When you are checking for tuberculosis in a human, you can examine them closely afterward, so you inject under the skin in the arm. If it is some monkey that is going to rip you to shreds at close quarters, you inject into the eyelid, so you can check it at a distance. Four days later, if the animal has been exposed previously to TB and formed anti-bodies, there will be an inflammatory response. Even from twenty meters away, the eyelid is visibly swollen closed. Swollen eye, you're dead.

It was a nightmare. You would dart some happy, healthy baboon while it was in the middle of grooming some relative or friend. Then it would sit there in your camp for four days, jammed in a tiny cage, one of half a dozen animals screaming and barking, shitting everywhere, making an incredible stench. Rotting cabbage, pools of urine, animals moaning at night in fear and unhappiness. Then, each morning there would be a couple due for their judgment. Maybe their eyes would be fine, and a moment later, they would be free, sprinting back to whoever had been grooming them, with an unlikely story to tell. And if the eyes were swollen shut, I'd somehow have to anesthetize them while they were flailing inside the cage. And then it would be to the other end of the field and the knife.

I was running out of everything. There weren't enough masks or gloves for the dissections; even though humans are pretty resistant to TB, it's not advisable to be passing your days with your face unmasked an inch from someone's terminal stage lungs, and I was getting worried for my own health.* There wasn't enough anesthetic to overdose the animals and, sickeningly, I was

---

*And years later, I discovered a possible answer as to why I never became infected—I turned out to be a genetic carrier for Tay-Sachs disease, which, amid its disadvantages, appears to confer resistance to TB.

beginning to have to give them just enough to anesthetize them and then slit their throats. My nights were now filled with the memory of the wet, sucking, heaving noise of baboons with no throats, trying to breathe. Then my knife disappeared.

I had continued to leave it in the crook of the tree that shaded my mortuary. I didn't have enough disinfectant anymore to clean it between animals, so at least I would sequester it to that corner of the camp. And one afternoon, it was gone.

I had another knife, that was not the problem. The disaster was that it had been taken by the Masai goat boys, passing through camp the day before. They were aware of what I was doing, had watched a dissection from afar, and had no doubt decided to filch it at some quiet point. It would be a great find for them, with a major use for the Masai—a good sharp knife was perfect for cutting the vein on the cow when bleeding it. Perfect, except that the knife was coated with tubercular lung, and cows are extremely susceptible, and those kids had just shoplifted a plague on their village.

So now, in addition to feeding my baboon prisoners, killing each day, and darting at two different ends of the reserve, I began negotiations. Rhoda and Soirowa quickly convinced me that no kids from their village had taken the knife. Instead, I was dealing with people from the adjacent villages, whom I didn't particularly know. I didn't care about the knife, I wasn't angry that someone had taken it, but they must understand me that it was dangerous, it could kill all the cows. I didn't even want the knife back, but they must throw it away. And the villagers indignantly denied it—steal something? Why, we Masai would never dream of something like that. Around and around, each day pleading with them to throw away the knife. It became a backdrop to the events, another layer of problems and anxiety.

After a week, there was yet to be a TB-positive animal in the distant troop, while the garbage dump animals were running around 50 percent positive. Firebreak, more and more inevitable. I was killing every day. Some just had nodules; others, nodules and lung decay. None as advanced as the initial horror cases; after all, these were all animals that looked healthy. Oddly, every one of them had the nodules in the digestive tract, sometimes even when the lungs were still clean. That was atypical, according to what I was now reading.

One day, I screwed up a garbage dump darting badly. I got a big male, and he crossed a stream before passing out, and, not knowing him, I had no idea how many enemies he had. By the time I had forded the stream and gotten to him, he was ripped open in a dozen places by canine slashes. I hauled him to camp and, overwhelmed by what a mess he was, I used some of the dwindling anesthetic to overdose him. And then, as I dissected him, I desperately hoped there would be pathology. Thank god, a small lesion in the left lung and the intestinal nodules—he would not have survived the judgment at the end of his four days in my cages anyway.

That night, acutely aware of the risks in darting strange animals, I resolved to finally start on my own troop. The next day, I darted Joshua and Devorah, along with two garbage dump animals. In the latter case, I wouldn't necessarily know who the animals were or just where to find them again, so they had to sit in the cages for the four days. With my troop, I would easily find the individual again, so there was no need to put them through the four days of waiting in captivity.

Instead, I waited. The next day, I got Jesse and Adam. The day after that, Daniel, and after that, Afghan and Boopsie. That night, I could barely sleep, waiting for the verdict about Joshua and Devorah, imagining what it would be like to have to slit their throats the next day, to saw through their ribs, to bury their bodies.

But they were clean. As was everyone else in my troop. I was euphoric, smiled for the first time in weeks. It took a few days to note that, suddenly, all the garbage dump animals were coming up negative as well on the tuber-culin test. Even one female who festered with the undeniable symptoms of TB over the course of the four days in the cage. Something was wrong.

The next day brought an explanation. I barreled into the house of the assistant manager at Olemelepo to get the tuberculin and discovered the room steward cleaning the place, including the refrigerator. Sitting on the windowsill, baking in the equatorial sun, were the milk, the cheese, the bottles of beer, and, of course, the tuberculin. He was new, had just started that week, would clean there every day. The tuberculin and the test results were useless. I waited for an airlift of more drug and dreamt of lava flows of lung.

I resumed darting, and the garbage dump positive rate climbed to close to 70 percent. I was being overwhelmed by autopsies. Two of the vets from the primate center, Ross Tarara and Mbaruk Suleman, came out to help and, probably, to try to convince me of the firebreak strategy. I prepared for their arrival—their help, their company, their commiseration, their professional insight into TB, which I sorely lacked. Then, the day before they were to arrive, Shem came up positive, the first of my animals to do so.

It is one of the sights that will always be with me. I had just had the nerve to start again on my troop, had darted Isaac, Rachel, then Shem. The first two were negative on days that garbage dump animals were positive, so I trusted the result. That morning, I entered the forest and immediately ran into Shem, sitting with an eyelid completely closed. I had wondered if there could ever be a borderline, disputable test result, but this was not it. He was TB positive.

I gave up on darting that day and spent the day with the baboons, my first quiet observational day with them in too long. I followed them, took distracted, mediocre behavioral data, sang to them, and felt near tears every time I saw Shem interact with someone—greet a male, groom a female, twist around to look at the goings-on in the neighborhood. All for the last time. And I kept passing up opportunities to dart him and slit his throat.

That night I fled to Laurence for advice and solace. I can never overemphasize how, during this insane period of my life, he was a constant source of sanity and big-brotherly stability. He listened and listened and did exactly as he should have—he reworded what I was telling him, and told it back as a command.

"Look, you know as well as I do that these vets don't know shit about TB out here, no one knows. If they're right, all of your animals are going to die anyway, so there is nothing gained by killing this guy now. And if they're wrong, maybe you'll save a few of the positive ones, maybe there is some resistance. Don't kill this one."

The next day, as I drove to the Olemelepo airstrip to meet Ross and Suleman, I spotted that Jesse had just come up positive as well. And I didn't say a word to the vets about him or Shem.

We went to work, and they were a tremendously positive force. Both Ross and Suleman were sweet, jovial men whom I already liked, and they readily fell into the "gee whiz, lookie what a mess those lungs are" mode of scientists having a good, detached time. I expected that this would infuriate me—my tragedy as their clinical pleasure—but it was surprisingly calming. Our pace increased as I shifted more to darting, something they didn't know how to do, and they did more of the autopsies, their specialty. We ground through more and more, I avoided questions about my troop, the distant troop continued with a 0 percent rate and the garbage dumpers about 70 percent. I would slip off during the day to do secret dartings and inspections of my own animals, and more positives there popped up—David, Jonathan. I darted Benjamin one day and found I did not have the resolve even to test him with tuberculin.

We worked in a numbing, distracting way, for which I was grateful. There was an analgesic effect to the sheer magnitude of the work, the repetition, the sleep deprivation. Darting, feeding the caged animals, reading test results, anesthetizing, cajoling at the Masai village, killing, dissecting, recording, passing the evenings discussing firebreaks. In some ways, that was academic, at least as far as the garbage dump animals were concerned; whether piecemeal or as a premeditated final solution, we were getting around to killing most of them anyway. The animals passed with exhausting labor, and each day's work ended with a sight that I now recall with the nostalgia wasted on long-ago nightmares that eventually end—a massive hole we had dug and the burning of baboon bodies doused with gasoline.

The repetitive peace of my death camp and crematorium, the calming sadness of smelling the burning, was suddenly interrupted by a radio-call from Jim Else. The microbiology result was in, and it was a shocker. It was bovine tuberculosis, not human.

TB is actually a hodgepodge of diseases. In all cases, it is due to a bacterium that runs amok in the body. Overwhelmingly, it lodges initially in the lungs, thanks to inhalation, after which it can be carried elsewhere via the bloodstream or lymphatics. You can have secondary TB in essentially any organ—central nervous system, genito-urinary system, bones. But it is usually the lungs. Most of the time, it is due to one type of bacteria, *Mycobacterium tuberculosis,* or human TB. But there are other, rarer kinds. *M. kansasii, M. scrofulaceum, M. fortuitum, M. bovis.* Some of them are "avian," some "bovine," some "soil" TB. The name does not indicate what it infects exclusively, but rather what species it was first found in or is most readily found in. There is even *M. marinum,* which is found in Infected swimming pools. But mostly, it is *M. tuberculosis,* and mostly it is in the lungs. But now, we had *M. bovis,* bovine tuberculosis, and it was primarily in the guts. The baboons weren't breathing TB from one another. They were eating it.

Work ground to a halt and we sat and scratched our heads. I poked around, asked some questions, had some wild theories that grew more plausible by the day. And then, one afternoon, a friend at Olemelepo suggested that I take him for a ride around the reserve a bit. Once we were away from the lodge, very circumspectly, he confirmed my suspicions.

He was frightened at being an informant, and I will not reveal his name or his identifying profession. He was of a tribe that was an enemy of the Masai and he was delighted to finger some of them. And, an educated man who had once worked as a veterinary assistant long ago, he knew what he was talking about.

It was obvious. The bovine tuberculosis was occurring in the bovids. The Masai could instantly spot when an occasional cow was becoming tubercular.

In the old days, cows were never killed. They were kept for blood and milk to drink, were honored, sung to, caressed, pampered. And if they became sick, they were nursed to the very end, at which point they might be eaten, but with great reluctance. But the Masai, pragmatic and adaptable even when it came to their beloved cows, had devised something new. All throughout Masai land surrounding the reserve, whenever a cow would get the first hint of TB, it would be loaded into a pickup truck that day, carted off to Olemelepo, and sold to Timpai, the Masai butcher at the staff quarters. After an appropriate bribe to the Masai meat inspector.

My friend knew what a tubercular cow looked like. He saw Timpai take the sick ones out to the far field, cut out the lungs and other infected organs, and toss them to the garbage dump baboons that would cluster around for scraps. And the remnants would be sold to the staff. Eventually, I would be able to observe the same ritual myself out in the field, take furtive, poor tele-photo pictures. I would watch Timpai, a beefy, avuncular man with massive butcher's forearms, whack away at a carcass, happily elbow deep in blood and gore (and no doubt tubercles and lesions), rummage around inside with the help of his bush Masai helpers, and toss something unsightly to the baboons waiting there. Big males would fight for the major chunks, females would rush in in between for pieces, scrappy infants would lunge for a snippet or two. Ensuring their deaths. And inevitably, now and then, I would spot Shem or Saul or Jesse, freelancing to try to grab a piece in the fray.

I indulged myself in a murderous anger at the Masai. I dropped any thought of going there to warn them about the tubercular knife they had stolen. Coals to Newcastle, they could go to hell. I was simply returning the bovine tuberculosis they had inflicted on my baboons. Mostly, I felt an odd relief. We had an explanation for the odd TB variant, the odd symptomatol-ogy. Mostly, we had an answer as to what to do. Get rid of the meat inspec-tor, clean up the operation, and maybe the TB would be stopped, maybe some animals could be saved. I edged on euphoria—an answer, an option, a hope.

Ross and Suleman had to leave, to return to their regular duties. I gave them a letter for Jim. In it, I detailed the butchery connection, outlined the obvious—we, maybe with Leakey, had to go immediately to the head of Safari Hotels, the chain that operated Olemelepo, get them to clean up their act, threaten a little bad publicity if they didn't, solve the problem.

The letter went off, and I was excited to get a radio-call from Jim by that evening, telling me to come to Nairobi immediately. I departed the next day, ready for us to leap into action, seeing the solution falling into place. And the next day, behind closed doors, Jim told me that nothing of the sort was going to happen.

Tourism is the biggest source of foreign currency in Kenya. It is bigger, proportionately, than the steel, automobile, and gasoline industries are in the United States, put together. Safari Hotels, owned by a prominent British-colonial family, was one of the bigger chains in the country; Olemelepo was one of their flagship hotels. And this was a region of the world where people with power did whatever they wanted. Where the widow of one government official was generally known to run the elephant poaching, where rangers with guns would shake down the hotel staff each payday, where a government minister once used his forecasts of a crop shortfall to buy up the entire crop with his own money and hoard it, engineering a profit-making famine among his own people. And, Jim informed me, neither I, nor he, nor even Richard Leakey, Kenya's best-known citizen internationally, was going to go see the head of Safari Hotels and tell him to clean up his meat operation. And we were not going to seek publicity about Olemelepo peddling tubercular meat. I pleaded, we went back and forth, and he told me to go back to the reserve, continue doing the TB science there, and he would see what could be done at his end.

Never in my life have I felt closer to drowning in anger, felt more poisoned, more lost in a corrosive sense of betrayal. I returned, as requested, withdrew into my fury, confided in no one except Laurence. I passed each day obsessing over fantasies of vengeance at everyone. I even began to lay the groundwork for some of the fantasies. I was going to protect my baboons, save them, I was going to protect myself, I was going to have my revenge. I went back to darting and methodically documenting the further spread of the disease for the data notebooks that seemed destined to sit in Jim's desk. But I also began doing other things. I photographed the animals clustering around the butchery, fighting over the refuse at the garbage dump. I spent a furtive morning shooting another roll of film, following one of the sick, terminal-stage baboons as he staggered along the edge of the stream that watered Olemelepo. He eventually passed out, and I photographed him lying there with the lodge in the background. I paid for a lodge lunch, the type of meal I would endlessly maneuver to get invited to by tourists; I sat there, barely eating, finding unlikely instances to spirit away pieces of the reddest beef to put into a small vat of formalin I had in a box with me. I bought meat for the same purposes from Timpai, left vats of formalin with my nervous informant for him to do the same when he spotted a particularly tubercular cow coming through. I was going to prove it, envisioned some headline in the States, "Premiere Kenyan Tourist Lodge Feeding Tubercular Food to Orthodontists from Akron"; I was going to have the information to save my baboons regardless of whatever powers that be, or, if I was going to lose my baboons, I was going to take everything down with them—Olemelepo, Safari Hotels and their owners, Timpai, the Kenyan tourist industry, the whole fucking country and its economy; my baboons were going to be avenged.

I tried a few of the logical things. For one, I went to talk to Timpai. If any one man single-handedly typified some of the stronger, more contradictory traits of Africans, it was he. He was a sweetheart of a man, charming, cherubic, the Tevye of the Masai community at Olemelepo. He was vastly too strong to be called fat. Instead, he had an anomalous, jiggly belly, an impish round face, and a chest and arms made of slabs of pig iron. He conjured up Thomas Hart Bentonesque images of capitalist realist men who carry anvils or railroad sidings or cows on their backs. Rare in the community, he had a full, well-shaped beard already shot through with flecks of white.

He was sweet, giggly, generous, one of the elders of the Masai community, always giving a place to stay to various Masai from the villages stranded at Olemelepo for lack of rides home, always serving tea to everyone. Incongruously, he even hugged people hello, an atypical gesture in those parts. He was the archetypally generous warm village character, the respected and required butcher, sage, and tea dispenser. Also, in a way that ultimately seems very African, he was utterly corrupt in a completely guileless, amoral fashion. His official job at Olemelepo was as the meteorologist, which meant he was supposed to check the rain gauge daily and write down the results. He had not done a stitch of meteorology in years, instead dumping the work on the minions of assistants that he had acquired through tearful letters to the government office. He devoted his working hours to his illegal butchering. He would happily cheat you and, conspiratorially, admit to it later with as much happiness. In one of his most flagrant outbursts of corruption, he came near to poisoning half the lodge staff. Some Masai out somewhere were bringing in an old, senile, near-comatose cow to meet Timpai's knife. They loaded the cow into the back of the truck they had hired, drove in, and, upon reaching their destination, discovered that said cow had died two hours before. It was already stiff. No problem. The Masai dropped their price for the cow, gave a little cash back to Timpai and the meat inspector, and the stiff was "slaughtered" out in the field. The meat was dutifully sold, everyone became sick. The police came to investigate and it was all straightened out after Timpai and the meat inspector paid the appropriate bribe.

So now I offhandedly asked Timpai, over his tea, whether it was possible that the cows were ever sick when they were slaughtered. Oh no. How do you know? Because the meat inspector tells me when they are good. How does he know? Oh, he knows. Then gesturing toward the glinting, half-naked Masai inspector, who was sitting on the floor in an alcoholic glaze, Timpai said one of the more memorable lines to nurture my black-humored moments. "When the cow comes here, he will look at its heart and stomach and liver and lungs and brain and intestines, and if there is anything wrong, then he will not let me kill the cow." Timpai gleamed happily. "That inspector is a good man and brings us much business because god is blessing he and the cattle to be so good."

So Timpai wasn't about to give up any of his business just to keep from killing some baboons. Perhaps even more logical would have been to make a stink at Olemelepo, to get everyone else to shut down the butchery. Climb up on a soapbox, folks, there's trouble here in River City, do you know your neighbors Timpai and the meat inspector are giving you TB? Frenzied vengeful crowds would develop, and that would be the last sick batch of meat foisted off on the community. You know what? It wouldn't work, because no one would give a damn. When Timpai poisoned everyone by slaughtering the dead cow, there was irritation, but little more than that. Nothing remotely resembling outrage. I would ask people, What happened then, aren't you upset? And they would say, "Well, Timpai and that inspector have learned, now they know that if they do that to us, they must be paying the police a lot of money, so maybe they will not do it again." Yeah, but he poisoned you, he could have killed you and your kids. "Yes, that is not good," and then they would say the archetypal resigned Swahili word, "dunia." "That's the world, that's how it is." Amid my wrestling during that period with the image of Timpai as pure evil and of Timpai as an old, generous acquaintance, I was aided by the insight implied by "dunia." It is not a notably evil thing to poison your neighbors if they themselves do not consider it to be much more than an irritant. People wouldn't give a damn if it turned out that Timpai and the inspector were giving them TB; it was almost as if they expected as much from them as part of their job.

At some point during this sickened period, I found something important. One of the healthy-looking lodge females came up positive. I slit her throat, did a dissection, and found nothing. There were no nodules in her gut or stomach. There were no lesions in the lungs. Alert, excited, I went over every inch of the lobes, and in the upper right corner, I found a single dried tubercle. There was no caseation, no liquefication, no adherences. It was a small pocket of rot, encased in a sort of cartilaginous package, sequestered from the rest of the lung. There was nothing else in her. It was possible to be exposed, to have the start of pathology, and to recover—there could be natural resistance in the wild.

I filed it away with all my other pieces, too cautious and soiled by now to feel hopeful about any particular fact. And it was time to go. It was the end of my season, I was due back for another nine months in the lab, everything would now have to run its course without me.

I collected my belongings and my facts:

- About 65 percent of the garbage dump troop was infected with the disease, and they were dropping like flies. No baboons were infected in the distant troop. And in my own troop, two thirds of my males either were TB positive or had been spotted by me to fight for a scrap of the meat during a foray over to the lodge for butchery lunches.

- In principle, all was not lost. The disease was working differently than in the laboratory. There could be (at least one case of) natural resistance and recovery or at least remission and, unlike with human TB, there did not appear to be much or any secondary transfer from baboon to baboon by coughing. Among the lodge baboons, there had not been a single case where there was only pulmonary infection and no gut lesions. Furthermore, in my troop, only animals that I had observed to go over to the butchery and fight for scraps were turning up positive—the females, the subadult and aged males all were clean. The baboons weren't giving TB to each other, at least not as rapidly as in the laboratory. The meat was the vector in all cases. If the source of the TB could be shut down, there would probably be no new infections. And some of those already infected just might survive. The key was to get rid of the meat inspector, to clean up the operation.

- There was no point to making a firebreak. If little or no secondary baboon-to-baboon transfer of the disease occurred in the wild, there was no fear of a massive epidemic running through all the baboons in the region. And even if secondary transfer did happen, if we annihilated the garbage dump troop, if we annihilated the adjacent troops, including my own, and still did not get rid of the tubercular meat, it was just a matter of time until the nearest baboon troop moved into the lodge to help Timpai with his irresistible leftovers. Again, we had to get rid of the meat inspector.

- But there was no indication that the inspector was going anywhere. Jim would see what he could do, but wouldn't promise much. He would push again to see if Leakey could do anything, but I was told not to hold my breath. Meanwhile, he gave me the go-ahead to begin writing up our reports about the TB outbreak, subject to Leakey's censoring for imprudent information. And he told me to keep quiet about the whole thing.

I spent a last morning with the baboons and, as always, with startling speed, I was back in my own world. As was the case each year, I luxuriated in the hot showers I had been missing, gorged on any food that was not rice and beans and mackerel, saw friends, whom I regaled with stories about the season's adventures while failing to mention tuberculosis. Slowly, life returned to normal; I began to analyze the blood samples from the baboons, I figured out the cheerful explanation I would give my funding agency to explain why I had gotten so little accomplished that season without mentioning the tubercular distraction, I managed to recall the muddle of experiments I had been doing in the lab prior to Kenya and got them going again. And I stewed with Lisa about the TB.

There was no news. Jim would respond to my barrage of letters and transcontinental phone calls with the occasional message that Leakey was working on it, but nothing had happened yet. My informant sent letters now and then, which, belying his role, were not informative. He made little mention of baboons or butchery and instead waxed poetic about the radio he wanted me to bring him.

I learned about tuberculosis, read the primate literature on the subject. The pathology papers focused on which types of lesions developed first where and taught me the technical terms for the rot I'd seen. The epidemiological papers were of the "As part of the Colonial Veterinary Survey of '47, we sampled [i.e., shot] umpteen monkeys in the upper Zambezi district and found TB in X percent of them" variety. These just confirmed that no one knew anything of the dynamics of the disease in the wild. The experimental papers focused on how a lab monkey gives TB to another one: take a primate and expose it to the food, or the water bottle, or the air of a sick animal; does it then get sick? These led irrefutably to opposing predictions: in the wild, TB should be less virulent than in the lab, because of the lower population density of the former. In the wild, TB should be more virulent than in the lab, because of the more intimate social interactions in the former. Who the hell knew.

Jim and his veterinarians and I began work on our own TB papers, detailing the pathology and epidemiology, with drafts sent to Leakey for approval. Exquisite care was given to the writing so that it was never clear what precise part of Kenya was being discussed, that there was a tourist lodge involved.

The papers eventually appeared in the *Journal of Wildlife Diseases* and in the *Journal of Medical Primatology*, two publications that, no doubt, grace every coffee table in America. I imagined that a careful reader would be able to detect the real story between the lines, that they would trigger outrage and action in the scientific community. Given that, instead, perhaps half a dozen readers bothered to glance at the title and summary of these obscure papers, the silence just confirmed my corrosive sense of anger and isolation.

I continued to spend far too much time obsessing on my revenge. In my fantasies, I managed to murder the meat inspector, to blackmail Safari Hotels into compliance. This was one of the lodges that the British royal family stayed at while on state visits (back in the jolly colonial days, the area had been one of the royal family's hunting grounds), and I considered trying to enlist Queen Elizabeth as an ally. I even had the first sentence of my letter planned: "Your Royal Highness might be interested to know of the possibility that you were fed tubercular food whilst on your recent visit to British East Africa." I knew damn well that her lunches weren't catered by Timpai the Butcher, but figured that would be a catchy opening anyway. I would offhandedly establish my credentials in order to get the letter past her minions of secretaries; she would be horrified and moved with compassion by my story (I became a Royalist during this time), she would command that the British owners of Safari Hotels and the meat inspector be placed in the Tower of London. I actually made drafts of a letter.

I had other plans. Laurence of the Hyenas' work had recently been profiled by a science writer for the *New York Times*. Now I planned to go to her and tell my story; I fantasized about the headlines. But I didn't go see her, I didn't write to the queen. I didn't do anything other than fret and call Jim for the news that there was no news. More and more, I had the restraining sense to realize that my baboon tragedy was pretty small change. Baboons are not endangered, they're no one's favorite species. The tubercular threat to the humans was minimal, and Africans are already rife with TB without the West being concerned. And the story was nothing more than a minor little piece of corruption in a very corrupt country. Instead, I waited and hoped and festered and, eventually, it was time to return for the next summer's season.

I always writhe with impatience when I am returning. I rush to the airport, I rush through my good-byes. Somehow, sitting in the airplane for endless hours, I manage an air of rushing. I barrel through the necessary chores in Nairobi, drive too fast through the outskirts of town and the Rift Valley and the dusty track leading to the reserve. I rush through the required hellos and

300 • Robert M. Sapolsky

endless handshakes and repeated conversations at the checkpoint and at the various lodges. I rush to finally smell my tent again and marvel that the mountains of the previous year are still there and to see the baboons.

If you are lucky, they oblige you the first day and move out into an open area, where you can gather them all in at once, revel in them. Just before, you wonder strange things—were there ever baboons here, did I imagine them, did I imagine this location? You decide you have forgotten critical but basic details in your time away—do baboons have tails, do they have antlers and I've forgotten? You wonder if you will recognize any of them and if any of them will recognize you.

And suddenly they are all around you and you choke up and swim in them—who looks exactly the same, who has aged, who has a new scar, who has new pubescent muscles. You look at the new infants and try to identify who their mothers are—just by looks—when they are off playing without Mom. You see how fast you can identify the new alpha male. You see what alliances are still intact, what friendships have solidified further, who is feuding with whom. You see what child from the previous year is now tortured with puberty and making a fool of herself in front of the males, which pipsqueak kid is now in the vile aggressive male adolescent stage. You try to assimilate the new males who have transferred in, individuate them, and convince yourself that they are not all villains simply because they are new and unfamiliar. You spend the coming weeks visiting the neighboring troops to see where last year's adolescent males have transferred to for their adult homes. And, of course, you see who is no longer there.

That year was no different. We shook hands at the lodge, sending greetings from every person in America, discussed the weather and crops at home, conversations that were endless and irritating and familiar and calming and necessary and delaying—rangers, wardens, waiters, mechanics, the assistant manager, the radio operator, the tour van drivers. And Timpai. And the meat inspector. We set up camp, fixed storage tents that had disintegrated in the previous year, dug the hole for the toilet, dug the drainage lines, tested the centrifuge, cleaned the blowgun, arranged the cans of mackerel, did all the conceivable chores until it was not possible to wait any longer.

The baboons once again gave me a return gift and marched at dawn into the most open field. And that day and in the coming weeks I learned how the year had been for them. I learned pretty conclusively that there is little secondary baboon-to-baboon transfer of TB like in the lab. It really doesn't spread like wildfire. And I gathered more evidence that there can be rare cases of natural resistance in the wild, just as my single case the previous year had suggested. And I learned that, nevertheless, tubercular meat as a primary infectious vector is rather virulent in olive baboons, Latin name *Papio anubis.*

And the plague took Saul, who died in my arms, as I described many stories ago.

And the plague took David.

And Daniel.

And Gideon.

And Absolom.

And the plague took Manasseh, who died writhing in front of a laughing crowd of staffers at the lodge.

And the plague took Jesse.

And Jonathan.

And Shem.

And Adam.

And Scratch.

And the plague took my Benjamin.

I write these words years later and I still have not found a Prayer for the Dead for the baboons. As a child, when I believed in the orthodoxy of my people, I learned the Kaddish. Once I said it in stunned, mechanical obeisance to my tradition at the open grave of my father, but it glorifies the actions and caprices of a god who does not exist for me, so that prayer does not come for these baboons. I have been told that in primate centers in Japan, Shinto prayers are offered to honor the monkeys that have been killed, and that the prayers are hybrids of the prayer for a dead animal offered by the successful hunter and the prayer for a dead enemy offered by the successful soldier. But even though I stalk these animals with my blowgun and I quicken at a darting, I swear that I have never been their hunter and they have never been my enemy. So that prayer does not come for these baboons. In a world already filled with so many words of lamentation, no words have come to me. And instead, these baboons only remain as ashes in my head. With the ashes of my father's dementia and my science that moved too slowly to help him. With the ashes of my ancestors in the death camps. With the ashes of Lisa's tears when I have been a monster to her. With the ashes of the rats dead in my lab. With the ashes of my depressions and my bad back that aches more each year. With the ashes of the hungry Masai children who watch me now as I type, wondering if they will be fed here today.

•   •   •

I have gained, as they say, some perspective with the years. I no longer rage at night with the memories of that period. I no longer keep mental lists of people whom I will hunt down someday. I do not write these words with the hope that they will collapse the Kenyan economy or destroy tourism there or even discomfort Olemelepo Lodge, whose managers still invite me to lunches and whose supply trucks still bring my longed-for mail and whose toilet paper I still steal regularly. As proof that I wish no malice, I have not even used the real names of Olemelepo Lodge and Safari Hotels. Both the meat inspector and Timpai have retired, and there hasn't been a TB outbreak since. The tidal waves of AIDS in Africa and desertification and war and hunger make my particular little melodrama seem self-indulgent and small potatoes, a tragedy for a whitey comfortable and privileged enough to be sentimental about animals on the other side of the globe. But still, I miss those baboons.

I began work on a new troop, in a remote, empty corner of the park. Richard slaved to habituate them, soon Hudson rejoined the project. Predictably, that corner of the park is now overrun with a new lodge and tourist campsites and by encroaching Masai. Already, a first male in that troop has died of TB, the first few have been killed for sport by bored guards at the campsites when the tourists are away. And the Masai have found a new sport, from which I have yet to find an escape. Just this week, a Masai came to us, telling how some rogue baboon had just leapt out of the bushes and killed a goat of his. We questioned him closely and found many contradictory details and concluded it couldn't have been one of our baboons and it probably didn't occur at all. But by afternoon, a collection of elders had arrived to tell us of the seriousness of the incident and to hint at how they could dissuade the man from a reprisal spearing for only so long. And inevitably, I will have to pay for the imaginary goat to save some baboons, and even then, the kids learning how to use their spears will still be practicing on the baboons and warthogs after I leave. We bickered over the price, I walled off the sense of rage that echoes from the time of the plague, and by afternoon, I had gone back to my work. And still, despite this pragmatism and detachment, I miss those baboons.

This new troop has allowed me to do some interesting science. I like these animals, but not much more than that, and each year I do less behavioral observation on them and more physiology, in part so that I will not know them well enough to get attached. I am a different person now and at a different point in life than when I started here. Once I was twenty and I feared nothing but buffalo and I came here to adventure and to exult and to defeat my depressions, and I had an infinity of love to expend on a troop of baboons. Now, more than twenty years later, I am almost as afraid of not balancing the budget on my grant, and I come here to think clearly about my lab work and to catch up on my sleep and to escape the demands of the endless academic committees. And despite still missing those baboons, the infinity of love I have now is for Lisa and our two precious children, our Benjamin and Rachel.

The original troop still exists, a small band of baboons who forage in a tight cluster and have remarkably low rates of aggression among themselves. They are too few in number for me to do much research on them, and I don't know who half of the animals are by now. Everyone from back then—Ruth, Isaac, Rachel, Nick—is gone, except for one last survivor from the beginning. Somehow, Joshua resisted the lure of tubercular meat and thus avoided the plague. And, except for his unlikely spring during the unstable years when he was briefly the alpha male and then supported Benjamin's alphaship, he avoided the fights and canine slashes and the piling up of injuries that ultimately do in a male baboon. And now he is an ancient ancient animal whose oldest child, Obadiah, must already be over the hill himself in some distant troop. Joshua sits as the infants play around him, he distractedly greets each female, he is left alone by the aggressive adolescent jerks, and he plods along methodically at the very back of each troop progression, making us worry that he is too exposed to predators. In his old age, he has started to fart staggering amounts. He is far from decrepit, and his lifelong tendency toward calmness has deepened with the years.

This season, very trepidant, very guiltily, we darted him, as it would be vital to get data from him. We fretted endlessly over him as he recovered from the anesthesia, snoring and drooling a bit and continuing to fart copiously. And when it was time to release him from the cage, he did something extraordinary. Normally, when I leap on top of the cage to pull up the door, the baboon inside roars and hammers and whirls like a dervish. And when the door is opened, he either sprints off at top speed or, on rare occasions, comes back to try to leap murderously at me.

The cage was angled behind a tree, and as I approached, Joshua peered calmly at me from one side of the tree and then from the other, like the paranoid peeking game he had played with Benjamin so long ago. As I leapt on top and started undoing the bungee cords, he didn't move, except to squeeze his hand out the side of the cage and upward in order to place his hand on my foot. And when the door opened, he merely walked out and sat down nearby.

Lisa and I did something rather unprofessional, but we didn't care. We sat down next to Joshua and fed him some cookies. English digestive biscuits. We ate some too. He went about it slowly, grasping the end of each delicately with his broken old fingers, chewing with small, fussy toothless bites, continuing to fart occasionally. We all sat in the sun, warming ourselves, eating cookies, watching the giraffes and the clouds.